CONCEPTS OF POWER IN KIERKEGAARD AND NIETZSCHE

The name Friedrich Nietzsche has become synonymous with studies in political power. The application of his theory that the vast array of human activities comprises manifestations of the will to power continues to influence fields as diverse as international relations, political studies, literary theory, the social sciences, and theology. To date, the introduction of Søren Kierkegaard into this discussion has been gradual at best. Long derided as the quintessential individualist, the social dimension of his fertile thought has been neglected until recent decades.

This book situates Kierkegaard in direct dialogue with Nietzsche on the topic of power and authority. Significant contextual similarities warrant such a comparison: both severely criticized state Lutheranism, championed the self and its imaginative ways of knowing against the philosophical blitzkrieg of Hegelianism, and endured the turbulent emergence of the nation-state. However, the primary justification remains the depth-defying prescience with which Kierkegaard not only fully anticipates but rigorously critiques Nietzsche's power position thirty years in advance.

ASHGATE NEW CRITICAL THINKING IN RELIGION, THEOLOGY AND BIBLICAL STUDIES

The *Ashgate New Critical Thinking in Religion, Theology and Biblical Studies* series brings high quality research monograph publishing back into focus for authors, international libraries, and student, academic and research readers. Headed by an international editorial advisory board of acclaimed scholars spanning the breadth of religious studies, theology and biblical studies, this open-ended monograph series presents cutting-edge research from both established and new authors in the field. With specialist focus yet clear contextual presentation of contemporary research, books in the series take research into important new directions and open the field to new critical debate within the discipline, in areas of related study, and in key areas for contemporary society.

Other Recently Published Titles in the Series:

Theosis *in the Theology of Thomas Torrance*
Myk Habets

Creativity, Spirituality, and Mental Health
Exploring Connections
Kelley Raab Mayo

Trusting Others, Trusting God
Concepts of Belief, Faith and Rationality
Sheela Pawar

What's Right with the Trinity?
Conversations in Feminist Theology
Hannah Bacon

Spirit and Sonship
Colin Gunton's Theology of Particularity and the Holy Spirit
David A. Höhne

Dalit Theology and Dalit Liberation
Problems, Paradigms and Possibilities
Peniel Rajkumar

Beyond Evangelicalism
The Theological Methodology of Stanley J. Grenz
Steven Knowles

Concepts of Power in Kierkegaard and Nietzsche

J. KEITH HYDE
University College of the North, Thompson, Manitoba, Canada

ASHGATE

Published by
Ashgate Publishing Limited
Wey Court East
Union Road
Farnham
Surrey, GU9 7PT
England

Ashgate Publishing Company
Suite 420
101 Cherry Street
Burlington
VT 05401-4405
USA

www.ashgate.com

British Library Cataloguing in Publication Data
Hyde, J. K.
Concepts of power in Kierkegaard and Nietzsche. – (Ashgate new critical thinking in religion, theology and biblical studies)
1. Nietzsche, Friedrich Wilhelm, 1844–1900. 2. Kierkegaard, Søren, 1813–1855. 3. Power (Philosophy) 4. Philosophy, Comparative.
I. Title II. Series
111–dc22

Library of Congress Cataloging-in-Publication Data
Hyde, J. K.
Concepts of power in Kierkegaard and Nietzsche / J.K. Hyde.
p. cm. – (New critical thinking in religion, theology, and biblical studies)
Includes bibliographical references (p.   ) and index.
ISBN 978-0-7546-6574-8 (hardcover: alk. paper) – ISBN 978-1-4094-1041-6 (ebook) 1. Power (Christian theology) 2. Kierkegaard, Søren, 1813–1855. 3. Nietzsche, Friedrich Wilhelm, 1844–1900. I. Title.
BT738.25.H93 2010
261–dc22

2010014661

ISBN 9780754665748 (hbk)

Mixed Sources
Product group from well-managed forests and other controlled sources
www.fsc.org Cert no. SA-COC-1565
© 1996 Forest Stewardship Council
FSC

Printed and bound in Great Britain by
MPG Books Group, UK

Dedicated to Professor Alan J. Torrance,
for exceptional guidance and friendship on many a dreich day.

[E]very great problem is like the precious stone which thousands walk over before one finally picks it up.[1]

—Nietzsche

The old Christian dogmatic terminology is like an enchanted castle where the most beautiful princes and princesses rest in a deep sleep—it needs only to be awakened, brought to life, in order to stand in its full glory.[2]

—Kierkegaard

But he said to me, "My grace is sufficient for you, for [my] power is made perfect in weakness." So, I will boast all the more gladly of my weaknesses, so that the power of Christ may dwell in me.

—II Corinthians 12:9 (NRSV)

---

[1]   Friedrich Nietzsche, *Untimely Meditations*, trans. R.J. Hollingdale (Cambridge, 1997), p. 214.

[2]   *Søren Kierkegaard's Journals and Papers*, trans. and ed. Howard V. Hong and Edna H. Hong (6 vols, Bloomington, [8 July 1837] 1975), vol. 4, p. 461.

Contents

Acknowledgements

This literary odyssey has taught me that it "takes a village" to raise a book, as well as a child. Many thanks to my parents, Jack and Hazel Hyde, without whose support and patient endurance I never would have come this far, my sisters Kari, Sharla, Dayna, and Tracey, who kept me well-fed on regular visits, and my darling Grandma, Eva Schwab, whose feisty pace until the age of 99 inspired us all!

I am deeply indebted to Prof. C. Stephen Evans, Prof. Trevor Hart, Dr. Michael Partridge, Dr. Robert L. Perkins, Prof. Murray Rae, and Prof. Nicholas Renger for helpful suggestions and scintillating discussion.

Thanks are also owed to my loyal band of Canadian moral supporters, including Dr. Jane Barter Moulaison, James Dean, Prof. Murray Evans, John Fondse, Jeff Henderson, Cam, Donna, Christine, and Kerry Hyde, Mike Kanski, Jim Kavanagh, Rev. Bob Kennedy, Dale Kohn, Karl McAllister, Dr. Kathryn McNaughton, Gordon Miller, Kevin Mueller, Nadine Powell, Lorena Rojas, Rev. Woody Ruten, the late Rev. A.C. Schindel, Rick Paddock Thiessen, and Trish Wiebe for helping to preserve any shred of sanity which still subsists.

During my time in St. Andrews, Scotland, fellow intellectual troubadour, Dr. Joachim Vette provided timely recharges and pinball breaks in Heidelberg humidity. Dr. Tony Clark, Dr. Don Collett, Dr. Oliver Crisp, Dr. Tracy Demmons, Dr. Sam Giere, Dr. Poul Guttesen, Dr. Matt Jenson, Kirstin Jeffrey Johnson, Dr. Don Yoon Kim, Dr. Steve Mason, Dr. Marilee Newell, Stephen Prokopchuk and family, Dr. Ed Russell, Drs Dave and Chelle Stearns, and Dr. David Wilhite generously contributed to long country-road walks, existential musings, adventures in cooking, English literature discussions, Faeroese flights, Munroe baggings, squash games, and multitudinous Chai-lattes at the Northpoint! As Nietzsche himself confessed, "I admire almost every man who does not lose faith in himself under a cloudy sky … . In Petersburg I should be a nihilist … ."[1]

Special thanks go out to my dear departed friend Ellen Johnson for regular Wednesday evening tea and biscuits at Balnacarron.

---

[1]   Georg Brandes, *Friedrich Nietzsche*, trans. A.G. Chater (London, 1914), p. 76.

Notes on the Text

Extracts throughout the text are from the following sources:

Kierkegaard, Søren. *Christian Discourses: The Crisis and a Crisis in the Life of an Actress*. Trans. and ed. Howard V. Hong and Edna H. Hong, 1997. © Reprinted by permission of Princeton University Press.

Kierkegaard, Søren. *The Moment and Late Writings*. Trans. and ed. Howard V. Hong and Edna H. Hong, 1998. © Reprinted by permission of Princeton University Press.

Kierkegaard, Søren. *Søren Kierkegaard's Journals and Papers* Vol IV. Trans. and ed. Howard V. Hong and Edna H. Hong, 1976. © Indiana University Press, reproduced with permission.

Kierkegaard, Søren. *Upbuilding Discourses in Various Spirits*. Trans. and ed. Howard V. Hong and Edna H. Hong, 1993. © Reprinted by permission of Princeton University Press.

Nietzsche, Friedrich. *Beyond Good and Evil: Prelude to a Philosophy of the Future*. Trans. R.J. Hollingdale, 1990. © Reproduced by permission of Penguin Books Ltd.

Nietzsche, Friedrich. *The Gay Science: With a Prelude in Rhymes and an Appendix in Song*. Trans Walter Kaufmann, 1974. © Reproduced by permission of Random House Inc.

Nietzsche, Friedrich. *On the Geneaology of Morals: A Polemic*. Trans. Douglas Smith, 1998. © Oxford University Press, Reproduced with permission.

Nietzsche, Friedrich, *Human, All Too Human: A Book for Free Spirits*. Trans. Marion Faber and Stephen Lehmann, 1986. © Reproduced by permission of the University of Nebraska Press.

Nietzsche, Friedrich. *Thus Spoke Zarathustra*. Trans. R.J. Hollingdale, 1976. © Reproduced by permission of Penguin Books Ltd.

Nietzsche, Friedrich. *Twilight of the Idols / The Antichrist*. Trans. R.J. Hollingdale, 1990. © Reproduced by permission of Penguin Books Ltd.

Abbreviations

Søren Kierkegaard

BA	*The Book on Adler*
CA	*The Concept of Anxiety: A Simple Psychologically Orienting Deliberation on the Dogmatic Issue of Hereditary Sin*
CD	*Christian Discourses: The Crisis and a Crisis in the Life of an Actress*
CI	*The Concept of Irony: With Continual Reference to Socrates*
CUP	*Concluding Unscientific Postscript*
EO	*Either/Or*
EUD	*Eighteen Upbuilding Discourses*
FS	*For Self-Examination/Judge For Yourself*
FT	*Fear and Trembling/Repetition*
JK	*The Journals of Kierkegaard: 1834–54*
JP	*Søren Kierkegaard's Journals and Papers* (6 vols.)
PC	*Practice in Christianity*
PF	*Philosophical Fragments/Johannes Climacus, or De Omnibus Dubitandum Est*
PV	*The Point of View*
SD	*The Sickness unto Death*
SW	*Stages on Life's Way: Studies by Various Persons*
TA	*Two Ages: The Age of Revolution and the Present Age: A Literary Review*
TC	*The Corsair Affair and Articles Related to the Writings*
TM	*The Moment and Late Writings*
UD	*Upbuilding Discourses in Various Spirits*
WA	*Without Authority: The Lily in the Field and the Birds of the Air*
WL	*Works of Love: Some Christian Reflections in the Form of Discourses* (1962)
WL [revised]	*Works of Love* (1995)

Friedrich Nietzsche

BG	*Beyond Good and Evil: Prelude to a Philosophy of the Future*
BT	*The Birth of Tragedy: Out of the Spirit of Music*
EH	*Ecce Homo: How One Becomes What One Is*
GM	*On the Genealogy of Morals: A Polemic*

GS	*The Gay Science: With a Prelude in Rhymes and an Appendix in Songs*
HA	*Human, All Too Human*
NR	*A Nietzsche Reader*
TI	*Twilight of the Idols/The Antichrist*
UM	*Untimely Meditations*
WP	*The Will to Power*
Z	*Thus Spoke Zarathustra: A Book for Everyone and No One*

Original dates are given in square brackets for journal and notebook entries. All emphases are the writer's own.

Chapter 1

Introduction: The Problem with Power

Is Power "Unchristian"?

Throughout the twentieth century, humankind has been preoccupied with the notion of power.[1] In the wake of philosophers such as Friedrich Nietzsche and Michel Foucault, this theme has spanned the conceptual "divide" between modernism and postmodernism, and has increasingly dominated such diverse academic fields as philosophy, economics, political science, English literature, anthropology, international relations, and the social sciences. Within the field of Christian theology, much attention has focused on power and its various manifestations within the world in general and the Church in particular. This emphasis has often been spearheaded by feminist, liberation, two-thirds world, and other theologians belonging to groups who have been historically marginalized from mainstream Christian scholarship. Theological responses to power can be loosely categorized under two headings: those which accept existing definitions and structural manifestations of power—or at least leave them significantly unchanged—seeking inversions and/or inclusions within "the powers that be"; and those who reject existing modes of power in search of a better or "more Christian" approach.[2]

In the Stob Lectures of 1989–90, Christian philosopher Alvin Plantinga challenged his audience to reconsider the Christian/non-Christian bifurcation of reality as it pertained to the area of academics: "Is there really such a thing as Christian scholarship—or is there only scholarship *simpliciter*, which can be practiced by Christians and non-Christians, though perhaps practiced in a Christian and in a non-Christian way?"[3] Using Plantinga's poignant wording, the purpose of this book is to investigate whether there is such a thing as "Christian power"—or whether there is only "power *simpliciter*," which may be exercised employing

---

[1]   The *Routledge Encyclopaedia of Philosophy* defines "power" as "the capacity to produce or prevent change." Leslie Green, "Power," in Edward Craig (ed.), *Routledge Encyclopaedia of Philosophy* (10 vols, London: 1998), vol. 7, p. 610.

[2]   Many of the latter focus on "mutual enhancement" (Rosemary Radford Ruether, *Sexism and Godtalk: Towards a Feminist Theology* [London, 1989], p. 30) or "enabling" models of power (Elizabeth Schüssler Fiorenza, *Bread Not Stone: The Challenge of Feminist Biblical Interpretation* [Boston, 1984], p. 143). See the brief overview in Elizabeth A. Johnson, *She Who Is: The Mystery of God in Feminist Theological Discourse* (New York, 1992), p. 270.

[3]   Alvin Plantinga, *The Twin Pillars of Christian Scholarship* (Grand Rapids, 1990), p. 6.

Christian and non-Christian methods towards explicitly Christian and non-Christian goals. To this end, this study will compare the respective concepts of power of two prominent thinkers, both of whom lived on the margins of nineteenth-century Christendom and were largely overlooked by their contemporaries. Both men were responding, in part, to a common threat—the dissimulation of all personal power and individuality through Hegel's systematic banishment of particularity in the evolutionary self-actualization of Spirit.[4] And yet, although Friedrich Nietzsche attacked Christianity as one of the direst obstacles to personal freedom and power, Søren Kierkegaard regarded the Christian faith as the only true refuge for the sanctity and liberation of the individual.[5]

The Two Dialogue Partners

Nietzsche's thought has provided an integral contribution to modern discussions on the topic of power, a conversation which he arguably initiated.[6] However, I will attempt to establish that Kierkegaard, facing similar pressures of Christendom's conformism, widespread spiritual lethargy, growing populist movements, and intellectual ostracism,[7] has equal claim as an authority on power. Part of the reason why Kierkegaard is easily overlooked in this regard is due to the non-systematic nature of his expansive corpus. His concept of power is not consolidated in one or two books, but rather unfolds throughout his entire body of writings. Hence, a significant challenge involves reconstructing a holistic account of his concept of power. Although Kierkegaard never wrote a comprehensive treatise on power, his entire life and corpus were diffused with issues concerning its uses and abuses.

On the political front, in 1848, Denmark went to war with Prussia over two important duchies, and their eventual loss led to national and financial impoverishment.[8] That same year, under immense pressure from rising populist

---

[4]   Georg W.F. Hegel, *The Phenomenology of Mind*, trans. J.B. Baillie (2 vols, London, 1910), vol. 1, p. 371.

[5]   Comparisons between Nietzsche and Kierkegaard are not novel. Thomas H. Brobjer acknowledges more than thirty studies which "extensively" examine them together ("Notes and Discussions of Nietzsche's Knowledge of Kierkegaard," *Journal of the History of Philosophy*, 41/2 [2003], p. 252).

[6]   Michel Foucault, *Religion and Culture by Michel Foucault*, ed. Jeremy R. Carrette (Manchester, 1999), p. 96.

[7]   Accordingly, both men regarded their thought as ahead of its time and, therefore, misunderstood by their contemporaries. See *TM*, p. 101 and *UM*, p. xlv.

[8]   *CD*, p. xi. Merold Westphal argues persuasively that Kierkegaard's political perspective was not merely a response to 1848 but developed over the course of his writing career ("Kierkegaard's Politics," *Thought*, 55/218 [1980], p. 325). The tumultuous events of 1848 also exerted a monumental impact on four-year-old Nietzsche, whose father, Pastor Karl Ludwig Nietzsche, a staunch monarchist who named his son after King Friedrich

movements, King Frederick VII ended the traditional monarchy by inaugurating a constitutional monarchy. As a self-financed author[9] and monarchist,[10] Kierkegaard reeled from the impact of these momentous events.

On the cultural and intellectual front, Kierkegaard wrestled valiantly against the epistemological juggernaut of Hegelianism, an all-inclusive system which threatened to assimilate all forms of individual expression—including faith— within the bounds of reason. For Kierkegaard, this philosophical "blitzkrieg" constituted an "objection" against Christianity. Climacus disdainfully described this systematic violence as being "world-historically butchered, salted, and packed in a paragraph."[11] Although Kierkegaard was not opposed to logic or logical systems as such, he mounted a blistering offensive against those that presumed to encapsulate all of existence: "[A] *logical system can be given ... but a system of existence cannot be given.*"[12]

The political, economic, and philosophical "power surges" during this period were paralleled by similar upheavals within the Danish state church. Had he believed that unawareness of Christian truth was the main problem plaguing the nineteenth-century Protestant church, Kierkegaard would likely have prescribed widespread dissemination of Christian teachings. Instead, he believed that the real problem was not ignorance of the truth but an active rebellion against truth that was known to all. Subsequently, authority became a pivotal issue within Kierkegaard's polemical attack on the Danish church.[13] He regarded the institutional church's growing political power and subsequent loss of spiritual authority with increasing dismay, and bitterly opposed the squelching of personal risk-taking and sacrifice by the oppressive conformity of false communitarianism which blighted Western Europe.

Kierkegaard's familiarity with power dynamics on macroscopic levels was accompanied by tremendous conflict and confrontation on a personal level. In addition to the guilt and fear which his profoundly devout but melancholic

---

Wilhelm IV of Prussia, grew "extremely despondent" following the political upheavals and died the following year (Lou Salomé, *Nietzsche*, trans. and ed. Siegfried Mandel [Urbana and Chicago, 2001], p. xii.).

[9]   *PV*, p. 208 [1849]: "In a matter of months I was in the situation where tomorrow, perhaps, I would not own a thing but be literally in financial straits. It was a severe drain on me. My spirit reacted all the more strongly. I wrote more than ever, but more than ever like a dying man."

[10]   Kierkegaard once instructed King Christian VIII on the threat of communism and how to be a king. See JK, pp. 155–7 [1849].

[11]   *CUP*, vol. 1, p. 107.

[12]   Ibid., p. 109.

[13]   See Walter Hong's sizable list of references to authority within Kierkegaard's writing (*BA*, pp. viii–x).

father had indelibly imprinted upon his childhood,[14] Kierkegaard's aloofness, pride, and eccentricities made him an irresistible target in one of the earliest and most celebrated examples of character assassination by the media. By bravely confronting the tyranny of *The Corsair*, whose slanderous accusations were protected from legalities by anonymous journalism, Kierkegaard unleashed an unrelenting onslaught of written and illustrated caricatures against himself.[15] As Walter Hong observes, the attack was devastatingly effective due to the "power of an unprecedented kind of journalism in a small city of 125,000 and the uncommon sensitivity of the object of the personal attack."[16] By the time it was over, the media circus had inspired no fewer than three Scandinavian plays featuring buffoon-like characters named "Søren," and Kierkegaard could no longer walk the streets of his beloved city in peace—one of his favorite and most fruitful pastimes—without being heckled by the people or mobbed by flocks of mocking children.

Following the furor, his public feud and ostracism by the Danish church accelerated after the death of his former mentor, Bishop Jacob Peter Mynster. Kierkegaard's own death ended a sophisticated polemical counter-offensive that incorporated irony, pseudonymous authors, and vigorous intellectual scrutiny.[17] All this time, Kierkegaard struggled to reconcile his physical and psychological torments with his Christian faith in a loving God. Mustering all of his considerable energies, he grappled with the foundational paradox of Christianity, the Incarnation—the greatest display of divine power which the world has never seen—and the radical impact which occurs when the rationality of the "autonomous" individual experiences a "head-on collision" with this divine truth. When he finally succumbed to his weakened constitution in 1855, Kierkegaard died a publicly and privately battle-scarred man. On account of all of these factors, Kierkegaard was spectacularly well-acquainted with the uses and abuses of power, and offers an extremely valuable and vital contribution to the ongoing discussion.

---

[14]   Kierkegaard once mused, "As a child, I was rigorously and earnestly brought up in Christianity, insanely brought up, humanly speaking ..." (*PV*, p. 79). Bruce Kirmmse also describes a lifelong struggle between the "little brother" and the eldest brother, Peter ("'Out With It!': The Modern Breakthrough, Kierkegaard and Denmark," in Alastair Hannay and Gordon D. Marino [eds], *The Cambridge Companion to Kierkegaard* [Cambridge, 1998], p. 35).

[15]   Kierkegaard emphasized that his decision to oppose the rising media power of *The Corsair* was carefully calculated: "As for myself, I believe that I have specific qualifications for this. I am single, I have no wife to grieve ..." (*TC*, p. 174 [1846]).

[16]   Ibid, p. xxxi. Over the better part of a year, this shameless assault lambasted his imagined treatment of women, his physical posture (the capital-K-like crease in his back caused by a spinal injury he suffered as a child), his supposed "God-like" supremacy placing himself in the centre of the cosmos around which everything revolved, and even the length of his trousers.

[17]   He was primarily inspired by Socrates' intellectual dismemberment of the Sophists of his day.

Preliminary Considerations

Towards a Provisional Definition of Power

In Kierkegaard's seminal discourse, "Purity of Heart is to Will One Thing," power may be defined as "the ability to implement one's desires, protect one's interests, or attain one's ends."[18] As such, power includes intellectual, spiritual, emotional, and not merely physical means.[19] Nietzsche would apparently concur, though he would add that the drive or instinct to exert and extend one's power constitutes the foundation for all life and organic growth.[20] As such, all cultural endeavors, ethical or religious enterprises, societal institutions, and personal involvements are reflections of power. According to Nietzsche, power is autonomous, amoral, self-serving, and innovative. In an elegy to architecture as the purest aesthetic expression of power, he asserted,

> The highest feeling of power and security finds expression in that which possesses *grand style*. Power which no longer requires proving; which disdains to please; which is slow to answer; which is conscious of no witness around it; which lives oblivious of the existence of any opposition; which reposes in *itself*, fatalistic, a law among laws: *that* is what speaks of itself in the form of grand style.[21]

The ability to accomplish one's chosen task is juxtaposed by what might be provisionally labelled "authority": the ability or right to ascertain and evaluate the task which is to be accomplished. Kierkegaard employed the analogy of a carriage and driver: while the "horses" serve as the locus of power, the will serves as the "driver." Just as the driver can lose control by allowing the diverse elements of power to dissipate through lack of coordination,

> so also are we distressed to see the same thing happen to a human being. He does not lack power—a person never really does—but he mismanages himself. The person who is to be the master (it is, of course, he himself) ruins it; such a person works with perhaps scarcely a third of his power in the right place and with more than two-thirds of his power in the wrong place or against himself. Now he gives up working in order to begin to deliberate all over again, now he

---

[18] *UD*, p. 32.

[19] Nietzsche distinguished *Macht* as "power of higher quality and greater vitality" from *Kraft* ["physical force"] (Jacob Golomb, "Nietzsche on Authority," *Philosophy Today* 34/3 [1990], p. 244). For the word's "construction" overtones with *machen*, see Richard Schacht, *Nietzsche* (London, 1983), p. 225, and Jürgen Habermas, *The Philosophical Discourse of Modernity*, trans. Frederick Lawrence (Cambridge, MA, 1987), p. 95.

[20] Nietzsche's view is somewhat amorphous, as reflected by passages where the will to power is one of several "grand affects." See, for example, *WP*, p. 62 [1887].

[21] *TI*, p. 85.

works instead of deliberating, now he pulls on the reins in the wrong way, now he wants to do both at the same time—and during all this he does not move from the spot.[22]

Hence, Kierkegaard concluded that power is powerless without the authority to harness and direct it properly.

Chapter Outline

It is a tantalizing mystery as to how well Nietzsche knew the writings of Kierkegaard, who died when Nietzsche was ten years old. R.J. Hollingdale contends that a diatribe against "afterworldsmen" in *Thus Spoke Zarathustra* contains several clues which suggest that Nietzsche was repudiating Kierkegaard's philosophy.[23] In a letter to Nietzsche dated 11 January 1888, Danish scholar Georg Brandes wrote: "There is a Nordic writer whose works would interest you. *Søren Kierkegaard*; he lived 1813–1855 and is in my view one of the most profound psychologists of all time ... ."[24] On 19 February, Nietzsche responded: "I have decided that during my next trip to Germany I want to study the psychological problem of Kierkegaard ..."; but, Walter Kaufmann adds, "[H]e never got around to reading Kierkegaard."[25] Consequently, any engagement between the two writers will necessarily be an imaginative reconstruction,[26] but one that will hopefully provide a fruitful cross-pollination on the topic of power while respecting and retaining the integrity of each man's original thought.

Because Nietzsche's concept of power is comparatively more formulated and familiar than Kierkegaard's, his position will be examined first in order to serve as a springboard and counterpoint to Kierkegaard's view. This order is also intended to highlight the extraordinary precision with which Kierkegaard anticipated and countered the latter's point of view. Chapters 2 and 3 will explore Nietzsche's concept of power within the broader context of his thought. Chapters 4 and 5 will reconstruct Kierkegaard's understanding of power from the multitudinous

---

[22]   *UD*, pp. 295–6.

[23]   Hollingdale argues that one statement in particular, "Weariness, which wants to reach the ultimate with a single leap, with a death-leap, a poor ignorant weariness, which no longer wants even to want: that created all gods and afterworlds" (*Z*, p. 59), strongly alludes to Kierkegaard, "who advocated a return to Christianity by means of a 'leap' from unbelief into belief" (ibid., p. 339, n. 6).

[24]   Georg Brandes, *Friedrich Nietzsche*, trans. A.G. Chater (London, 1914), p. 69.

[25]   *WP*, p. 53, n. 48. Brobjer, p. 253, lists six books which would have likely exposed Nietzsche to key tenets of Kierkegaard's thought.

[26]   In addition to shared similarities of historical and cultural context, this dialogue is partially informed by the attitudes both men displayed when interacting with the other's intellectual "kindred spirits": Kierkegaard's engagement with Feuerbach and the "free-thinkers," and Nietzsche's response to Pascal.

fragments and references which proliferate his corpus. Chapters 6 and 7 will then compare the two concepts of power. The final chapter will contain a brief summary of the strengths and weaknesses of both perspectives and articulate their relevance for contemporary discussion on issues of power. I contend that Kierkegaard's theory of power is more coherent and consistent than Nietzsche's position, which he foresaw and "forswore" with uncanny accuracy.

Methodological Limitations

Scope

In *The Gay Science*, Nietzsche exclaimed, "[T]here are truths that are singularly shy and ticklish and cannot be caught except suddenly—that must be *surprised* or left alone."[27] Both Nietzsche and Kierkegaard shared a remarkable sensitivity and child-like wonder towards the subtle complexities of existence. Subsequently, they employed a rich array of narrative strategies and techniques to portray its iridescent "flutterings" without impaling its intricate dynamics within the intellectual "display cases" of abstract thought. On account of their sophisticated analyses and creative formats, I will focus exclusively on primary sources, both published and unpublished during the writers' lifetimes. Although this strategy is intended to provide a holistic account of their concepts of power, this approach invites certain risks. Some scholars contend that the amorphous and fragmentary nature of Nietzsche's writing seriously jeopardizes any attempt to construct a coherent account of his cosmology or anthropology.[28] However, in a letter to his publishers in the mid-1880s, Nietzsche wrote: "I now need profound tranquility,

---

[27] *GS*, p. 345.

[28] See Karl Löwith, *From Hegel to Nietzsche: The Revolution in Nineteenth-Century Thought*, trans. David E. Green (London, 1965), p. 192, and Michael Tanner, *Nietzsche* (Oxford, 1994), pp. 4, 64. Nevertheless, Tanner posits that it is possible to trace "the underlying unity of his concerns" (ibid., p. 8). There is widespread disagreement on the degree to which Nietzsche's perspective shifted during his life. Maudemarie Clark contends that motifs such as "will to power," eternal recurrence, and the *Übermensch* were downplayed and/ or abandoned towards the end of his career ("Nietzsche, Friedrich," in Edward Craig (ed.), *Routledge Encyclopaedia of Philosophy* [10 vols, London, 1998], vol. 6 , pp. 856–9). By contrast, Maurice Mandelbaum argues that "there was a considerable degree of unity in Nietzsche's thought" (*History, Man & Reason: A Study in Nineteenth-Century Thought* [Baltimore and London, 1974], p. 338), while Karl Löweth compliments Nietzsche's former companion, Lou Salomé, for observing "clearly worked out lines of a 'system'" in his thought (p. xi). See also Stephen Houlgate, *Hegel, Nietzsche and the Criticism of Metaphysics* (Cambridge, 1986), pp. 38, 54, and Nicholas Davey, "Nietzsche, Friedrich," in Stuart Brown, Diané Collinson and Robert Wilkinson (eds), *One Hundred Twentieth-Century Philosophers* (London, 1998), p. 142.

for many, many years to come, because I am facing the elaboration of my entire system of thought ... ."[29]

Kaufmann warns of the editorial tampering which transpired when Nietzsche's notebooks were published by his anti-Semitic sister, Elisabeth Forster-Nietzsche.[30] However, rather than abandon the *Nachlass* altogether, Kaufmann cogently suggests that they can offer great insights by allowing glimpses into "the workshop of a great thinker."[31]

The situation with Kierkegaard is complicated on account of the rather contested relation between his pseudonymous writings and his signed works. He famously forbade readers from attributing pseudonymous quotations to himself.[32] Furthermore, scholars have argued that his use of irony and hyperbolic polemics similarly frustrate any attempts to elucidate his "true" position on a given topic.[33] However, Kierkegaard regarded his authorship as a coherent whole under the direction of "religious" concerns, and was careful to maintain a balance between pseudonymous publications and "directly" authored works.[34] He once predicted

---

[29]   Rüdiger Safranski, *Nietzsche: A Philosophical Biography*, trans. Shelly Frisch (New York, 2003), p. 158. As late as 24 March 1887, Nietzsche felt compelled "to build up a coherent structure of thought over the next few years" (ibid., p. 284). Houlgate states that although Nietzsche "cannot develop an ontology," he "sketches a hypothetical ontology using the scientific notion of force (*Kraft*) and the analogy of human will" (*Hegel, Nietzsche and the Criticism of Metaphysics*, p. 60). John Richardson, however, insists that Nietzsche retains all of the categories and structures integral to an ontology (*Nietzsche's System* [New York and Oxford, 1996], p. 65). On Nietzsche's "essentialism" and "foundationalism," see Stephen Houlgate, "Power, Egoism and the 'Open' Self in Nietzsche and Hegel," *Journal of the British Society for Phenomenology* 22/3 (1991), p. 123. On his "metaphysics of conflict, see Ian Burkitt, "Overcoming Metaphysics: Elias and Foucault on Power and Freedom," *Philosophy of the Social Sciences*, 23/1 (1993), p. 63, and Keith Ansell-Pearson, *An Introduction to Nietzsche as Political Thinker* (Cambridge, 1997), p. 161.

[30]   For a useful synopsis, see *WP*, pp. xiii–xv. Tanner, p. 5, states that these "undeveloped" thoughts allow unscrupulous interpreters to project their own thoughts into his writing.

[31]   *WP*, p. xvi. See also Clark, p. 848.

[32]   *FS*, pp. 240–41 [1851]; *CUP*, vol. 1, p. 625; *TC*, p. 5.

[33]   For example, Roger Poole criticizes a "blunt reading" which reduces Kierkegaard to didactic, propositional truth-statements and downplays the ironic, dialectical, and playful dimensions of his writing ("The Unknown Kierkegaard: Twentieth-Century Receptions," in Alastair Hannay and Gordon D. Marino (eds), *The Cambridge Companion to Kierkegaard* (Cambridge, 1998), pp. 60–61).

[34]   *FS*, p. ix, *PV*, pp. 6–7, 30; *CD*, p. 415 [1848]. Kierkegaard, however, admitted that he did not possess this comprehensive understanding of his authorship at the time of writing the early pseudonymous works (*CUP*, vol. 2, pp. 166–7 [1850]). Patrick Gardiner doubts whether his initial purposes for writing were as straightforward as purported in his overview (*Kierkegaard: A Very Short Introduction* [Oxford, 2002], p. 43). For a contrasting view, see Michael Plekon, "Kierkegaard the Theologian: The Roots of His Theology in *Works of Love*," in George B. Connell and C. Stephen Evans (eds), *Foundations of*

that there would be no completed analysis of his work during his lifetime, "for no one has sufficient faith in it, or time or competence to look for a comprehensive plan in the entire production."[35] Though the pseudonyms personify perspectives which Kierkegaard did not personally endorse, Murray Rae advises, "[W]e should not assume that there is nothing in the pseudonymous works to which Kierkegaard himself might consent."[36] In response to the aforementioned scholarly concerns, I will endeavor to support unpublished or pseudonymous statements with citations from published or signed works when possible, in order to emphasize the continuity of thought in each man's corpus.[37] Moreover, this approach respects both writers' expressed desire to sentence their readers to hermeneutical "hard labour" and invite them to participate in rigorous engagement with their texts.[38]

Finally, it is important to reiterate that I will be concentrating primarily upon the writings of Nietzsche and Kierkegaard themselves. This study in no way purports to undertake a comprehensive overview of the staggering plethora of secondary material on these vastly popular thinkers.[39] Rather, it is a concerted attempt to crystallize the core concepts behind their respective understanding of power and contrast their strengths and weaknesses via a creative dialogue between the two

---

Kierkegaard's Vision of Community: Religion, Ethics, and Politics in Kierkegaard (New Jersey and London, 1992), p. 3, and Carl Pletsch, "The Self-Sufficient Text in Nietzsche and Kierkegaard," *Yale French Studies*, 66 (1984), p. 169.

[35]   *BA*, pp. 323–4 [19 February 1849].

[36]   Murray Rae, *Kierkegaard's Vision of the Incarnation: By Faith Transformed* (Oxford, 1997), p. x. See also C. Stephen Evans, *Kierkegaard's "Fragments" and "Postscript": The Religious Philosophy of Johannes Climacus* (New Jersey, 1983), p. 7. Gardiner contends that pseudonymous books where he appears as editor "expressed views that were basically his own" (p. 240).

[37]   Quotations will typically be ascribed to the pseudonyms themselves. In light of his importance to the present topic, a brief clarification is necessary for the pseudonym H.H., "author" of "Two Ethical-Religious Essays," which Kierkegaard was reluctant to include within his "authentic" canon (*WA*, p. xv). Kierkegaard explained that his reluctance stemmed not from fundamental disagreement with H.H's perspective, but through misgivings that readers may misinterpret him to be presenting himself as an "apostle" rather than a "genius" (ibid., pp. 237–40 [1849]). Kierkegaard wrote of H.H.: "He rightly understood and explained perhaps the most important ethical-religious concept: authority" (Stephen N. Dunning, "Who Sets the Task? Kierkegaard on Authority," in George B. Connell and C. Stephen Evans [eds], *Foundations of Kierkegaard's Vision of Community: Religion, Ethics, and Politics in Kierkegaard* [New Jersey and London, 1992] p. 19).

[38]   One of Kierkegaard's favourite images for the truth-seeker was that of a relentless detective pursuing his quarry. See *TM*, p. 130; *CUP*, vol. 1, p. 239; *TA*, p. 80; *SW*, p. 311. For the hermeneutical demands which Nietzsche's aphorisms place upon readers, see *Z*, p. 67 and *GM*, p. 10.

[39]   Tanner claims of Nietzsche that "more books appear on him each year than on any other thinker" (p. 2).

perspectives. This endeavor will hopefully illuminate issues of authority within contemporary debate and enhance our theological understanding of power.

Structure

In light of the rich complexities and organic nature of the thought-worlds of two tried and tested anti-systematicians such as Nietzsche and Kierkegaard,[40] it is impossible to impose a systematic framework without accusations of theoretical violence and arbitrary dissection. For the purposes of analysis, I have adopted a three-tiered structure. The cosmological tier will address the overall workings of the universe at large, according to each man. In the anthropological tier, the focus will then concentrate more specifically on how humankind fits within this broader context. Finally, each man's concept of power will be further examined in the tier of authority.

The inadequacies of this model are readily apparent, since certain articulations on the nature of power—such as Nietzsche's principle of universal conflict, or Kierkegaard's account of the Incarnation—could easily be included under all three categories. However, the purpose of this structure is two-fold: first, to underscore the importance of situating their statements on power within the broader context of their (a)theological world views in order to gain a deeper understanding of the subtleties and elegance of their thinking; second, to illustrate how vitally the topic of power resonates within their corpora at all levels. Due to the organic, almost nodal nature of their thought-worlds, the investigation will often proceed in a spiralling rather than strictly linear progression in an attempt to preserve the reticular interconnectedness of their concepts with a minimum of repetition.[41] The three-fold structure will hopefully admit greater insights than impediments into comprehending the writings of these two extraordinary thinkers.

---

[40]   Compare *CUP*, vol. 1, p. 107, cited above, with *TI*, p. 35: "I mistrust all systematizers and avoid them. The will to a system is a lack of integrity."

[41]   Although, given the predominance of repetition/recurrence in their thinking, this may be somewhat apropos.

Chapter 2

For the Taking:
Nietzsche's View of the Universe

The Cosmological Tier

Nietzsche's "Natural" Monism[1]

The theme of power resonates throughout the entirety of Nietzsche's thought and attains key prominence in the articulation of his cosmology. One fundamental tenet of Nietzsche's view of the universe is literally, "What you see is what you get": the natural universe in all of its wondrous beauty is all there is to behold and be held. Like the ancient Greeks, Nietzsche cherished an attitude of reverent wonder towards the natural world:

> But to stand in the midst of this *rerum concordia discors* [the discordant harmony
> of circumstances] and of this whole marvellous uncertainty and rich ambiguity
> of existence *without questioning*, without trembling with the craving and the
> rapture of such questioning, without at least hating the person who questions,
> perhaps even finding him faintly amusing—that is what I feel to be *contemptible*,
> and this is the feeling for which I look first in everybody.[2]

However, Nietzsche vociferously denied the existence of any divine creator, higher metaphysical reality, or implicit structure in the universe—whether moral or otherwise—because "nature is always value-less."[3] He insisted, "There are no moral phenomena at all, only a moral interpretation of phenomena ... ."[4] Truth itself is a human construct, a "necessary lie" which enables humans to project their own standards of order upon an essentially amoral universe, an equally enchanting yet foreboding environment which remains majestically indifferent to

---

[1]   Stephen Houlgate observes that Nietzsche rejects monism in so far as it posits a "comprehensive unity" [*übergreifende Einheit*], but espouses it as an expression of the "wholeness" of the universe. See *Hegel, Nietzsche and the Criticism of Metaphysics* (Cambridge, 1986), p. 42.

[2]   *GS*, pp. 76–7.

[3]   Ibid., p. 242. See also *HA*, p. 16. For the development of Nietzsche's naturalism, see Maudemarie Clark, "Nietzsche, Friedrich," in Edward Craig (ed.), *Routledge Encyclopaedia of Philosophy* (10 vols, London, 1998), vol. 6, p. 847.

[4]   *BG*, p. 96.

human existence: "Think of a being such as nature is, prodigal beyond measure, indifferent beyond measure, without aims or intentions, without mercy or justice, at once fruitful and barren and uncertain … ."[5] *Homo sapiens* thus becomes "*homo hermeneuticus.*"[6] Furthermore, Nietzsche deprivileged humankind as the pinnacle of this monistic universe by denying any preferential gazes from "the cruel and desolate face of nature":[7]

> Man is absolutely not the crown of creation: every creature stands beside him at the same stage of perfection … . And even in asserting that we assert too much: man is, relatively speaking, the most unsuccessful animal, the sickliest, the one most dangerously strayed from its instincts—with all that, to be sure, the most *interesting*![8]

Against a world devoid of providential guidance or teleological direction, human culture in general and philosophy in particular launch their brave formulations, striving to bind nature to will: "[P]hilosophy is this tyrannical drive itself, the most spiritual will to power, to 'creation of the world,' to *causa prima*."[9] Notions of metaphysics and "truth" represent previous human attempts to gain mastery, all of which must be constantly challenged and overcome in order to expand human potential. In a very real sense, cosmology must elide into anthropology according to Nietzsche:

> [T]hat every elevation of man brings with it the overcoming of narrower interpretations; that every strengthening and increase of power opens up new perspectives and means believing in new horizons—this idea permeates my writings. The world with which we are concerned is false, i.e., is not a fact but a fable and approximation on the basis of a meager sum of observations; it is "in flux," as something in a state of becoming, as a falsehood always changing but never getting near the truth: for—there is no "truth."[10]

Even science falls under Nietzsche's censure of objectivity:

---

[5]   Ibid., p. 39.

[6]   Karen L. Carr, "Nietzsche on Nihilism and the Crisis of Interpretation," *Soundings*, 73/1 (1990): p. 87.

[7]   *UM*, p. 149.

[8]   *TI*, p. 136. See also *WP*, p. 169 [1888]: "[M]an a little, eccentric species of animal, which—fortunately—has its day … something of no importance to the general character of the earth … ." Nietzsche did not, however, want to denigrate humankind to mere animal status, since humans alone seek to perfect the species by "conscious willing" (*UM*, p. 164).

[9]   *BG*, p. 39.

[10]   *WP*, p. 330 [1885–86].

We operate only with things that do not exist: lines, planes, bodies, atoms, divisible time spans, divisible spaces. How should explanations be at all possible when we first turn everything into an *image*, our image! It will do to consider science as an attempt to humanize things as faithfully as possible ... .[11]

He once contested that belief in a rationally constructed, coherent universe brings the scientist uncomfortably close to the role of "shaman," since "[t]he thinking of men who believe in magic and miracles is bent on *imposing a law on nature* ... ."[12] Subsequently, he advised, "Let us beware of saying that there are laws in nature. There are only necessities: there is nobody who commands, nobody who obeys, nobody who trespasses."[13]

Such a cosmos constitutes a realm of terror and uncertainty for the weak, but a veritable playground for the "gods."[14] God himself, however, remains a chimerical projection, whose death is famously announced in Nietzsche's "Parable of the Madman": "God is dead. God remains dead. And we have killed him."[15] By this, he meant that the idea of God is becoming no longer tenable, though this radical notion is only just "beginning to cast its first shadows over Europe."[16] Although Nietzsche praised the Greek and Roman pantheons as reflections of "healthy" human self-confidence and self-projection,[17] he vehemently attacked the nonsensical banalities of the Christian God, who supersedes and simultaneously devalues the material world, and denigrates humankind's natural powers:

> A god who conceives children with a mortal woman; a wise man who calls upon us to work no more, to judge no more, but to heed the signs of the imminent apocalypse; a justice that accepts the innocent man as a proxy sacrifice; someone who has his disciple drink his blood; prayers for miraculous interventions; sins against a god, atoned for by a god; fear of the afterlife, to which death is the gate; the figure of the cross as a symbol, in a time that no longer knows the purpose and shame of the cross—how horridly all this wafts over us, as from the grave of the ancient past! Are we to believe that such things are still believed?[18]

---

[11] *GS*, pp. 172–3. For the "arbitrary" nature of alleged causality, see ibid., p. 210; *HA*, p. 22.

[12] Ibid., p. 82.

[13] *GS*, p. 168. Nietzsche employed the notion of "necessity" with extreme caution to avoid implying an implicit imperative within nature. See *WP*, pp. 229–300 [1887].

[14] For Nietzsche's rejection of a correspondence theory of truth in favor of epistemological courage, see Maurice Mandelbaum, *History, Man & Reason: A Study in Nineteenth-Century Thought* (Baltimore and London, 1974), p. 341.

[15] *GS*, p. 181. See also *HA*, p. 4.

[16] *GS*, p. 279.

[17] *HA*, p. 85; *GS*, p. 195.

[18] *HA*, pp. 84–5. See also *EH*, p. 21: "God is a crude answer, a piece of indelicacy against us thinkers— fundamentally even a crude *prohibition* to us: you shall not think!"

In contrast to the chaotic vitality of the Greek gods, "these magnificent child-minds with the courage of lions,"[19] Nietzsche deplored a God who ruled over every jot and tittle of the universe— "some spider of finality and morality which is supposed to exist behind the great net and web of causality"—[20] and paradoxically pandered to the slavish whims of the plebeian masses. "What sets *us* apart is not that we recognize no God, either in history or in nature or behind nature—but that we find that which has been reverenced as God not 'godlike' but pitiable, absurd, harmful, not merely an error but a *crime against life* … ."[21] In place of a disembodied "spiritualized God," reflecting humanity's vain attempts to devalue the "evil" world of nature, Nietzsche lauded the anthropomorphized deities which were forged by "the Greeks of the strongest epoch, who were not afraid of themselves but rejoiced in themselves, brought their gods close to all their own affects—."[22] Although the idea of "God" as a self-celebration of "master" values would prove useful to his philosophical project, Nietzsche possessed no personal belief in a transcendent deity. Hence, in his "autobibliography," *Ecce Homo*, Nietzsche wrote: "I have absolutely no knowledge of atheism as an outcome of reasoning, still less as an event: with me it is obvious by instinct."[23]

Space: Nature's Telos

In place of belief in a fictitious deity, Nietzsche advocated an ecstatic embrace of the natural world in its entirety. This closed universe does not possess "laws," "principles," "purposes," or other value-laden "facts" as such. He countered:

> This entire teleology is predicated on the ability to speak about man of the last four thousand years as if he were eternal, the natural direction of all things in the world from the beginning. But everything has evolved; there are *no eternal facts*, nor are there any absolute truths. Thus *historical philosophizing* is necessary henceforth, and the virtue of modesty as well.[24]

Humankind must, therefore, become accustomed to the role of a "wanderer" who delights in "change and transitoriness," instead of "a traveller *towards* a final goal, for this does not exist."[25] According to Nietzsche, no element in the natural universe is stable or static in itself: everything is in a perpetual state of flux—changing,

---

[19]   *GM*, p. 74.

[20]   Ibid., p. 92.

[21]   *TI*, pp. 174–5.

[22]   *WP*, p. 308 [1888].

[23]   *EH*, p. 21.

[24]   *HA*, pp. 14–15.

[25]   Ibid., p. 266. For the fecund suggestion of Nietzsche's epistemological "homelessness," see Lou Salomé, *Nietzsche*, trans. and ed. Siegfried Mandel (Urbana and Chicago, 2001), p. 15.

growing, destroying or being destroyed.[26] And so it should be, he exclaimed, once a person grasped the "Dionysian" truth that the natural order is in constant spin, producing astonishing new configurations and then indifferently smashing them into atoms while engendering an infinite array of alternatives. Humans are merely swept up in the *"bellum omnium contra omnes"*—"the war of all against all."[27] Unlike classical notions of fate, which accepted such cosmic "cruelty" with an air of noble resignation or tragedy, Nietzsche regarded this "reality" as a cause for celebration—"the will of life rejoicing in its own inexhaustibility through the *sacrifice* of its highest types."[28] The strange vicissitudes and variances recorded by human history reinforce that humankind is simply a product of nature:

> But the strange fact is that all there is or has been on earth of freedom, subtlety, boldness, dance and masterly certainty, whether in thinking, or in ruling, or in speaking and persuasion, in the arts as in morals, has evolved only by virtue of the "tyranny of such arbitrary laws"; and, in all seriousness, there is no small probability that precisely this is "nature" and "natural … ."[29]

However, Nietzsche did not banish all traces of teleology from his world view— merely those teleologies which contradicted the observably "natural" universe.[30] In a notebook entry, he once stated that an accurate theory must account for the universe in its entirety: "In order to understand what 'life' is, what kind of striving and tension life is, the formula must apply as well to trees and plants as to animals."[31] The German philosopher fervently argued that the will to power, the intractable desire to expand one's boundaries against the holdings of all others, constitutes the necessary foundation of life: "[L]ife itself is *essentially* appropriation, injury, overpowering of the strange and weaker, suppression, severity, imposition of one's own forms, incorporation and, at the least and mildest, exploitation … ."[32] Nietzsche carefully qualified the amorality of this "exploitation": "'Exploitation' does not pertain to a corrupt or imperfect or primitive society: it pertains to the

---

[26] Nietzsche was influenced by Heraclitus in these matters (*UM*, p. 242). For a summary of Nietzsche's views on the pre-Socratics, see Tracy B. Strong, *Friedrich Nietzsche and the Politics of Transfiguration* (Berkeley, Los Angeles and London, 1975), pp. 152–61.

[27] *UM*, p. 30. See also ibid., p. 214.

[28] *EH*, p. 50. See also *BG*, p. 99: "A people is a detour of nature to get to six or seven great men.— Yes: and then to get round them."

[29] Ibid., pp. 110–11.

[30] See Philip J. Kain, "Nietzschean Genealogy and Hegelian History in *The Genealogy of Morals*," *Canadian Journal of Philosophy* 26/1 (1996): 136.

[31] *WP*, p. 374 [1887–88].

[32] *BG*, p. 194.

essence of the living thing as a fundamental organic function, it is a consequence of the intrinsic will to power which is precisely the will to life."[33]

By identifying life with the will to power, Nietzsche regarded all forms of moral and religious restraints as provisional blockages of the grand universal "drive"which encompasses everything from bacteria to baccalaureates:

> To talk of right and wrong *as such* is senseless; *in themselves*, injury, violation, exploitation, and destruction can of course be nothing "wrong," in so far as life operates *essentially*—that is, in terms of its basic functions—through injury, violation, exploitation, and destruction, and cannot be conceived in any other way. One is forced to admit something even more disturbing: that, from the highest biological point of view, legal conditions may be nothing more than *exceptional states of emergency*, partial restrictions which the will to life in its quest for power provisionally imposes on itself in order to serve its overall goal: the creation of *larger* units of power.[34]

Furthermore, he strongly disagreed with Darwin's "erroneous" presupposition concerning the primary instinct of biological life: "Physiologists should think again before postulating the drive to self-preservation as the cardinal drive in an organic being. A living thing desires above all to *vent* its strength—life as such is will to power—: self-preservation is only one of the indirect and most frequent *consequences* of it."[35]

---

[33]   Ibid. Houlgate writes, "[T]here is overwhelming evidence that Nietzsche rejected the idea that will to power constitutes a unified monistic principle," maintaining that such a formulation would reek of metaphysics and veer towards Hegel's unholy *Geist*. Thus, he regards it as "an anthropomorphic metaphor for what Nietzsche calls the 'pathos' within existing forces" (*Hegel, Nietzsche and the Criticism of Metaphysics*, p. 66). See also Walter Kaufmann, *Nietzsche: Philosopher, Psychologist, Antichrist*, 4th edn (Princeton, 1974), p. 420. Most scholars devote major sections to the "pivotal notion" of will to power (Jacob Golomb, "Nietzsche on Authority," *Philosophy Today*, 34/3 [1990]: 244). See also Ian Burkitt, "Overcoming Metaphysics: Elias and Foucault on Power and Freedom," *Philosophy of the Social Sciences*, 23/1 (1993): 65, and Rüdiger Safranski, *Nietzsche: A Philosophical Biography*, trans. Shelly Frisch (New York, 2003), p. 185: "The ominous 'will to power' ... builds up to a cosmic explanation and directive of grand-scale politics in Nietzsche's later years." According to Richard Schacht, Nietzsche developed the will to power as a means to avoid agency while explaining "the tendency to organization" in the natural world as "some characteristic rooted in the specific nature of force itself" (*Nietzsche* [London, 1983], p. 212). For a contrary view, see Clark, pp. 857–8. Despite its metaphysical "baggage," the word "will" arguably served Nietzsche's purposes for inspiring human efforts towards greatness while simultaneously relegating metaphysical objections to the fundamentally "egoistical" nature of all living forces (Houlgate, *Hegel, Nietzsche and the Criticism of Metaphysics*, p. 67) through use of a pivotal and familiar term.

[34]   *GM*, pp. 56–7.

[35]   *BG*, p. 44. See also *Z*, p. 138: "[L]ife sacrifices itself—for the sake of power!"

According to Nietzsche, his comprehensive theory of power possesses an unparalleled explanatory scope which can even explain natural life on the cellular level: "Is it virtuous when a cell transforms itself into a function of a stronger cell? It has no alternative. And is it evil when the stronger cell assimilates the weaker? It also has no alternative; it follows necessity, for it strives for superabundant substitutes and wants to regenerate itself."[36] As "[t]he most universal and basic instinct in all doing and willing," Nietzsche explained that the will to power has gone largely unnoticed by theorists "because *in praxi* we always follow its commandments, because we *are* this commandment."[37]

Time: Eternal Recurrence

Although he intended to write a book on eternal recurrence, Nietzsche never completely formulated this concept.[38] One notebook entry illuminates how the tenet flowed naturally from his belief in a universe devoid of metaphysical telos:

> If the world had a goal, it must have been reached. If there were for it some unintended final state, this also must have been reached. If it were in any way capable of a pausing and becoming fixed, of "being," if in the whole course of its becoming it possessed even for a moment this capability of "being," then all becoming would long since have come to an end, along with all thinking, all spirit. The fact of "spirit" as a form of becoming proves that the world has no goal, no final state, and is incapable of being.[39]

The concept of eternal recurrence was first introduced as part of the essential "psychosophical" makeup of the "preparatory" human being who provides the foundation for the *Übermensch*: "[T]here is no longer any reason in what happens, no love in what will happen to you; no resting place is open any longer to your heart, where it only needs to find and no longer to seek; you resist any ultimate peace; you will the eternal recurrence of war and peace ... ."[40] In *Thus Spoke*

---

[36] *GS*, pp. 175–6. See also *WP*, p. 345 [1885–86]; ibid., p. 403 [1882].

[37] Ibid., p. 356 [1887–88].

[38] For a planned outline, see ibid., p. 544 [1883–88].

[39] Ibid., p. 546 [1885].

[40] *GS*, p. 230. This later becomes a curse uttered by a demon (ibid., 273). The idea is not original to Nietzsche. Parallels include the Pythagorean notion that terrestrial events recur when celestial configurations are repeated (*UM*, p. 70), Schopenhauer, the myth of Dionysus, the natural science of Julius Robert Mayer (Safranski, pp. 223–5) and poet Heinrich Heine: "Now, however long a time may pass, according to the eternal laws governing the combinations of this eternal play of repetition, all configurations that have previously existed on this earth must yet meet, attract, repulse, kiss, and corrupt each other again ... ." (cited in *GS*, p. 16).

Zarathustra, existence is portrayed as an indestructible, perpetually inverted "hourglass":

> But the complex of causes in which I am entangled will recur—it will create me again! I myself am part of these causes of the eternal recurrence. I shall return, with this sun, with this earth, with this eagle, with this serpent—*not* to a new life or a better life or a similar life: I shall return eternally to this identical and self-same life, in the greatest things and the smallest, to teach once more the eternal recurrence of all things, to speak once more the teaching of the great noontide of earth and man, to tell man of the Superman once more.[41]

It is a dizzying piece of logic to conceive of someone who is "the first" to proclaim the infinite repetition of existence! Maudemarie Clark posits that eternal recurrence should be considered as a hermeneutical ideal or "philosophical test case" for evaluating the vitality of new values, as opposed to a cosmological statement.[42] However, Nietzsche's erstwhile companion and commentator Lou Salomé maintains, "[I]n fact, Nietzsche's logic, ethics, and aesthetics must be regarded as building blocks for his teaching of the eternal recurrence."[43] It is important to situate the doctrine of eternal recurrence within Nietzsche's enthusiasm to embrace unconditionally all of life in its entirety: "To me ... everything seems far too valuable to be so fleeting: I seek an eternity for everything: ought one to pour the most precious salves and wines into the sea?—My consolation is that everything that has been is eternal: the sea will cast it up again."[44] The emphases on "anti-telos" and unconditional embrace are united in the figure of "the suprahistorical man, who sees no salvation in the process and for whom, rather, the world is complete and reaches its finality at each and every moment."[45]

Because all events are inextricably interconnected, Nietzsche argued that a person cannot nullify any "negative" without negating all of existence. Hence, Zarathustra proclaimed, "All things are chained and entwined together, all things are in love; if ever you wanted one moment twice, if ever you said, 'You please me, happiness, instant, moment!' then you wanted *everything* to return!"[46] While "lower" individuals shun suffering and loss, the "higher-minded" comprehend that

---

[41]   *Z*, pp. 237–8.

[42]   Clark, pp. 858–9. Michael Tanner contends that Nietzsche's musings on the topic are too obtuse to form a comprehensive cosmological theory (*Nietzsche* [Oxford, 1994], p. 53), while Kaufmann argues that it is "less an idea than an experience," a state of "arrival" wherein man "gives meaning to his own life by achieving perfection and exulting in the moment" (*Nietzsche: Philosopher, Psychologist, Antichrist*, pp. 323–4).

[43]   Salomé, p. 129.

[44]   *WP*, p. 548 [1887–88].

[45]   *UM*, p. 66.

[46]   *Z*, p. 332.

"[a]ll joy wants the eternity of all things … ."[47] Contrary to the "life-deprecating" tenets of Christianity or Stoicism, Nietzsche declared,

> My formula for greatness in a human being is *amor fati*: that one wants nothing to be other than it is, not in the future, not in the past, not in all eternity. Not merely to endure that which happens of necessity, still less to dissemble it—all idealism is untruthfulness in the face of necessity—but to *love* it … .[48]

In theory, eternal recurrence allowed Nietzsche to relish the kaleidoscope of variations in existence without resorting to a stultifying teleology which negates variables deemed "unnecessary" or "undesirable." Hence, he compared the joyous "strains" of existence to a "music box" that "repeats eternally its tune which may never be called a melody."[49]

The Anthropological Tier

In a letter written on 25 October 1874, Nietzsche expressed his desire to comprehend "the whole highly complex system of antagonisms that make up the 'modern world.'"[50] He once explained his major thrust as follows: "My task is the dehumanization of nature and then the naturalization of humanity once it has attained the pure concept of 'nature' … ."[51] Having outlined Nietzsche's understanding of the universe in broad strokes, it is necessary to focus more specifically upon how humankind responds to its decidedly decentred position in the cosmos.

Epistemology as Power

Reality under construction
One of Nietzsche's primary principles is the notion that "notion" itself is not based upon external "truth" but rather stems from the socio-political and psychological needs and desires of the truth-sayer.[52] Because humankind inhabits a world of hostile indifference devoid of a universal Caretaker, cultures and civilizations strive for mastery by remaking the world in their own imagery:

> That which we now call the world is the result of a number of errors and fantasies, which came about gradually in the overall development of organic beings, fusing

---

47 Ibid.
48 *EH*, pp. 37–8.
49 *GS*, p. 168.
50 Cited in Safranski, p. 156.
51 Ibid., p. 227.
52 *BG*, p. 39; *Z*, p. 136; *WP*, p. 267 [1883–88].

with one another, and now handed down to us as a collected treasure of our entire past—a treasure: for the *value* of our humanity rests upon it.[53]

Nietzsche contended that, despite their variety and contradictions with one another, the diverse systems of thought, metaphysics, and morality are united in their self-presumed "goodness": "Socrates and Plato are right: whatever man does, he always acts for the good; that is, in a way that seems to him good (useful) according to the degree of his intellect, the prevailing measure of his rationality."[54] However, rather than sinking into a despairing agnosticism over epistemological relativism, by classifying the will to truth as will to power[55] Nietzsche possessed a universal standard by which to measure all human "truths": a precept is good, "natural" and therefore "healthy" to the extent that it expresses or augments one's degree of power—primarily by liberating specific instincts—and embraces life in the material world.

> Every philosophy that ranks peace above war, every ethic with a negative definition of happiness, every metaphysics and physics that knows some *finale*, some final state of some sort, every predominantly aesthetic or religious craving for some Apart, Beyond, Outside, Above, permits the question whether it was not sickness that inspired the philosopher. The unconscious disguise of physiological needs under the cloaks of the objective, ideal, purely spiritual goes to frightening lengths ... .[56]

In *The Gay Science*, Nietzsche observed, "Gradually, man has become a fantastic animal that has to fulfill one more condition of existence than any other animal: man *has to* believe, to know, from time to time *why* he exists; his race cannot flourish without a periodic trust in life—without faith in *reason in life*."[57] Furthermore, he advised humanity to renounce its "childish ways" and shed any cognitive "exoskeletons" which formerly protected life but now constrict it:

---

[53] *HA*, p. 24.

[54] Ibid., p. 71.

[55] Nietzsche cautiously approved of will to truth "[o]nly insofar as the truthful man possesses the unconditional will to justice ... whereas in the eyes of less clear-sighted men a whole host of the most various drives—curiosity, flight from boredom, envy, vanity, the desire for amusement, for example—can be involved in the striving for truth ..." (*UM*, pp. 88–9). As John Richardson thoroughly points out, Nietzsche's life work as a philosopher reflects his personal endorsement of the will to truth (*Nietzsche's System* [New York and Oxford: 1996], pp. 220–31).

[56] *GS*, p. 34. See also *HA*, p. 213. For genuine "truth" as "life-enhancing," see *UM*, p. 71.

[57] *GS*, p. 75.

But perhaps this error [repressing vital instincts] was as necessary for you then, when you were still a different person—you are always a different person—as are all your present "truths," being a skin, as it were, that concealed and covered a great deal that you were not yet permitted to see. What killed that opinion for you was your new life and not your reason: *you no longer need it*, and now it collapses and unreason crawls out of it into the light like a worm.[58]

For Nietzsche, the problem of epistemology is simply the over-vaunted, untenable position of "truth" itself, which plagues scientists and salvationists alike: "the same overestimation of the truth (more accurately: the same belief that the truth is *above* evaluation and criticism)."[59] Subsequently, Nietzsche unleashed his "battle cry": "[T]he value of truth must for once, by way of experiment, be *called into question* … ."[60] Nietzsche was not, however, proposing nihilistic relativism, but merely opposing those traditional formulations of truth which he regarded as "diseased" or "life-inhibiting," instead advocating openness to a multiplicity of perspectives. Hence, he could still exclaim with near-evangelical fervor: "Truth has had to be fought for every step of the way, almost everything dear to our hearts, on which our love and our trust in life depend, has had to be sacrificed to it. Greatness of soul is needed for it: the service of truth is the hardest service."[61]

Dis-ontologizing Being

Because "truth" is ineluctably conditioned by the conscious and unconscious drives of the truth-seeker, Nietzsche contended that it is impossible to distinguish appearances from "things-in-themselves," "for we do not 'know' nearly enough to be entitled to any such distinction."[62] The elision of ontology into human subjectivity was announced by Zarathustra: "And whatever may yet come to me as fate and experience—a wandering and a mountain-climbing will be in it: in the final analysis one experiences only oneself."[63] For this reason, Nietzsche once sketched in his notebook that a self-critical stance is illusory:

> The intellect cannot criticize itself, simply because it cannot be compared with other species of intellect and because its capacity to know would be revealed only in the presence of "true reality," i.e., because in order to criticize the intellect we should have to be a higher being with "absolute knowledge."[64]

---

[58]   Ibid., p. 246.

[59]   *GM*, p. 128.

[60]   Ibid. Nietzsche even suggested that the "will to truth" "might be a concealed will to death" (*GS*, p. 282).

[61]   *TI*, p. 179.

[62]   *GS*, p. 300. See also *HA*, p. 13 and *UM*, p. 27.

[63]   *Z*, p. 173.

[64]   *WP*, p. 263 [1886–87].

Without an Archimedean point to comprehend "being," there can be no absolute certainty of human knowing.[65] The appeal to "fact" is a cultural fable because, "All meaning is will to power (all relative meaning resolves itself into it)."[66] Facticity merely entails what previous generations have found useful to their specific contexts and agendas.[67]

For Nietzsche, existence consists of a never-ending swirl of force and counter-force, an orgiastic, eternally dynamic—if restless—endless stream of "becomings," which humankind has purposefully ossified into "beings" for the purposes of societal stability.[68] "Being," therefore, lacks ontological status: objects do not exist in and of themselves; value-laden "editors" have merely dissected the reel-to-reel "film" of becoming into motionless "freeze-frames" of being: "In the world of becoming, 'reality' is always only a simplification for practical ends, or a deception through the coarseness of organs, or a variation in the tempo of becoming."[69] Nietzsche endeavored to prevent his emphasis on "becomings" from being assimilated within traditional teleological categories:

> Becoming must be explained without recourse to final intentions; becoming must appear justified at every moment (or incapable of being evaluated; which amounts to the same thing); the present must absolutely not be justified by reference to a future, nor the past by reference to the present ... . More strictly, one must admit nothing that has being—because then becoming would lose its value and actually appear meaningless and superfluous.[70]

To summarize, a fundamental tension characterizes Nietzsche's thought with regards to the notion of truth. While he adamantly sought to deny an ontology of being, which presupposes a greater, metaphysical Being or higher reality to which humanity and nature must submit, he approved of truth claims insofar as they represent manifestations of humankind's will to power: "To impose upon becoming the character of being—that is the supreme will to power."[71] His response to "fossilized" ontologies of being was to advocate journeys without arrivals and joyfully acknowledge the endless flux of cosmic synergy without nailing

---

[65]   Ibid., p. 269 [1885–86]: "One would have to know what *being* is, in order to decide whether this or that is real (e.g., 'the facts of consciousness'); in the same way, what *certainty* is, what *knowledge* is, and the like.—But since we do not know this, a critique of the faculty of knowledge is senseless: how should a tool be able to criticize itself when it can use only itself for a critique? It cannot even define itself!"

[66]   Ibid., p. 323 [1885–86].

[67]   *GS*, p. 300.

[68]   *WP*, p. 288 [1885–86].

[69]   Ibid., p. 312 [1887].

[70]   Ibid., p. 377 [1887–88]. See also ibid., p. 546 [1885] where teleology implied an exhaustion of becoming, an end to "all thinking, all 'spirit.'"

[71]   Ibid., p. 330 [1883–85].

"becomings" and potentialities onto the "crosses" of brute facts and ideologies: "That *everything recurs* is the closest *approximation of a world of becoming to a world of being*:—high point of the meditation."[72]

Philosophical Eugenics

Countering nihilism

"What are man's truths ultimately?" Nietzsche once thundered. "Merely his *irrefutable errors*."[73] While weaker individuals panic at the notion of a semantic abyss separating the "knower" from the objective world, Nietzsche rejoiced: "There is no 'reality' for us—not for you either, my sober friends."[74] This freedom from ontology allows humanity to modify the world at will by altering one's interpretative lenses: "[I]t is enough to create new names and estimations and probabilities in order to create in the long run new 'things.'"[75] Although many human "truths" are fallacious, they are still useful for human mastery of the environment:

> The falseness of a judgment is to us not necessarily an objection to a judgment: it is here that our new language perhaps sounds strangest. The question is to what extent is it life-advancing, life-preserving, species-preserving, perhaps even species-breeding; and our fundamental tendency is to assert that the falsest judgments (to which synthetic judgments *a priori* belong) are the most indispensable to us ... .[76]

Such "necessary lies" include the beliefs "that there are enduring things; that there are equal things; that there are things, substances, bodies; that a thing is what it appears to be; that our will is free; that what is good for me is also good in itself."[77] For Nietzsche, the history of ideas, like the history of the universe, is a saga of strife and insurrection: "Woe to him who seeks to darken it [a "cherished idea"]; unless it itself should one day become suspicious to us:—then, unwearying king-makers in the history of the spirit that we are, we hurl it from the throne, and immediately raise its opponents in its place."[78]

Nihilism is one response to the fallaciousness of "truth" and nature's ongoing dissolution of existing power configurations. Nietzsche once identified three

---

[72]   Ibid.

[73]   *GS*, p. 219.

[74]   Ibid., p. 121.

[75]   Ibid., p. 122.

[76]   *BG*, p. 35. Though one's capacity for new ideas is limited by one's capacity for power: "One hears only those questions for which one is able to find answers" (*GS*, p. 206). This is how Nietzsche explained the poor reception of his own writings (*EH*, p. 40).

[77]   *GS*, p. 169.

[78]   *NR*, p. 31. See also *HA*, p. 154.

"psychological states" which give rise to nihilism: the awareness that "becoming" has no goals; the awareness that there are no "grand unities" or cosmic schemes in which humankind participates; and a disbelief in the existence of truth.[79] However, rather than regarding nihilism as a theoretical irruption, he viewed it as a natural and necessary outcome of humanity's "fatal" will to get to the bottom of things: "The faith in the categories of reason is the cause of nihilism. We have measured the value of the world according to categories *that refer to a purely fictitious world*."[80] For Nietzsche, the philosophical "therapy" for humankind's epistemological pathology is obvious: in order to appreciate the world of "becoming," the world of "being" must be sublated: "*Overcoming of philosophers* through the destruction of the world of being: intermediary period of nihilism: before there is yet present the strength to reverse values and to deify becoming and the apparent world as the only world, and to call them good."[81] Thus, nihilism was endorsed by Nietzsche as a temporary means of demolition to clear the ground for new philosophical constructions, but never as an end in itself.[82]

The philosopher's role
The intricate organicism of Nietzsche's thought parallels the intrinsic interconnectedness of every element in the natural universe. The role of philosophy is, consequently, to facilitate an unconditional acceptance and exuberance for all aspects of nature. In his notebooks, he once wrote, "In the actual world, in which everything is bound to and conditioned by everything else, to condemn and think away anything means to condemn and think away everything. The expression 'that should not be,' 'that should not have been,' is farcical."[83] However, Nietzsche's concept of a universe "closed off" from any transcendent interference invoked an ardent conservationism. Because there is no infusion of new energy from "beyond," no creation *ex nihilo*, all of nature's resources are limited; therefore, new "becomings" are founded on the demise and reconstitution of older forms. Such hermeneutical recycling is pivotal to the role of philosopher as Nietzsche conceived it. Like a Norse god standing warily victorious over his slain foes, he must carefully ensure that every metaphysical "rib" and drop of semantic "blood" is judiciously employed to fashion new creations from the corpses of the vanquished "titans." Subsequently, a form of "epistemological cannibalism" becomes the hallmark of the genealogical approach to history:

> [A]nything which exists, once it has somehow come into being, can be reinterpreted in the service of new intentions, repossessed, repeatedly modified

---

[79] *WP*, p. 13 [1887–88].

[80] Ibid.

[81] Ibid., p. 319 [1887, 88].

[82] R.J. Hollingdale claims that Nietzsche's ultimate aim was "the transcendence of modern nihilism" (*Nietzsche* [London and Boston, 1973], p. 115).

[83] *WP*, p. 316 [1888].

to a new use by a power superior to it; that everything which happens in the organic world is part of a process of *overpowering, mastering*, and that, in turn, all overpowering and mastering is a reinterpretation, a manipulation, in the course of which the previous "meaning" and "aim" must necessarily be obscured or completely effaced.[84]

According to Nietzsche's "First Law of Spiritual Thermodynamics," nothing can disappear—it can merely be re-circulated.[85] Hence, the great philosophical mission is to counter the "powers that be" in order to make way for the "powers that become."[86]

It is noteworthy that Nietzsche did not promulgate a specific societal blueprint or government model.[87] Such undertakings may have been considered too banal or ineffectual for implementing his epistemological revolution—an overturning of conventional formulations of truth in order to expand both the imaginational frontiers of the species and surpass the bounds of what it means to be human.[88] Therefore, to establish another creed or political system would merely be to fall into the trap of petrifying "becomings" into "beings" beneath the Medusan glare of "objective truth." What he sought, rather, was to alter the definitions and existential parameters of what it means to be human. In an essay on philosophical education, Nietzsche contended that the true educator's role is neither to nurture

---

[84]   *GM*, pp. 57–8.

[85]   *WP*, p. 323 (1883–86)]: "There is no struggle for existence between ideas and perceptions, but a struggle for dominion: the idea that is overcome is not annihilated, only driven back or subordinated. There is no annihilation in the sphere of spirit—."

[86]   Concerning the concepts of "God," "progress," "eternity," and "truth," Zarathustra proclaimed, "All that is intransitory—that is but an image! And the poets lie too much. But the best images and parables should speak of time and becoming: they should be a eulogy and a justification of all transitoriness" (*Z*, p. 111).

[87]   In this qualified sense, Kaufmann is correct in calling attention to Nietzsche's "antipolitical" nature regarding his relentless opposition of "the idolatry of the state," political liberalism, and sectarianism (*Nietzsche: Philosopher, Psychologist, Antichrist*, p. 412). Perhaps Nietzsche's political "silence" is a Zarathustran move, reminiscent of Plotinus' view of Heraclitus: "[H]e leaves us to conjecture and omits to make his argument clear to us, no doubt because we should inquire for ourselves as he himself inquired and found" (Julian Barnes, *Early Greek Philosophy* [London, 1987], p. 117). For a fascinating overview of how Nietzsche was appropriated by the "purely power-political interests" or *Machtpolitik* which he rigorously opposed, see Keith Ansell-Pearson, *An Introduction to Nietzsche as Political Thinker* (Cambridge, 1997), pp. 29–32.

[88]   See Jacob Golomb and Robert Wistrich's distinction between *Macht* ["spiritual power"] and *Kraft* ["brute political force"] (*Nietzsche, Godfather of Fascism? On the Uses and Abuses of a Philosophy* [Princeton, 2002], p. 8), and Golomb's essay, "How to De-Nazify Nietzsche's Philosophical Anthropology?" in the same volume, pp. 20–24. Golomb writes: "The distinction between 'force' and 'power' is based on the assumption that that *power is a sublimated force*" (ibid., p. 21).

a pupil's greatest strength to the neglect of all other faculties, nor to strengthen all of one's forces and coral them into a harmonious order, but to identify "the central force" in each pupil and "prevent its acting destructively on the other forces: ... to mould the whole man into a living solar and planetary system and to understand its higher laws of motions."[89]

Nietzsche's understanding of humankind is characterized by a significant degree of ambivalence. As a species which is intractably embedded in the cosmic surge towards greater units of power, humankind involuntarily participates in the great "*telos*" of nature. Like a vibrant tree, humankind must grow in all directions at once, pressing downwards into the subterranean murk while clutching at the stratosphere of ethereal excellence.[90] Happily, the tree can be pruned. Hence, Zarathustra declared, "Our way is upward, from the species across to the superspecies."[91] The notion of "human becomings" energized Nietzsche and preserved him from nihilistic despair, particularly when viewing his German contemporaries:

> So far they are nothing: that means, they are all sorts of things. They will become something: that means, they will stop some day being all sorts of things. The latter is at bottom a mere wish, scarcely a hope; fortunately, a wish on which one can live, a matter of will, of work, of discipline, of breeding, as well as a matter of annoyance, of desire, of missing something, of discomfort, even of betterment ... .[92]

Nietzsche's timely appearance boded well for the development of the species, which had fallen prey to certain life-enervating obstructions: "I take it for a piece of good fortune of the first rank to have lived at the right time, and to have lived precisely among Germans, so as to be *ripe* for this work ... ."[93] Philosophy's greatest service to humankind lies in determining which part of the world is unalterable and then "*improving that part of it recognized as alterable* with the most ruthless courage."[94] In *Untimely Meditations*, he wrote, "The best we can do is to confront our inherited and hereditary nature with our knowledge, and through a new, stern discipline combat our inborn heritage and implant in ourselves a new habit, a new instinct, a second nature, so that our first nature withers away."[95] By altering the spiritual "genome" of the human race, the role of the philosopher is compared to that of "breeder":

---

[89] *UM*, p. 131.
[90] *GS*, pp. 331–2.
[91] *Z*, p. 100.
[92] *WP*, p. 68 [1885].
[93] *EH*, p. 31.
[94] *UM*, p. 208.
[95] Ibid., p. 76.

The philosopher as *we* understand him, we free spirits—as the man of the most comprehensive responsibility who has the conscience for the collective evolution of mankind: this philosopher will make use of the religions for his work of education and breeding, just as he will make use of existing political and economic conditions.[96]

This task incorporated the philosopher within the ideal focus of human civilization: "to promote the production of the philosopher, the artist and the saint within us and without us and thereby to work at the perfecting of nature."[97]

Comprehending the Universal: The Fallacy of Free Will

After examining the implications of Nietzsche's thought for epistemology, ontology, and the task of philosophy, it is necessary to explore further his views on humankind. Nietzsche's comprehension remains consistent with his universal rubric of nature as the ceaseless conflict of "all against all."[98] As Rüdiger Safranski notes, a person is not regarded as an "individuum" but a "dividuum."[99] Subsequently, a person represents a conglomeration of drives and instincts waging perpetual warfare for mastery of the self, wherein a "sovereign instinct" emerges which temporarily subordinates the weaker instincts as "tools."[100] Even self-knowledge becomes a dubious prospect at best.[101] Nietzsche did not, however, allow individuals to excuse their self-anarchy, but rather urged his reader to "organize the chaos within him by thinking back to his real needs."[102] Human "health"—a significant theme in light of Nietzsche's recurring bouts with illness—is predicated upon one of the "dominating passions" governing the "multiplicity of 'souls in one breast.'"[103] Nietzsche contended that such drives

---

[96] *BG*, p. 86.

[97] *UM*, p. 160. Nietzsche's enthusiasm towards the saint as the paradigm for personal transformation from the base to the glorious (Ibid., p. 161) waned in later years. See Kaufmann, *Nietzsche: Philosopher, Psychologist, Antichrist*, p. 280.

[98] *UM*, p. 30.

[99] Safranski, p. 184.

[100] *WP*, p. 203 [1883–88]; *BG*, p. 37. Such passages do not quite entail "the nuclear fission of the individual" *per se*, as pithily phrased by Safranski, p. 26, but do reflect the dissolution of the individual as postulated by certain traditional metaphysical and ethical systems. Oddly, the divided-self theme finds a parallel in certain Christian formulations, and self as struggle was a familiar motif in Paul, Augustine, and Luther.

[101] *UM*, p. 129. In *Daybreak*, he claimed, "If we would wish and dare to construct an architecture corresponding to the nature of our soul we would have to take the labyrinth as a model" (cited in Salomé, p. 22).

[102] *UM*, p. 123.

[103] *WP*, p. 408 [1888]. In a bizarre "biologization" of the will, he traced contemporary weakness of will to the intermingling of races and classes: "The man of an era of dissolution

"have all at some time or other practiced philosophy—and ... each one of them would be only too glad to present *itself* as the ultimate goal of existence and as the legitimate *master* of all the other drives."[104] Thought itself is an artifice welded by and wielded over the instincts:

> "Thinking," as epistemologists conceive it, simply does not occur: it is a quite arbitrary fiction, arrived at by selecting one element from the process and eliminating all the rest, an artificial arrangement for the purpose of intelligibility— The "spirit" something that thinks: where possible even "absolute, pure spirit"— this conception is a second derivative of that false introspection which believes in "thinking": first an act is imagined which simply does not occur, "thinking," and secondly a subject-substratum in which every act of thinking, and nothing else, has its origin: that is to say, both the deed and the doer are fictions.[105]

Even "freedom" for Nietzsche represents the domination of certain instincts:

> For what is freedom? That one has the will to self-responsibility. That one preserves the distance which divides us. That one has become more indifferent to hardship, toil, privation, even to life. That one is ready to sacrifice men to one's cause, oneself not excepted. Freedom means that the manly instincts that delight in war and victory have gained mastery over the other instincts—for example, over the instinct for "happiness."[106]

The necessity of a centralized will or "master drive," which entails "an end to fumbling, straying, to the proliferation of secondary shoots," came to Nietzsche's attention in the music of Wagner: "[W]ithin the most convoluted courses and often daring trajectories assumed by his artistic plans there rules a single inner law, a will, by which they can be explained ... ."[107] Like the will, Wagner's

---

which mixes the races together and who therefore contains within him the inheritance of a diversified descent, ... such a man of late cultures and broken lights will, on average, be a rather weak man: his fundamental desire is that the war which he *is* should come to an end; happiness appears to him, in accordance with a sedative (for example Epicurean or Christian) medicine and mode of thought, pre-eminently as the happiness of repose, of tranquility, of satiety, of unity at last attained, as a 'Sabbath of Sabbaths' ..." (*BG*, p. 121).

[104]   Ibid., p. 37.

[105]   *WP*, p. 264 [1887–88]. See also *BG*, p. 47.

[106]   *TI*, p. 103.

[107]   *UM*, p. 200. A psychology of "counterpoints" resonates with Nietzsche's rejection of ontological "opposites," contending rather that there are merely gradations of "becomings" rather than clear-cut dualities in existence. With regards to ontological "opposites," metaphysical philosophies are most guilty of "denying the origin of the one from the other" and "assuming for the more highly valued things some miraculous origin" (*HA*, p. 13).

"overwhelming symphonic intelligence" becomes a "sorcerer's apprentice," which temporarily secures a harmony of the elements and "out of all this conflict brings forth concord."[108] Such respites among the instincts are fleeting, for the most part, in light of Nietzsche's conception of the "storm" of self.[109] Initially, Nietzsche used the term "spirit" to express "a force wholly pure and free" which can direct "the precipitate current of a vehement will which as it were strives to reach up to the light through every runway, cave and crevice, and desires power."[110] This central direction or "higher self"[111] does not merely repress the tumultuous instincts in the manner of Freud's "superego," but exhibits "loyalty out of free and most selfless love, the creative, innocent, more illuminated sphere to the dark, intractable and tyrannical."[112]

Contrary to thousands of years of intellectual endeavor, Nietzsche believed that humanity owes its existence to instinct rather than to consciousness or rationality.[113] Nietzsche traced the rise of consciousness to the need to communicate dangers and desires to others. As a result, consciousness became a communal canopy of desires and insecurities:

> This is the essence of phenomenalism and perspectives as *I* understand them: Owing to the nature of *animal consciousness*, the world of which we can become conscious is only a surface- and sign-world, a world that is made common and meaner; whatever becomes conscious *becomes* by the same token shallow, thin, relatively stupid, general, sign, herd signal ... .[114]

---

[108]   *UM*, p. 242. He continued, "Wagner's music as a whole is an image of the world as it was understood by the great Ephesian philosopher [Heraclitus]: a harmony produced by conflict, the unity of justice and enmity." For Heraclitus' views on the universality of conflict and the transformation of opposites, see Julian Barnes, *Early Greek Philosophy* (London, 1987), pp. 102–7.

[109]   The "master drive" provided a parallel to "the *ruling idea*" (*UM*, p. 227), which will gain importance in Nietzsche's later thought. See *BG*, p. 171.

[110]   *UM*, p. 201. Although the "spirit" was elevated above the "will" which "raged below," Nietzsche identified them as "two drives or spheres" in Wagner. The Christian and Hegelian "baggage" associated with the former term likely led to its absence in later writings.

[111]   Ibid., p. 228.

[112]   Ibid., p. 203.

[113]   *GS*, pp. 84–5: "If the conserving association of the instincts were not so very much more powerful, if it did not serve on the whole as a regulator, humanity would have to perish of its misjudgements and its fantasies with open eyes, of its lack of thoroughness and its credulity—in short, of its consciousness ... ."

[114]   Ibid., pp. 299–300. See also *WP*, p. 357 [1883–88]: "We learn to think less highly of all that is conscious; we unlearn responsibility for ourselves, since we as conscious, purposive creatures, are only the smallest part of us."

As one of the most recent innovations of evolution, consciousness contains the most glitches in humanity's biological "software."[115] Knowledge itself is the product of the instincts, the "white flag" of a temporary truce hoisted above the subliminal shadows into the rays of conscious thought.[116] Maintaining purity of instinct and avoiding "the many lower and more shortsighted drives which are active in so-called selfless actions" comprise "the test, the final test perhaps, which a Zarathustra has to pass—the actual *proof* of his strength... ."[117] By contrast, repressed dominant instincts vent their fury in acts of self-dissolution and "bad conscience."[118]

Nietzsche was, however, extraordinarily wary of using the term "will" on account of its metaphysical associations. In a journal entry, he once wrote:

> *Weakness of the will*: that is a metaphor that can prove misleading. For there is no will, and consequently neither a strong nor a weak will. The multitude and disgregation of impulses and the lack of any systematic order among them result in a "weak will"; their coordination under a single predominant impulse results in a "strong will": in the first case it is the oscillation and the lack of gravity; in the latter, the precision and clarity of the direction.[119]

At the same time, however, Nietzsche wanted to avoid the despair arising from volitional entropy—a flaw in Schopenhauer's thought—so he emphasized that the will can be modified regardless of its unconscious content.[120] This carefully nuanced term allowed him to consolidate the illusory polarities of subject and object, chaos and order, world and *Weltanschauung*, reflecting the power which

---

[115]   *GS*, p. 84.

[116]   Ibid., p. 261: "Since only the last scenes of reconciliation and the final accounting at the end of this long process rise to our consciousness, we suppose that *intelligere* must be something conciliatory, just and good—something that stands essentially opposed to the instincts, while it is actually nothing but a *certain behavior of the instincts towards one another*." For "reason" as "a system of relations between various passions and desires," see *WP*, p. 208 [1887–88].

[117]   *EH*, p. 14. Failure to do so resulted in "a man of profound mediocrity" (*WP*, p. 359 [1883–88]).

[118]   *GM*, pp. 65–7.

[119]   *WP*, pp. 28–9 [1888].

[120]   *GM*, p. 7. He criticized Schopenhauer for this excess in *WP*, p. 52 [1887]: "*Schopenhauer's* basic misunderstanding of the *will* (as if craving, instinct, drive were the *essence* of will) is typical: lowering the value of the will to the point of making a real mistake ... . Great symptom of the *exhaustion* or the *weakness* of the *will*: for the will is precisely that which treats cravings as their master and appoints to them their way and measure."

"transforms moments of pathos into interpretations and perspectives through which they become enduring creations."[121]

In *Beyond Good and Evil*, Nietzsche identified three components in human volition. First, there is a physiological component, "a plurality of sensations, namely the sensation of the condition we *leave*, the sensation of the condition towards which we *go*, the sensation of this 'leaving' and 'going' itself, and then also an accompanying muscular sensation ... ." Second, there is an unconscious psychological component, an intersection of diverse emotions and thoughts which coalesce to form "the commanding thought." Third, there is "the affect of command," the conscious attribution of action to personal volition, the glorious—if, at times, specious—self-proclamation, "I willed it thus."[122] The person who attributes intentionality to an action thus bolsters a particular "dominating instinct." Nietzsche concluded, "He who wills adds in this way the sensations of pleasure of the successful executive agents, the serviceable 'under-wills' or under-souls—for our body is only a social structure composed of many souls—to his sensations of pleasure as commander."[123]

It is within this third component of willing that the notion of domination is rooted. According to Nietzsche, "What is called 'freedom of will' is essentially the affect of superiority over him who must obey: 'I am free, "he" must obey.'"[124] Zarathustra asserted that belief in a governable body, whether one's own or one's subordinate, is vital to the quality of human life:

> All *feeling* suffers in me and is in prison: but my *willing* always comes to me as my liberator and bringer of joy. Willing liberates: that is the true doctrine of will and freedom—thus Zarathustra teaches you. No more to will and no more to evaluate and no more to create! Ah, that this great lassitude may ever stay far from me![125]

However, the German philosopher at times doubted whether a person can ever be said to will an action intentionally without engaging in hermeneutical gymnastics:

> A quantum of force is also a quantum of drive, will, action—in fact, it is nothing more than this driving, willing, acting, and it is only through the seduction of language (and through the fundamental errors of reason petrified in it)—language

---

121 Golomb, "Nietzsche on Authority," p. 255.

122 *BG*, p. 48.

123 Ibid., p. 49.

124 Ibid., 48.

125 *Z*, p. 111.

which understands and misunderstands all action as conditioned by an actor, by a "subject"—that it can appear otherwise.[126]

Nietzsche believed that the will to will within every individual is dictated by generations of biological and behavioural elements: "But at the bottom of us, 'right down deep,' there is, to be sure, something unteachable, a granite stratum of spiritual fate, of predetermined decision and answer to pre-determined selected questions."[127] However, he was able to smuggle a volitional "file" into the dungeon of spiritual determinism: though the instincts themselves are "constants," the hierarchies among the instincts are transitional and established primarily through the imaginative faculties.[128] Since knowledge issues from the instincts, it is possible to reverse the flow:

> To this day the task of *incorporating* knowledge and making it instinctive is only beginning to dawn on the human eye and is not yet clearly discernible; it is a task that is seen only by those who have comprehended that so far we have incorporated only our errors and that all our consciousness relates to errors.[129]

This imaginative category of "willing" provides a means whereby humankind may be moulded and influenced by a cunning philosopher, provided that the species can be liberated from certain sociological and metaphysical "shackles" which currently restrain the instincts. One cannot but marvel at the audaciousness of a man who fiercely contended: "You know these things as thoughts, but your thoughts are not your experiences, they are an echo and an after-effect of your experiences: as when your room trembles when a carriage goes past. I however am sitting in the carriage, and often I am the carriage itself."[130] But there were still several potholes which jolted both rider and carriage.

Combatting the Christian Obstruction

Nietzsche blamed many pernicious movements within the nineteenth century for smothering the instincts which benefit the species,[131] attacking any politic, creed, or ideology which appeared "not as a means in the struggle between power-

---

126   *GM*, p. 29. See also *TI*, p. 60: "The 'inner world' is full of phantoms and false lights: the will is one of them … . Merely a surface phenomenon of consciousness, an accompaniment to an act, which conceals rather than expresses the *antecedentia* of the act."

127   *BG*, pp. 162–3.

128   *WP*, pp. 263–4 [1887–88].

129   *GS*, p. 85.

130   *Z*, p. 12.

131   It is essential to emphasize that Nietzsche did not desire an unleashing of all instincts, but merely those that he deemed "ascending instincts" (*WP*, p. 217 [1888]).

complexes, but as a means *against* struggle itself … ."[132] Such principles deemed "hostile to life" were embodied in communism,[133] socialism,[134] liberalism,[135] democracy,[136] utilitarianism,[137] populist-driven nationalism,[138] women's movements,[139] and most contemporary forms of ethics and religion.[140] However, Nietzsche was a particularly vociferous opponent of Christianity and its doctrine of free will.[141] He first theorized that the doctrine had originated as "an invention of *ruling classes*," who merely projected their personal socio-political freedoms onto the metaphysical domain.[142] Nietzsche attributed the widespread dissemination of this most powerful illusion to human pride:

> [M]an is the free being in a world of unfreedom, the eternal *miracle worker* whether he does good or ill, the astonishing exception, the superbeast and almost-god, the meaning of creation which cannot be thought away, the solution of the cosmic riddle, the mighty ruler over nature and the despiser of it, the creature which calls *its* history *world history*!—*Vanitas vanitatum homo.*[143]

However, he eventually regarded the concept as a corrupted tool in the hands of the rabble for the primary aim of ritual condemnation: "One has deprived becoming of its innocence if being in this or that state is traced back to will, to intentions, to accountable acts: the doctrine of will has been invented essentially for the purpose of *finding guilty*."[144]

---

[132]   *GM*, p. 57.

[133]   Ibid.

[134]   *WP*, p. 77 [1885]. Nietzsche regarded socialism as "despotic" since it desires a "despotic" degree of executive power and seeks to destroy the individual by reducing him to "an expedient *organ of the community*" (*HA*, p. 226).

[135]   *BG*, p. 52; *WP*, p. 462 [1888].

[136]   *GM*, p. 129.

[137]   *TI*, p. 80. He similarly attacked the Rousseauian view of social contract, arguing that no two actions can have equal value, thus obviating any exchangeability (*WP*, p. 489 [1887–88]).

[138]   *BG*, p. 171.

[139]   Ibid., p. 166.

[140]   *GM*, p. 129.

[141]   In his introduction to Salomé's book, Siegfried Mandel helpfully situates Nietzsche's views of Christianity within the turmoil that followed his father's death. The family relocated to Naumburg, whose "terrifying bourgeois conventionality, conformism, and religious conservatism seeped into his being as afflictions he called '*Naumburger Tugend*,' a superficial decorum or respectability …" (Salomé, p. xiv).

[142]   *NR*, p. 57.

[143]   Ibid., p. 199.

[144]   *TI*, p. 64.

Nietzsche maintained that the "core" Christian doctrines of sin and guilt, reward and punishment, were constructed upon the false attribution of causal relations between man's actions and his conscious will—"a magically effective force"[145]—without due consideration for the intractable nature of human instincts,[146] the inescapable biases of the injured person who judges the "perpetrator," the unalterable variables of biological lineage and culture, and the "pinball" erratics of any given action on account of conflicting wills and unpredictable consequences in the natural world,[147] not to mention the duplicitous means by which the "righteous" victim gains power over the "sinner."[148] Contending that "the history of moral feelings is the history of an error, an error called 'responsibility,' which in turn rests on an error called 'freedom of the will,'"[149] Nietzsche declared that the very act of judging is, itself, the greatest injustice.[150] Since Nietzsche's philosophical project to exhume "evil" instincts and return the species to a more "natural" evolutionary trajectory conflicted with the conventional morality of the nineteenth century, he sought to undermine the transcendental truth claims of Christian ethics.[151] Hence, he argued,

> Between good and evil actions there is no difference in type; at most, a difference in degree. Good actions are sublimated evil actions; evil actions are good actions become coarse and stupid. The individual's only demand, for self-enjoyment (along with the fear of losing it), is satisfied in all circumstances: man may act as he can, that is, as he must, whether in deeds of vanity, revenge, pleasure, usefulness, malice, cunning, or in deeds of sacrifice, pity, knowledge.[152]

Because Nietzsche regarded Christianity as the venom of *réssentiment* spat by the masses against the privileged classes,[153] he exclaimed, "I call Christianity the *one* great curse, the *one* great intrinsic depravity, the *one* great instinct for revenge

---

145   *GS*, p. 183.

146   *BG*, p. 63.

147   *HA*, pp. 43–4.

148   "Oh, how much superfluous cruelty and vivisection have proceeded from those religions which invented sin! And from those people who desired by means of it to gain the highest enjoyment of their power!" (cited in Golomb, "How to De-Nazify Nietzsche's Philosophical Anthropology?," p. 33).

149   *HA*, p. 43.

150   *UM*, p. 35; *HA*, p. 44.

151   *The Genealogy of Morality* exposed the relativity and transience of seemingly "timeless" values. See also *NR*, p. 91: "Whoever has overthrown an existing law of custom has hitherto always first been accounted a *bad man*: but when, as did happen, the law could not afterwards be reinstated and this fact was accepted the predicate gradually changed;—history treats almost exclusively of these *bad men* who subsequently became *good men*!"

152   *HA*, p. 75.

153   Ibid., pp. 68–9.

for which no expedient is sufficiently poisonous, secret, subterranean, *petty*—I call it the *one* immortal blemish of mankind .... ."[154]

By contrast, Nietzsche forbade men from judging the will to power: "For this is the doctrine preached by life itself to all that has life: the morality of development. To have and to want to have more—*growth*, in one word—that is life itself."[155] Because of the close interrelationality of the world and its events, one cannot condemn an action without condemning the entire man,[156] or even the world itself:

> The concept "reprehensible action" presents us with difficulties. Nothing that happened at all can be reprehensible in itself: for one should not want to eliminate it: for everything is so bound up with everything else that to want to exclude something means to exclude everything. A reprehensible action means: a reprehended world.[157]

In contradistinction to an exuberant acceptance of the world and all of its contingencies, Christianity sacrifices the temporal for the eternal, thus "depriving life as such of its centre of gravity."[158] This "myth" of the afterlife is merely "a moral optical-illusion," a metaphysical asylum from the natural world whereby "we *revenge* ourselves on life by means of the phantasmagoria of 'another,' a 'better' life."[159] Subsequently, Nietzsche deplored Christianity for possessing a "thoroughly thought-out method of psychological counterfeiting":[160] "Nothing but imaginary *causes* ('God,' 'soul', 'ego,' 'spirit,' 'free will'—or 'unfree will'): nothing but imaginary *effects* ('sin,' 'redemption,' 'grace,' 'punishment,' 'forgiveness of sins')."[161]

Concerning the Particular: Nietzsche's "Magnificent Monsters"[162]

In light of his dismissal of "obstructive" societal conventions and his emphasis on liberating the instincts, it is easy to portray Nietzsche as a histrionic revolutionary, bent on civilization's plunge into anarchy. However, Nietzsche's rallying cries were intended for a select audience only, his calls for freedom limited to "nobler" ears.[163]

---

[154] *TI*, p. 199.

[155] *WP*, p. 77 [1885].

[156] Ibid., p. 180 [1887–88].

[157] Ibid., p. 165 [1888].

[158] *TI*, p. 167. See also *Z*, p. 42.

[159] *TI*, p. 49.

[160] *WP*, p. 212 [1887–88]. See also *HA*, pp. 85, 94, 230.

[161] *TI*, p. 137. See also *EH*, p. 67.

[162] "The 'great man' is great owing to the free play and scope of his desires and to the yet greater power that knows how to press these magnificent monsters into service" (*WP*, p. 492 [1887]).

[163] *EH*, p. 24; *Z*, p. 299.

Within any human society, he identified three distinct yet interdependent ranks of individuals: "the most spiritual human beings," who break old barriers to found new religions, customs, and mores; "the guardians of the law," who safeguard a culture's venerated traditions and typically include both royalty and the nobility; and the working classes, who engage in "[t]he crafts, trade, agriculture, *science*, the greater part of art, in a word the entire compass of *professional* activity," who would be "out of place among the elite."[164] The last and most populous class uniformly seeks happiness through service, "the kind of *happiness* of which the great majority are alone capable, which makes intelligent machines of them. For the mediocre it is happiness to be mediocre; mastery in one thing, specialization, is for them a natural instinct."[165]

Attempts to impose universal standards and mores over all humankind regardless of rank constitute the ultimate injustice for Nietzsche, since different people are subject to different standards and "necessities":

> Over one man *necessity* stands in the shape of his passions, over another as the habit of hearing and obeying, over a third as a logical conscience, over a fourth as caprice and a mischievous pleasure in escapades. These four will, however, seek the *freedom* of their will precisely where each of them is most firmly fettered .... How does this happen? Evidently because each considers himself most free where his *feeling of living* is greatest; thus, as we have said, in passion, in duty, in knowledge, in mischievousness respectively.[166]

Furthermore, he especially repudiated the "misapplication" of lower-class mores to the strong:

> Just as the common people distinguish lightning from the flash of light and take the latter as *doing*, as the effect of a subject which is called lightning, just so popular morality distinguishes strength from expressions of strength, as if behind the strong individual there were an indifferent substratum which was at *liberty* to express or not to express strength. But no such substratum exists; there is no "being" behind doing, acting, becoming; "the doer" is merely a fiction imposed on the doing—the doing itself is everything.[167]

Because people erroneously believe that a transgressor could have chosen not to commit the infraction, Nietzsche wrote, "This belief in his choice arouses hatred,

---

[164]   *TI*, p. 191. Zarathustra compared the three classes to "camels" [society's "beasts of burden"], "lions" [society's rulers], and a "child" [society's mavericks]—"innocence and forgetfulness, a new beginning, a sport, a self-propelling wheel, a first motion, a sacred Yes" (*Z*, pp. 54–5).

[165]   *TI*, p. 191.

[166]   *NR*, p. 57.

[167]   *GM*, p. 29.

thirst for revenge, spite, the whole deterioration of our imagination; whereas we get much less angry at an animal because we consider it irresponsible."[168]

As a result of "class" distinctions, Nietzsche's philosophy is pervaded by a sociological and ethical conservatism which prohibits movement beyond one's natural rank and advocates different laws for different echelons of society.[169] Humankind must come to the conclusion that "it is *immoral* to say: 'What is good for one is good for another.'"[170] This way, humanity realigns itself with what Nietzsche observed in the natural world. "Order of rank among capacities; distance; the art of dividing without making inimical; mixing up nothing, 'reconciling' nothing; a tremendous multiplicity which is none the less the opposite of chaos—this has been the precondition, the protracted secret labour and artistic working of my instinct."[171] In an effort to shape the future, Nietzsche identified the discipline and skills he cherished within the elevated caste of the past, whose members "inherited and cultivated a proper mastery and subtlety in conducting a war against oneself, that is to say self-control, self-outwitting … ."[172] We will now examine Nietzsche's interpretations of the aristocracy in order to elucidate the plight of the slave-dominated present and Nietzsche's hope for the future, the arrival of the *Übermensch*.[173]

Masters of the past
Throughout his writing career, Nietzsche identified the creation of new values as the primary task of the philosopher. However, he prescribed different labors to different classes within a spiritual hierarchy:

> It is the duty of these scholars ["philosophical labourers and men of science"[174]] to take everything that has hitherto happened and been valued, and make it clear, distinct, intelligible and manageable, to abbreviate everything long, even

---

[168]   *HA*, p. 69.

[169]   *TI*, p. 134; *GS*, p. 84; *WP*, p. 162 [1883–88]: "My philosophy aims at an ordering of rank: not an individualistic morality. The ideas of the herd should rule in the herd—but not reach beyond it: the leaders of the herd require a fundamentally different valuation for their own actions, as do the independent, or the 'beasts of prey,' etc." This social conservatism is traceable to Plato: "Plato explained … it should be impossible ever to mingle or confound the order of castes …" (*UM*, p. 119).

[170]   *BG*, p. 151.

[171]   *EH*, p. 35.

[172]   *BG*, p. 122.

[173]   I will follow Ken Gemes in employing the untranslated term, *Übermensch*, with its emphasis on "overcoming," rather than the phrase "higher man" ("Postmodernism's Use and Abuse of Nietzsche," *Philosophy and Phenomenological Research*, 62/2 [2001]: p. 358, n. 34).

[174]   Nietzsche unflatteringly referred to scholars as "the spiritual middle-class"! (*GS*, p. 334). Scholarship represented the nadir of creativity: "Like those who stand in the street

"time" itself, and to *subdue* the entire past ... . *Actual philosophers, however, are commanders and law-givers*: they say "thus it *shall* be!," it is they who determine the Wherefore and Whither of mankind, and they possess for this task the preliminary work of all the philosophical labourers, of all those who have subdued the past—they reach for the future with creative hand, and everything that is or has been becomes for them a means, an instrument, a hammer. Their "knowing" is *creating*, their creating is a law-giving, their will to truth is—*will to power*.[175]

In keeping with this creative task, Clark explains that Nietzsche's attitude toward history is revisionist, not restorational: he seeks to free the future from the fundamental valuational errors of the past.[176] In effect, Nietzsche's revaluational mastery of history desires the elevation of what is truly exemplary. Although all humans instinctively pursue the furtherance of their personal power, history testifies to men of refinement who cultivated that pursuit to the level of an artform, men who lived "contemporaneously with one another ... across the desert intervals of time" like Schopenhauer's "republic of genius."[177] Such "proud" men

> feel good only at the sight of unbroken men who might become their enemies and at the sight of all possessions that are hard to come by. Against one who is suffering they are often hard because he is not worthy of their aspirations and pride; but they are doubly obliging toward their *peers* whom it would be honourable to fight if the occasion should ever arise. Spurred by the good feeling of *this* perspective, the members of the knightly caste became accustomed to treating each other with exquisite courtesy.[178]

According to Nietzsche, the actions of a "healthy" gentility clearly embody the natural will to power:

---

and stare at the people passing by, so they too wait and stare at thoughts that others have thought" (*Z*, p. 147).

[175]   *BG*, pp. 142–3.

[176]   Clark, p. 859.

[177]   *UM*, p. 111. Salomé, p. 46, contends that "the cult of genius"—that is, "[t]he representation of the single, noble solitary, for whose sake alone the remaining 'mass products of nature' exist"—is a Schopenhauerian theme which Nietzsche "never relinquished," though it was greatly truncated during his period of disaffection from Wagner (ibid., p. 66). For "[h]is basic principle of anthropodicy, according to which mankind and history are justified only by the birth of a genius," see Safranski, p. 191. Peter Bergmann attributes the rise of the "cult of the superior man" to the collapse of "the liberal dream of an enlightened public opinion guided by the educated element in society" following the upheavals of 1848 (*Nietzsche: The Last Antipolitical German* [Bloomington and Indianapolis, 1987], p. 181).

[178]   *GS*, p. 87.

Even that body within which, as was previously assumed, individuals treat one another as equals—this happens in every healthy aristocracy—must, if it is a living and not a decaying body, itself do all that to other bodies which the individuals within it refrain from doing to one another: it will have to be the will to power incarnate, it will want to grow, expand, draw to itself, gain ascendancy—not out of any morality or immorality, but because it *lives*, and because life *is* will to power.[179]

Nietzsche posited that the existence of a ruling elite over the majority is essential for the development of "high" culture.[180] In a preface to an unpublished work entitled, "The Greek State," he wrote, "In order to have a broad, deep and fertile soil for artistic development, the overwhelming majority must be slavishly subjected to the necessities of life in order to serve a minority beyond the measure of its individual needs … ."[181] Through his philological excavations, Nietzsche uncovered an ancient value system which reflects an impenetrable class boundary:[182]

The judgement "good" does *not* derive from those to whom "goodness" is shown! Rather, the "good" themselves—that is, the noble, the powerful, the superior, and the high-minded—were the ones who felt themselves and their actions to be good—that is, as of the first rank—and posited them as such, in contrast to everything low, low-minded, common, and plebeian.[183]

The strength of this "master-based" value system stemmed from the physical and psychological potency of the upper echelons of society: "The knightly-aristocratic value-judgments presuppose a powerful physicality, a rich, burgeoning, even over-flowing health, as well as those things which help to preserve it—war, adventure, hunting, dancing, competitive games, and everything which involves strong, free, high-spirited activity."[184] In summary, master morality encapsulated an unrestrained, unapologetic lust for life, and the nobility itself came to personify "a complete automatism of instinct" which, for Nietzsche, constitutes "the precondition of any kind of mastery."[185]

---

[179] *BG*, p. 194.

[180] *HA*, p. 216.

[181] Cited in Safranski, p. 74.

[182] Mandel highlights a monograph Nietzsche wrote on the Greek oligarch Theognis, who praised the morality of his fellow leaders as "good" versus the "bad" morality of the commoners (Salomé, p. xvii).

[183] *GM*, p. 12. See also *HA*, p. 47. Like Hegel's master-slave dialectic, Nietzsche did not locate this morality clash within a specific historical context. Rather, he ascribed it to "those extended periods of the 'morality of custom' which preceded 'world history'" (*GM*, p. 93).

[184] Ibid., p. 19.

[185] *TI*, p. 189.

According to Nietzsche, the aristocratic ideal was preserved by a combination of careful cultural nurturing—"the accumulatory labour of generations"[186]—and sudden, unexpected avatarial emergences. In addition to the gentry's attempts to cradle a small flicker of human excellence within the "cupped hands" of "the pathos of distance,"[187] a "phoenix" like Napoleon could rise inexplicably from the plebeian ashes of post-Revolution France.[188] As a result, the great men who heralded momentous changes in the species were not confined to the hereditary gentry, and included men like Goethe, Beethoven, Stendhal, Heine, Schopenhauer, and—at times—Wagner.[189] Furthermore, Nietzsche did not consider all aristocrats to be higher types of men. Rather, the aristocratic institutions acted as an "incubator" for those rare and exceptional, era-embodying specimens, whom he regarded as "suddenly emerging late ghosts of past cultures and their powers—as atavisms of a people and its *mores* … ."[190] Instead of focusing on the aristocrats themselves, Nietzsche valued the ideal they represented, a "spiritual nobility" which seeks to embrace and master life with all of its vicissitudes.

Throughout his writings, Nietzsche highlighted several distinctive traits of the aristocratic ideal, which would become pivotal in his formulations of the masters of the future. First, members of the nobility embody a leisurely principle towards life; nothing "forces" their hand, whether decadence or duty, country or courtesan.[191] This insouciance bolsters a second essential attribute, genuine independence: "Few are made for independence—it is a privilege of the strong. And he who attempts it, having the completest right to it but without being *compelled* to, thereby proves that he is probably not only strong but also daring to the point of recklessness."[192]

---

[186]   Ibid., p. 112.

[187]   Nietzsche defined "pathos of distance" as "the chasm between man and man, class and class, the multiplicity of types, the will to be oneself, to stand out," and claimed that it "characterizes every *strong* age" (ibid., p. 102). He later described it as the mark of a "gentleman," the "first thing in which I 'test the reins' of a person" (*EH*, p. 93).

[188]   *GM*, p. 36.

[189]   *BG*, p. 189. Examples of "the *strong* German type" included Handel, Leibniz, and Bismarck (*WP*, pp. 471–2 [1887]). Houlgate observes, "When he does praise political figures, however, it is usually because of their 'heroic' style, rather than because of specific political achievements …" (*Hegel, Nietzsche, and the Criticism of Metaphysics*, p. 245, n. 180).

[190]   *GS*, p. 84. However, preserving class and cultural boundaries becomes essential, since "[i]t is preeminently in the generations and castes that *conserve* a people that we encounter such recrudescences of old instincts while such atavisms are improbable wherever races, habits, and valuations change too rapidly." In contrast to northern Europe, Nietzsche identified a contemporary "nobility" in Italy which transcended class. He wrote of Genoa: "But what you find *here* upon turning any corner is a human being … who knows the sea, adventure, and the Orient; a human being who abhors the law and the neighbor as a kind of boredom and who measures everything old and established with envious eyes" (ibid., p. 234).

[191]   *WP*, p. 479 [1887].

[192]   *BG*, p. 60.

These two attributes culminate in a third aspect, a super-abundance of power which is its own justification and has nothing to prove:

> The born aristocrats of the spirit are not overeager; their creations blossom and fall from the trees on a quiet autumn evening, being neither rashly desired, not hastened on, nor supplanted by new things. The wish to create incessantly is vulgar, betraying jealousy, envy, and ambition. If one is something, one does not actually need to do anything—and nevertheless does a great deal. There is a type higher than the "productive" man.[193]

Based on these traits, the spiritual aristocracy will transcend conventional morality and metaphysics, giving free range to their instincts at the expense of societal mores, religion, and reason itself.[194] Hence, members will act as existential "frontiersmen" of the human spirit, blazing new trails across previously untraveled regions of politics, aesthetics, and experience, "preserving the species" from the banalities of the staid and stagnant "farmers of the spirit":

> The strongest and most evil spirits have so far done the most to advance humanity: again they relumed the passions that were going to sleep—all ordered society puts the passions to sleep—and they re-awakened again and again the sense of comparison, of contradiction, of the pleasure in what is new, daring, untried; they compelled men to pit opinion against opinion, model against model. Usually by force of arms, by toppling boundary markers, by violating pieties—but also by means of new religions and moralities.[195]

In this way, the aristocratic class will cultivate autonomous, instinctual spiritual innovators, the "noble type of man" who "feels *himself* to be the determiner of values; he does not need to be approved of, he judges 'what harms me is harmful in itself,' he knows himself to be that which in general first accords honour to things, he *creates values*."[196] Ultimately, he will arrive at the pinnacle of

---

[193]   *HA*, p. 126. Since the true nobleman has nothing to prove by either creation or destruction, he becomes neither an anti-hero nor a poster-boy for nihilism. Kaufmann observes that this non-revolutionary thrust is commonly misapprehended in many expositions of Nietzsche (*WP*, p. 468, n. 5).

[194]   *GS*, p. 77. His indebtedness to Machiavelli is most evident here. In a notebook entry, he wrote: "Now, no philosopher will be in any doubt as to the type of perfection in politics; that is Machiavellianism" (*WP*, p. 170 [1887–88]). Like Machiavelli, he advocated the usefulness of an external allegiance to religious convention when beneficial to ruling (*BG*, p. 86). See Niccoló Machiavelli, *The Prince*, trans. George Bull (London, 1981), p. 56.

[195]   *GS*, p. 79.

[196]   *BG*, p. 195.

human development, the banishment of all hatred in place of the creator-god's unconditional love for the natural universe:[197]

> [T]hat enormous, overflowing certainty and health which cannot do without even illness itself, as an instrument and fishhook of knowledge; ... that excess of vivid healing, reproducing, reviving powers, the very sign of *great* health, an excess that gives the free spirit the dangerous privilege of being permitted to live *experimentally* and to offer himself to adventure: the privilege of the master free spirit![198]

The present plight: the herd is the word

The image of the noble spirit reaches titanic heights in Nietzsche. After asking what makes a person "noble," he answered: "[T]he feeling of heat in things that feel cold to everybody else; the discovery of values for which no scales have been invented yet; offering sacrifices on altars that are dedicated to an unknown god; a courage without any desire for honors; a self-sufficiency that overflows and gives to men and things."[199] Because these noble spirits are rare indeed, no tenet or principle must be allowed to squelch the sheer exceptionality of such persons. In an intriguing "marriage" of physiological and cultural determinants, Nietzsche regarded the aristocracy's will to power as something inherited, preserved, and concentrated from generation to generation, provided that classes and races are not diluted through interbreeding.[200] Hence, he derided the contemporary malaise of European scepticism as

> [t]he most spiritual expression of a certain complex physiological condition called in ordinary language nervous debility and sickliness; it arises whenever races or classes long separated from one another are decisively and suddenly crossed. In the new generation, which has as it were inherited varying standards and values in its blood, all is unrest, disorder, doubt, experiment; the most vital forces have a retarding effect, the virtues themselves will not let one another grow and become strong, equilibrium, centre of balance, upright certainty are lacking in body and soul. But that which becomes most profoundly sick and degenerates in such hybrids is the *will* ... . Our Europe of today, the scene of a senselessly sudden attempt at radical class—and *consequently* race—mixture, is as a result sceptical from top to bottom ... .[201]

---

[197]   *GM*, p. 24.

[198]   *HA*, pp. 7–8.

[199]   *GS*, p. 117.

[200]   Contrary to Nazism, however, Nietzsche did not restrict "noble races" to Arians, but included "Roman, Arab, German, Japanese nobility, Homeric heroes, Scandinavian Vikings" (*GM*, p. 26).

[201]   *BG*, pp. 136–7. See also ibid., pp. 152, 199; *GM*, p. 109. Zarathustra likewise denounced "the herd" for its interbreeding: "Rabble-hotchpotch: in that everything is mixed

Nietzsche argued that, originally, the "masses" were significant for three reasons: "first as faded copies of great men produced on poor paper with worn-out plates, then as a force of resistance to great men, finally as instruments in the hands of great men ... ."[202] However, in an ironic twist of feat, the millennia-old political and cultural supremacy of the aristocracy was overthrown. As the historical aristocracy brought more power to bear upon their vassals, "a vast quantity of freedom" was "forcibly made latent" and began compounding across the centuries.[203] In addition, the slaves' "natural" faith in the superiority of the masters was undermined by certain corrupt Roman emperors: "For at bottom the masses are willing to submit to slavery of any kind, if only the higher-ups constantly legitimize themselves as higher, as *born* to command—by having noble manners."[204] Consequently, the slaves were ripe for revolt, despite that their ongoing subjugation "benefited" both the species in general[205] and the slaves themselves.[206]

In an apparent excerpt from the sermon dossier of Dostoyevsky's Grand Inquisitor, Nietzsche once declared that the majority of men covet the collective security which a hierarchical society offers: "To be alone, to experience things by oneself, neither to obey nor to rule, to be an individual—that was not a pleasure but a punishment; one was sentenced 'to individuality.'"[207] Moreover, slaves need to be mastered—both physically and spiritually—in order to thrive, a craving which manifests itself particularly in religiosity among slaves: "If one considers what need people have of an external regulation to constrain and steady them, how compulsion, *slavery* in a higher sense, is the sole and final condition under which the person of weaker will, woman especially, can prosper; then one also understands

---

up with everything else, saint and scoundrel and gentleman and Jew and every beast out of Noah's Ark" (*Z*, p. 258). Kaufmann argues against accusations of "biologism," citing Nietzsche's belief that "race mixture might favor the attainment of culture—both in nations and individuals" (*Nietzsche: Philosopher, Psychologist, Antichrist*, p. 288). He also contends that Nietzsche's claim to have Polish ancestry reflects his desire to be of mixed blood. However, Nietzsche's growing aversion to all things German likely motivated the Polish myth. Furthermore, his passion for purity and abhorrence of hybrids are recurrent themes. See, for example, *Z*, p. 258; *BG*, pp. 40, 136–7, 182; *WP*, p. 461 [1888]; *EH*, pp. 14, 18.

[202]   *UM*, p. 113.

[203]   *GM*, p. 67.

[204]   *GS*, p. 107. See also *WP*, p. 468 [1884]: "When Nero and Caracalla sat up there, the paradox arose: 'the lowest man is worth more than that man up there!' And the way was prepared for an image of God that was as remote as possible from the image of the most powerful—the god on the cross!"

[205]   *BG*, p. 168.

[206]   On the "joy" that ensues for "the weaker that wants to become a function," see *GS*, p. 176.

[207]   Ibid., p. 175. See Fyodor Dostoyevsky, *The Brothers Karamazov*, trans. David McDuff (London, 1993), p. 295, where the Inquisitor argues that the crowds begged the clergy to remove the "horrific" freedom which Christ unleashed upon them.

the nature of conviction, 'faith.'"[208] His peculiar conception of "spiritual heredity," whereby one inherits psychological habits from one's ancestors, approximated a subtle strand of "spiritual predestination." Hence, Nietzsche wrote,

> That which his ancestors most liked to do and most constantly did cannot be erased from a man's soul ... . It is quite impossible that a man should *not* have in his body the qualities and preferences of his parents and forefathers: whatever appearances may say to the contrary. This constitutes the problem of race.[209]

Both politically and biologically, it would seem, slavery is an inexorable necessity. This rendered the slaves' strategic victory over the aristocratic ideal that much more disturbing. Because slavery is presupposed in the amoral "natural" universe in which humankind dwells, Nietzsche regarded the cultural and political slave uprising as inherently "unnatural" and inimical to life itself.[210] In addition to numerical advantages, the slave revolution received crucial assistance from the nobles themselves when a disenfranchised group of aristocrats, crippled by physical and/or political weakness, sought power in a new way.[211] Initially, the religious sphere was derived from the political following "the rule that the political concept of rank always transforms itself into a spiritual concept of rank ... ."[212] However, at some point, the priests unleashed devastating, psychological warfare upon their own class by instigating an ethical revolution: the denigration of master values (strength, power, pride, vengeance, autonomy) as "evil," and the elevation of slave values (subjugation, humility, compassion, industriousness, weakness) as "good."[213] Furthermore, the priests abolished the previous valuational boundaries which had formerly restricted master virtues to masters and slave virtues to

---

[208]   *TI*, p. 185. For master power as the necessary locus of faith for the slaves, see *GS*, p. 289.

[209]   *BG*, p. 203. Nietzsche listed three traits—"untoward intemperance," "narrow enviousness," and "obstinate self-assertiveness"—as endemic to "the plebeian type," asserting that "qualities of this sort must be transferred to the child as surely as bad blood; and the best education and culture will succeed only in *deceiving* with regard to such an inheritance" (ibid.). For Nietzsche and "the Lamarckian notion of the biological heritability," see Richard Schacht, *Nietzsche* (London, 1983), p. 335, and Kaufmann *Nietzsche: Philosopher, Psychologist, Antichrist*, p. 304.

[210]   Slaves were useful to society, so long as they remembered their place. Slavery provided a vital historical counter-weight to the excess of will to power which threatened to destroy sixteenth-century Europe (*BG*, p. 144). Furthermore, the prosperity of the nobility and "every higher culture" depended upon the well-being of the lower classes (ibid., p. 168); thus, Nietzsche forbade "the exception" from trying to become the rule (*GS*, p. 131).

[211]   On the direct connection between priesthood and ill health, see *HA*, p. 88; *GM*, p. 18.

[212]   Ibid., p. 17.

[213]   Ibid., p. 18.

slaves.[214] In place of this two-tier system, the priests advocated slave morality as an absolute, universal moral code regardless of rank or class. Consequently, the priest rose to supremacy and the "herd" became the word throughout Europe:

> [M]en not noble enough to see the abysmal disparity in order of rank and abysm of rank between men and man—it is *such* men who, with their "equal before God," have hitherto ruled over the destiny of Europe, until at last a shrunken, almost ludicrous species, a herd animal, something full of good will, sickly and mediocre has been bred, the European of today … .[215]

Nietzsche was infuriated by this "unfortunate" turn of events, particularly since it constituted a nonsensical rejection of the "natural" order: "To demand of strength that it should *not* express itself as strength, that it should *not* be a will to overcome, overthrow, dominate, a thirst for enemies and resistance and triumph, makes as little sense as to demand of weakness that it should express itself as strength."[216] Moreover, the actions of the priests were not motivated by extreme munificence—like those of the higher nobles—but by disease, frailty, and the most sordid hatred of life and health.[217] This *ressentiment* was concentrated in the ultimate weapon against instinct and one of the purest manifestations of will to power, though one deplorably directed against life itself, the ascetic ideal:

> The ascetic ideal has a *goal*—and this goal is sufficiently universal for all other interests of human existence to seem narrow and petty in comparison; it relentlessly interprets periods, peoples, men in terms of this goal, it allows no other interpretation, no other goal, … it subordinates itself to no other power, it believes rather in its prerogative over all other powers, in its absolute *seniority of rank* with respect to all other powers … .[218]

---

214   It is important to reiterate that slave morality, when confined to slaves, is good and proper for the well-being of civilization, according to Nietzsche: "As soon as there is a desire to take this principle further, however, and if possible even as the *fundamental principle of society*, it at once reveals itself for what it is: as the will to the *denial* of life, as the principle of dissolution and decay" (*BG*, pp. 193–4).

215   Ibid., p. 89. He also blamed universal education—"[I]f one wants slaves, one is a fool if one educates them to be masters" [*TI*, p. 106]—for providing commoners with the opportunity to pee in the intellectual gene pool: "Life is a fountain of delight; but where the rabble also drinks all wells are poisoned" (*Z*, p. 120). When properly administered, however, education is useful in converting men into "intelligent tools" by divorcing pleasure from duty and inculcating the "sublime monotony" of routine, repetitive tasks (*WP*, p. 474 [1887, 88]).

216   *GM*, p. 29.

217   Hence, he exclaimed, "Priests are, as is well-known, the *most evil enemies*—but why? Because they are the most powerless. From powerlessness their hatred grows to take on a monstrous and sinister shape, the most cerebral and most poisonous form" (ibid., p. 19).

218   Ibid., pp. 123–4. When an instinct "seeks not to master some isolated aspect of life but rather life itself, its deepest, strongest, most fundamental conditions … ," then it must

Nietzsche concluded that this "morality of unselfing" is an atrocity against nature which must be extirpated at all costs.[219] In light of these developments, Nietzsche lamented, "The declining instincts have become master over the ascending instincts—The will to nothingness has now become master over the will to life!"[220]

The priests' legacy both haunted and inspired Nietzsche by unequivocally demonstrating that actual power can be overcome by something even greater—the desire for unpossessed power. Hence, he could not help but grudgingly admire the "morality manoeuvre," which had led to the banishment of his beloved aristocratic ideal and blighted Europe with the mediocrity of Christendom: "In comparison with the ingenuity of priestly revenge, all other intelligence scarcely merits consideration. Human history would be a much too stupid affair were it not for the intelligence introduced by the powerless."[221] But all was not lost. In addition to highlighting the value of revaluation and the explosive potential of desire, religion had assisted the aristocracy both by instilling self-discipline, honor, and the ability to keep promises—the better to rule—and also by cultivating a more compliant "herd" of humanity—the better to be ruled.[222] With Machiavellian optimism, even the ascetic ideal can be useful in purifying the will to power, protecting society from nihilistic despair, pooling the societal reservoir of available physical and spiritual resources, and thus preparing the way for the radical redaction of the *Übermensch.*[223]

The hope of the future: rise of the Übermensch

Throughout human history, Nietzsche had observed a miasma of mediocrity. Penetrating this spiritual smog, however, the towering figures of great men rose mountainous above the tumult, forming "a kind of bridge across the turbulent stream of becoming."[224] These giants transcended their "Lilliputian" forebears, participating in an "exalted spirit-dialogue" with their equals which is "undisturbed by the excited chattering dwarfs who creep about beneath them."[225] This great "chain" of human exemplars serves to unite the species and supply "the fundamental idea of faith in humanity."[226] Despite the current domination of "the lower species,"[227] Nietzsche envisioned a being who was—along Anselmian lines—simply too good not to be real:

---

be opposed (ibid., p. 97).

[219]   *EH*, p. 67.

[220]   *WP*, p. 217 [1888].

[221]   *GM*, p. 19.

[222]   Ibid., p. 41.

[223]   Ibid., pp. 105–6, 136; *WP*, pp. 9–10 [1886–87].

[224]   *UM*, p. 111. Nietzsche employed similar images of an archipelago of greatness in describing Wagner's growing "chain" of great operatic characters (ibid., p. 202).

[225]   Ibid., p. 111.

[226]   Ibid., p. 68.

[227]   *WP*, p. 19 [1887].

Conversely, one could conceive of such a pleasure and power of self-determination, such a *freedom* of the will that the spirit would take leave of all faith and every wish for certainty, being practiced in maintaining himself on insubstantial ropes and possibilities and dancing even near abysses. Such a spirit would be the *free spirit* par excellence.[228]

The concept of "spiritual evolution" provided another metaphorical means of linking the erratic yet spectacular specimens of the past—like Caesar and Napoleon—to a future which overshadowed the present plight.[229] Though it would be a gross inaccuracy to accuse Nietzsche of seeking to return to a "Golden Age" in light of his constant urge to "press ahead," there is no shortage of sentiment when he gazes at the past.[230] As Michael Tanner points out, Nietzsche sought to combine the "incorrigible health" of the rather "simplistic" master [*Herr*] with the cleverness and complexity of the slave [*Sklave*].[231] However, attempts to interpret Nietzsche's vision of humanity as a message of interior self-overcoming for a general audience seem strained.[232] Instead, "selective" evolution safeguarded the spiritual *status quo*.

---

[228]   *GS*, pp. 289–90. Hollingdale argues that this vision is, in part, how Nietzsche personally resisted the will to nihilism (*Z*, p. 25).

[229]   *WP*, p. 470 [1887, 88]: "[I]t is perhaps part of the economy of human evolution that man should evolve piece by piece."

[230]   Tanner, p. 46. Ansell-Pearson states: "Nietzsche's aristocratism seeks to revive an older conception of politics, one which he locates in the Greek *agon* …" (pp. 33–4). Richard White contends that Nietzsche is attempting "to inspire us with an urgent longing for 'the Master's return'" ("The Return of the Master: An Interpretation of Nietzsche's 'Genealogy of Morals,'" *Philosophy and Phenomenological Research*, 48/4 [1988]: p. 685). Bruce Detwiler observes a marked absence of aristocratic politics and "more sympathetic" treatment of democracy during Nietzsche's "middle period" (*Nietzsche and the Politics of Aristocratic Radicalism* [Chicago and London, 1990], p. 16).

[231]   Tanner, p. 71. However, Tanner argues that Nietzsche "gave up on the *Übermensch*," turning increasingly to Goethe as a model for the 'higher man'" (ibid., p. 79).

[232]   I disagree with commentators like Philip Kain who attempt to argue for a "kinder, gentler *Übermensch*." who thereby becomes a paragon of "self-repression, sublimation and self-overcoming" ("Nietzschean Genealogy and Hegelian History in *The Genealogy of Morals*," *Canadian Journal of Philosophy*, 26/1 [1996]: 134). See also Kaufmann, *Nietzsche: Philosopher, Psychologist, Antichrist*, pp. 309–10; Hollingdale, *Nietzsche*, pp. 97–9; Golomb and Wistrich, *Nietzsche, Godfather of Fascism? On the Uses and Abuses of a Philosophy*, p. 8. Such theorizing hinges, in part, upon an exaggerated dichotomy between "private" and "political"; for example, Hollingdale insists: "[T]he consequences following from the theory of will to power are, in fact, not social at all, … they are concerned with what takes place within a single 'soul'" (*Nietzsche*, p. 95). Kain, p. 135, goes on to acknowledge that the *carte blanche* "poetic license" which the *Übermensch* receives, combined with Nietzsche's silence on specified exercises of that power is, indeed, foreboding. He writes, "The only kind of power Nietzsche is after, the sort of power the *Übermensch* must have, is the power to create meaning—a new heaven, a new vision, new cultural values" (ibid., p. 143). It is one thing to extol the "creation of new values,"

The German philosopher relished Danish scholar Georg Brandes' assessment: "The expression 'aristocratic radicalism,' which you employ, is very good. It is, permit me to say, the cleverest thing I have yet to read about myself."[233]

In order to escape from a world of plebeian pettiness, Nietzsche strove to captivate the imagination with an artistic model for emulation,[234] a new image of human destiny, "a higher type that arises and preserves itself under different conditions from those of the average man."[235] Although Zarathustra stated that such a being has yet to appear in human history,[236] Nietzsche placed his hope in nature's serendipitous production of "exceptions":

> One does not reckon with such beings, they arrive like fate, without motive, reason, consideration, pretext, they arrive like lightning, too fearful, too sudden, too convincing, too "different," even to be hated. Their work is an instinctive creation and impression of form, they are the most involuntary, most unconscious artists there are—wherever they appear, something new quickly grows up, a *living* structure of domination, in which parts and functions are demarcated and articulated, where only that which has first been given a "meaning" with respect to the whole finds a place.[237]

Nietzsche viewed entire civilizations, races, classes, and religions as useful means to this end—the emergence of a "superspecies." In a notebook entry, he once summarized his philosophical project as follows:

> My ideas do not revolve around the degree of freedom that is granted to the one or to the other or to all, but around the degree of *power* that the one or the other should exercise over others or over all, and to what extent a sacrifice of freedom, even enslavement, provides the basis for the emergence of a *higher type*. Put in the crudest form: *how could one sacrifice the development of mankind* to help a higher species than man to come into existence?[238]

---

but whose meanings and for whom do they apply? For a longer rebuttal of attempts to ameliorate the theme of domination in Nietzsche, see Detwiler, pp. 157–62.

[233]   Brandes, p. 3. This letter was written on 2 December 1887.

[234]   Jacob Golomb, "Nietzsche on Authority," *Philosophy Today*, 34/3 (1990): 255. William Irwin suggests that Nietzsche's treatment of human history parallels the Renaissance artists' use of Hellenistic culture, "drawing inspiration from the Greeks, but also allowing themselves enough freedom and forgetting to produce truly great and original art" ("Philosophy and the History of Philosophy: On the Advantage of Nietzsche," *American Catholic Philosophical Quarterly*, 75/1 [2001]: 42–3).

[235]   *WP*, p. 463 [1887–88].

[236]   *Z*, p. 117.

[237]   *GM*, pp. 66–7.

[238]   *WP*, p. 458 [1883–88]. See also ibid., p. 464 [1887–88]. Salomé, p. 19, argues that, for Nietzsche, "'victory' equals self-destruction of mankind to make possible the creation

Despite the unpredictability of an *Übermensch* appearance, other people can be instrumental in their arrival. Regarding the "man of science," Nietzsche once stated:

> The objective man is an instrument, a precious, easily damaged and tarnished measuring instrument and reflecting apparatus which ought to be respected and taken good care of; but he is not an end, a termination and ascent, a complementary man in whom the *rest* of existence is justified, a conclusion … but rather only a delicate, empty, elegant, flexible mould which has first to wait for some content so as "to form" itself by it … .[239]

This "termination and ascent" is the *Übermensch*: the "superman" or "overman" which, Kaufmann contends, was inspired by the concept of the "over-soul" from an essay by Ralph Waldo Emerson.[240] Safranski identifies Nietzsche's first usage of the term when he was a teenager, describing Byron's "Manfred" as an "*Übermensch* who commands the spirits."[241] "*I teach you the Superman*," a post-transfigurational Zarathustra announced: "Man is something that should be overcome. What have you done to overcome him?"[242] However, Nietzsche did not envision a literal vanquishing of humankind. The *Übermensch* is dependent upon the human masses which comprise the very "power generators" from which the super-individuals "spike," so long as society is not inhibited by metaphysical "surge protectors":

> Great men, like great epochs, are explosive material in whom tremendous energy has been accumulated; their prerequisite has always been, historically and physiologically, that a protracted assembling, accumulating, economizing and preserving has preceded them—that there has been no explosion for a long time. If the tension in the mass has grown too great the merest accidental stimulus suffices to call the "genius," the "deed," the great destiny, into the world.[243]

Like the idealized nobleman, the *Übermensch* radiates cool indifference from a glacial core of invulnerable superabundance after defeating his strongest foes:

---

of a superior mankind."

[239]   *BG*, p. 135. See also *Z*, p. 44: "What is great in man is that he is a bridge and not a goal; what can be loved in man is that he is a *going-across* and not a *going-down*."

[240]   *GS*, p. 11. Brandes, p. 36, contends that Nietzsche's vision was strongly influenced by Renan's *Dialogues Philosophiques*, while Kaufmann highlights parallels with Aristotelian "greatness of soul" (*Nietzsche: Philosopher, Psychologist, Antichrist*, pp. 382–4). Kaufmann dates the word back to second-century C.E. usage by Lucian, and lists occurrences in Heinrich Müller, J.G. Herder, Jean Paul, and Goethe (ibid., pp. 307–8).

[241]   Safranski, p. 35.

[242]   *Z*, p. 41.

[243]   *TI*, p. 108.

"What is best about a great victory is that it liberates the victor from the fear of defeat. 'Why not be defeated some time, too?' he says to himself; 'Now I am rich enough for that.'"[244] The *Übermensch* will remain impervious to opposing forces, whether external or internal, and will thereby epitomize true freedom.[245] Unlike the self-negation of Christianity, the *Übermensch*'s self-conquering will merely be a means to higher feats of mastery.[246] He will implement new values and revaluations while simultaneously inspiring them.[247] Contrary to fascist appropriations of Nietzsche's writings, Houlgate states: "The epitome of Nietzschean strength and self-expression is thus not to be conceived as the crude, material manifestation of physical or political power, but rather as an internalized, spiritualized (*vergeistigt*) form of aesthetic wholeness and creativity."[248] Moreover, this ultra-human can soar over the darkest abysses like a bird, tear through human values faster than a speeding bullet, boldly go into the vast realms of undiscovered human experience,

---

[244]   *GS*, p. 199.

[245]   *TI*, p. 104. Nietzsche's vision of autonomy bears a strong resemblance to Hegel's description of the "two modes of consciousness": "The one is independent whose essential nature is to be for itself, the other is dependent whose essence is life or existence for another. The former is the Master, or Lord, the latter the Bondsman" (*The Phenomenology of Mind*, trans. J.B. Baillie [2 vols, London, 1910], vol. 1, p. 182).

[246]   *NR*, p. 233.

[247]   One may either argue that Nietzsche conflated the role of philosopher with the *Übermensch* or that, despite obvious overlap in function, the coveted "new philosopher" remains a distinct yet crucial role which prepares the way for the coming *Übermensch*. Because Nietzsche never identified himself as an *Übermensch*, I favor the latter interpretation.

[248]   Houlgate, *Hegel, Nietzsche and the Criticism of Metaphysics*, p. 74. I concur with Ansell-Pearson, p. 33, in dismissing J.P. Stern's assertion that Hitler was the closest embodiment of Nietzsche's anthropological idea. This does not, however, distance Nietzsche entirely from the fascist politics which commandeered his thoughts. As Detwiler, p. 113, observes, "Nietzsche's artistic vision carries with it a willingness to aestheticize politics in ways that suggest distinct affinities with fascism." See also Gemes, p. 356: "While Nietzsche scholars may believe that his many positive accounts of mixtures, his continual disparagement of German nationalism, and his many positive comments about Jews exonerate him from responsibility ... I think those who take seriously Nietzsche's dictum that a thing is the sum of its effects and understand how destructive the biologistic rhetoric of degeneration has been for Europe will find little solace here." Nietzsche's bellicose attitude towards perceived agents of "weakness" is, likewise, unsettling. See, for example, *TI*, p. 128: "The weak and ill-constituted shall perish: first principle of *our* philanthropy. And one shall help them to do so." For a fascinating collection of essays on the relations of Nietzsche and fascism, see Golomb and Wistrich, *Nietzsche, Godfather of Fascism? On the Uses and Abuses of a Philosophy*. The editors conclude: "While almost any philosophy can be propagandistically abused (as Hans Sluga has shown, Kant was a particular favourite among academic philosophers of the Third Reich!), Nietzsche's pathos, his imaginative excesses as well as his image as a prophet-seer and creator of myths, seems especially conducive to such abuse by fascists" (ibid., p. 4).

resisting the black holes of nihilism, probing the nebulae of "evil," and emerging victorious, cold and distant as a god, torn and bloodied as only a man can be:

> [T]he ideal of a human, superhuman well-being and benevolence that will often appear *inhuman*—for example, when it confronts all earthly seriousness so far, all solemnity in gesture, word, tone, eye, morality, and task so far, as if it were their most incarnate and involuntary parody—and in spite of all of this, it is perhaps only with him that *great seriousness* really begins, that the real question mark is posed for the first time, that the destiny of the soul changes, the hand moves forward, the tragedy *begins*.[249]

A deliberate elision of the human and the "divine" lies at the heart of Nietzsche's vision, the energy of heaven flung in playful, childlike fury upon the earth.[250] For the German philosopher, the heavens are empty because the earth is full. He concluded,

> It is richness in personality, abundance in oneself, overflowing and bestowing, instinctive good health and affirmation of oneself, that produce great sacrifice and great love: it is strong and godlike selfhood from which these affects grow, just as surely as do the desire to become master, encroachment, the inner certainty of having a right to everything.[251]

Unlike the universal message of Christianity or the egalitarian auspices of liberal and utilitarian ethics,[252] the promulgation of a "dangerous knowledge"[253] which reveals the "true" meaning of appearances—religious and otherwise—to a select readership[254] and remains shrouded from the vast majority of people suggests

---

[249]   *GS*, p. 347.

[250]   Zarathustra thus styled himself "a prophet of the lightning … called *Superman*" (*Z*, p. 45). Hollingdale argues, "The superman is not man's successor but rather God's" (*Nietzsche*, p. 98). See also Richardson, p. 66, n. 103.

[251]   *WP*, p. 209 [1887].

[252]   See Ansell-Pearson, p. 55: "Nietzsche's anti-humanist political thinking does not give equal value to every individual human life, but assesses the value of an individual life in terms of whether it represents an ascending or descending mode of life … . If individuals cannot attain greatness, they should at least serve it. This is the essence of Nietzsche's aristocratism, as well as the principle on which he bases his unorthodox, illiberal, and anti-Christian notion of justice." See also Detwiler, p. 113.

[253]   *BG*, p. 53.

[254]   Ibid., p. 61; *Z*, p. 299; *EH*, p. 24.

an affinity between Nietzsche's philosophical project and the Greek Mystery religions.[255] For Nietzsche, individualism clearly isn't for everyone.[256]

It is difficult to overestimate the value which the *Übermensch* ideal injected into life for Nietzsche. As Zarathustra proudly proclaimed, "The Superman is the meaning of the earth. Let your will say: The Superman *shall be* the meaning of the earth!"[257] The *Übermensch* became a mote of meaning in the swirling vortex of eternal recurrence, redeeming his vision from eternal redundancy: "I do not want life *again*. How did I endure it? Creating. What makes me stand the sight of it? The vision of the overman who *affirms* life. I have tried to affirm it *myself*— alas!"[258] Ironically, the *Übermensch* constitutes both motivational exemplar as well as "biological product of deliberate breeding."[259] Like an alpine lake, humankind needs to be "eternally dammed" in order to be deepened, or so Nietzsche dared to dream: "[P]erhaps man will rise ever higher as soon as he ceases to *flow out* into a god."[260] To this end, Nietzsche labored vigorously. In light of his vision of the past, present, and future of humankind, the next chapter will examine more closely Nietzsche's validations of power "properly exercised."

---

[255]   See Owen Barfield, *History in English Words* (London, 1962), p. 99: "[T]hey revealed in some way the inner meaning of external appearances, and secondly, that the 'initiate' attained immortality in a sense different from that of the uninitiated."

[256]   See Detwiler, p. 105: "Nietzsche champions the individualism of the highest type but not that of all man."

[257]   *Z*, p. 42.

[258]   *GS*, p. 19. Salomé, p. 139, insightfully observes that the *Übermensch* is an intensely personal and stylized man, dubbing him an "*Über-Nietzsche*."

[259]   Safranski, p. 271. In keeping with Nietzsche's rejection of body/soul dichotomies, Kaufmann observes that "'breeding' is at least as spiritual as it is physical" (*Nietzsche: Philosopher, Psychologist, Antichrist*, p. 326).

[260]   *GS*, p. 230.

Chapter 3
Appropriating Power:
Nietzsche's Concept of Power

The Tier of Authority: Valid Exertions of Power

A brief survey of the secondary literature confirms the observation of Keith Ansell-Pearson: "Inquiry into the political dimension of Nietzsche's thought still remains the most contentious and controversial aspect of Nietzsche studies."[1] Peter Bergmann states that, whereas "his accusers have placed him outside his time" by deeming him "unpolitical," "his defenders have placed him above his time" by regarding him as "antipolitical."[2] It is highly significant that Nietzsche did not articulate key roles for particular positions in society. With an aloofness from contextualized particulars, Nietzsche endorsed no specific political models— whether monarchy, oligarchy, etc. Instead, he cited Machiavelli's claim that "the form of governments is of very slight importance, although semi-educated people think otherwise. The great goal of politics should be *permanence*, which outweighs anything else, being much more valuable than freedom."[3] He then added, "Only when permanence is securely established and guaranteed is there any possibility of constant development and ennobling inoculation, which, to be sure, will usually be opposed by the dangerous companion of all permanence: authority."[4]

Because he was preoccupied with humankind as a species and not individual contexts *per se*, Nietzsche refrained from providing elaborate measures for societal reconfiguration. The masters must merely be allowed to rule as masters, supplying conducive "canvases" for artistic endeavors. The slaves must continue to serve as slaves, comprising the stable "easel" upon which the master-pieces will be displayed. And all must be subject to the "aesthetic" authority of the *Übermensch*, whenever one should grace the studio of human history.

Nietzsche did, however, articulate the importance of exemplary enactments of the will to power. In *The Gay Science*, Nietzsche attributed all actions to the drive

---

[1]   Keith Ansell-Pearson, *An Introduction to Nietzsche as Political Thinker* (Cambridge, 1997), 2. For a brief overview, see Bruce Detwiler, *Nietzsche and the Politics of Aristocratic Radicalism* (Chicago and London, 1990), pp. 1, 200, n. 13.

[2]   Peter Bergmann, *Nietzsche: The Last Antipolitical German* (Bloomington and Indianapolis, 1987), p. 2.

[3]   *HA*, p. 139.

[4]   Ibid. He once contended that the contemporary state's desire for absolute authority parallels the loyalty commanded by the medieval church (*UM*, p. 150).

for power enhancement: "Benefiting and hurting others are ways of exercising one's power upon others; that is all one desires in such cases. One hurts those whom one wants to feel one's power, for pain is a much more efficient means to that end than pleasure ... ."[5] Despite the apparent amorality of all human action, there are at least two general manifestations of power which Nietzsche opposed. The first is any thought or action which transgresses the "natural" categories of class, race, and "blood," and blurs all gradations of distinction into one dispiriting herd. The second is any thought or action which obstructs the ongoing development of the species by miring it within the "stasis-quo" of "being," antiquated conventionality, and/or religious domestication. To "freeze" such valuable assets—human and otherwise—can scarcely be tolerated within a closed universe where former values and truths must be sacrificed for new ones to take their place in the epistemological "food chain."[6] No metaphysical or religious truths can be privileged in this god-eat-god world in which mastery of the other is the primary, inescapable goal and means of life. Hence, Nietzsche announced,

> [W]e are delighted with all who love, as we do, danger, war, and adventures, who refuse to compromise, to be captured, reconciled, and castrated; we count ourselves among conquerors; we think about the necessity for new orders, also for a new slavery—for every strengthening and enhancement of the human type also involves a new kind of enslavement.[7]

Zarathustra thus commanded that peace should be loved "as a means to new wars. And the short peace more than the long."[8]

On account of Nietzsche's faith in the constructive role of conflict in "natural" growth,[9] he generally sanctioned those actions which destabilize old "orders" and re-establish new and more powerful ones in their wake: "For wherever the great architecture of culture developed, it was its task to force opposing forces into harmony through an overwhelming aggregation of the remaining, less incompatible powers, yet without suppressing or shackling them."[10] Once again, it is important to emphasize that Nietzsche did not glorify "mindless" destruction

---

[5]   *GS*, p. 86.

[6]   In keeping with his predilection for biological imagery, Nietzsche once compared the spirit to a "stomach," amorally ingesting whatever agreed with it and disgorging the rest (*BG*, p. 161).

[7]   *GS*, p. 338. See also *WP*, p. 193 [1888]; *TI*, p. 31. On the virtue of slavery, see *BG*, p. 112, where he described it as "the indispensable means also for spiritual discipline and breeding."

[8]   *Z*, p. 74.

[9]   See, for example, *EH*, p. 17: "[E]very growth reveals itself in the seeking out of a powerful opponent—or problem: for a philosopher who is warlike also challenges problems to a duel."

[10]   *HA*, p. 168.

or epistemological anarchy as an end in itself. The hammer strokes he directed at the hallowed edifices of civilization were aimed and delivered with calculated precision. The vaunted higher species to which humankind is being urged will not resort to brute force, but will personify the richness and gracefulness of a meticulously measured self-control. Hence, Zarathustra exclaimed,

> To stand with relaxed muscles and unharnessed wills: that is the most difficult thing for all of you, you sublime men! When power grows gracious and descends into the visible: I call such descending beauty. And I desire beauty from no one as much as I desire it from you, you man of power: may your goodness be your ultimate self-overpowering.[11]

In a notebook entry describing "him that has turned out well," Nietzsche declared:

> He enjoys the taste of what is wholesome for him; his pleasure in anything ceases when the bounds of the wholesome are crossed; he divines the remedies for partial injuries; he has illnesses as great stimulants of his life; he knows how to exploit ill chances; he grows stronger through the accidents that threaten to destroy him; he instinctively gathers from all that he sees, hears, experiences, what advances his main concern—he follows a principle of selection—he allows much to fall through; he reacts with the slowness bred by a long caution and a deliberate pride—he tests a stimulus for its origins and its intentions, he does not submit; he is always in his *own company*, whether he deals with books, men, or landscapes; he honors by choosing, by admitting, by trusting.[12]

The genuine hero must not define himself exclusively based on external conflict "under the impulse of a moment," but must personify the keenest potency under the sway of no occipital goals or mores.[13]

This chapter will examine six general actions endorsed by Nietzsche in the performance of his vital task of salvaging humankind from its current existential plight. These six dispensations of power contain at least one unifying factor—they presuppose Nietzsche's fundamental motto from "the military school of life": "What does not kill me makes me stronger."[14] He argued:

> A new creation in particular, the new *Reich* for instance, has more need of enemies than friends: only in opposition does it feel itself necessary, only in opposition does it *become* necessary ... . We adopt the same attitude towards the "enemy within": there too we have spiritualized enmity, there too we have

---

[11] Z, p. 141.

[12] *WP*, p. 520 [1888].

[13] Ibid., p. 490 [1887–88].

[14] *TI*, p. 33.

grasped its *value*. One is *fruitful* only at the cost of being rich in contradictions; one remains *young* only on condition the soul does not relax, does not long for peace … . One has renounced *grand* life when one renounces war … .[15]

The major manifestations which Nietzsche endorsed include the determination of new values, the destruction of antiquated mores, the embracing of suffering, the employment of cruelty, the aestheticizing of the world, and the breeding of the species.[16]

The Task of Revaluation

As the events of World War II have shown, it is frightfully easy to caricature Nietzsche's will to power as a maudlin endorsement of brute strength and overlook the subtler nuances of his thought.[17] In a notebook entry, Nietzsche once criticized the futility of unleashing brute force: "[W]hile a crude injury done him [an adversary] certainly demonstrates our power over him, it at the same time estranges his will from us even more—and thus makes him less easy to subjugate."[18] Nietzsche harbored little optimism that something as ubiquitous and amorphous as the will to power can be encapsulated within a specific empire, nation, or political system. For this reason, the surging military might of the Prussian Empire under Otto von Bismarck elicited scant attention from the philosopher. He viewed such "grand politics" as a prescription of "blood and iron" to combat German cultural

---

[15]   Ibid., p. 54.

[16]   This list admittedly neglects "lighter" exercises such as celebration (*BT*, p. xviii; *Z*, pp. 98–9), play (*GS*, p. 347; *EH*, pp. 37, 72; *WP*, p. 419 [1885–86]), joy (*Z*, pp. 111, 332; *WP*, p. 62 [1887]), dancing (*GS*, pp. 164, 289–90; *Z*, p. 227; *BG*, p. 110), and laughter (*GS*, pp. 163–4, *Z*, p. 68, *GM*, p. 79), which he also condoned as expressions of abundant strength. Such activities are omitted on account of space limitations, although they may elide into the above mentioned "darker" activities: for example, "the eternal joy of becoming—that joy which also encompasses *joy in destruction* …" (*TI*, p. 121). See Babette E. Babich, "Self-Deconstruction: Nietzsche's Philosophy as Style," *Soundings*, 73/1 (1990): 114: "For Nietzsche, the few are those individuals physically and spiritually constituted with power to face what is no ultimate vision of truth but only the emptiness behind the masks of culture, to see reality and to savor this raw reality in the moment purchased by laughter and delight, until, as it eternally recurs, the balance of life shudders and decays." Ansell-Pearson identifies in Nietzsche a lesser-known "'politics of survival,' which consists not of legislating new values and law-tables for men, but of playing in parodic and ironic fashion with the ideals of humanity," in addition to his "politics of cruelty." However, due to the fragmentary nature of his final writing, he argues that it is impossible to determine which politics Nietzsche favored more and, thus, identifies the latter as "the only overt or explicit politics which it is possible to associate with him" (Ansell-Pearson, p. 147).

[17]   I owe this timely exhortation to Dr. Leslie Stevenson following a paper delivered at the University of St. Andrews on 23 October 2002.

[18]   *WP*, p. 404 [1888].

"anemia," "a dangerous therapeutic which has certainly taught me how to wait but has not yet taught me how to hope."[19]

Although the fickle crowds may worship at "another Tower of Babel, some monstrosity of empire and power," Nietzsche espoused "the old belief that it is the great idea alone which can bestow greatness on a deed or a cause."[20] The real struggle for supremacy takes place on the battlefield of the mind. Invoking the symbolism of Christopher Columbus' brave forages beyond the horizons of Europe, Nietzsche exclaimed:

> *Embark!*—Consider how every individual is affected by an overall philosophical justification of his way of living and thinking: he experiences it as a sun that shines especially for him and bestows warmth, blessings, and fertility on him; it makes him independent of praise and blame, self-sufficient, rich, liberal with happiness and good will; incessantly it re-fashions evil into good, leads all energies to bloom and ripen, and does not permit the petty weeds of grief and chagrin to come up at all. In the end one exclaims: How I wish that many such new suns were yet to be created! Those who are evil or unhappy and the exceptional human being—all these should also have their philosophy, their good right, their sunshine! What is needful is not pity for them ... what is needful is a new *justice*! And a new watchword. And new philosophers. The moral earth, too, is round. The moral earth, too, has its antipodes. The antipodes, too, have the right to exist. There is yet another world to be discovered—and more than one. Embark, philosophers![21]

The "ruling idea"[22] became central to Nietzsche's species-shifting project, entrusted to the apostolic zeal of likeminded thinkers: "To prepare a *reversal of values* for a certain strong kind of man of the highest spirituality and strength of will and to this end slowly and cautiously to unfetter a host of instincts now kept in check and calumniated—whoever reflects on this becomes one of us, the free spirits ... ."[23]

Because there are no transcendent or privileged "truths,"[24] Nietzsche regarded the creation of values as a highly sophisticated mode of the will to self-empowerment. Hence, he once exclaimed, "The great epochs of our life are the occasions when we gain the courage to rebaptize our evil qualities as our best

---

[19]   *BG*, p. 187.

[20]   Ibid., p. 171. This is one reason why Nietzsche denigrated the false-triumphalism surrounding Germany's victory in the Franco-Prussian War of 1870–71. The ensuing celebration of Germany's "cultural superiority" and the stupor of smugness constituted "the power to extirpate the German spirit" (*UM*, p. 4).

[21]   *GS*, pp. 231–2.

[22]   *UM*, p. 227.

[23]   *WP*, p. 503 [1885].

[24]   *HA*, p. 45.

qualities."[25] This sentiment lay at the heart of his summons for a new breed of philosophers, "spirits strong and original enough to make a start on antithetical evaluations and to revalue and reverse 'eternal values ... .'"[26] However, Zarathustra's maxim, "Nothing is true, everything is permitted," is a privilege reserved only for these "higher" types of men.[27] The German philosopher did not advocate a value-free world, but rather a world in which values are pragmatically subordinated to the expansion of personal power bases. Nietzsche's "prince," like Machiavelli's, is characterized by a radical "objectivity"

> understood not as "disinterested contemplation" (which is a non-concept and a nonsense), but as the capacity to have all the arguments for and against *at one's disposal* and to suspend or implement them at will: so that one can exploit that very *diversity* of perspectives and affective interpretations in the interests of knowledge.[28]

The primary objective behind Nietzsche's strategy of revaluation is to enhance existential commitment to and aspirations for the material world in keeping with his monistic dismissal of the supernatural.[29] Hence, Zarathustra sought to repatriate those "natural" instincts which more fully embody the universal drive towards building larger power units: sensual pleasure, the lust for power, and selfishness.[30] Such summarily dismissed "sins" as "hatred, envy, covetousness, and lust for domination" are re-transcribed as healthy and natural, "life-conditioning" instead of life-effacing.[31] Ironically, the slaves adopted the proper methodology in overthrowing the masters—unfortunately for Nietzsche, they toppled the wrong target.

Destroying Antiquated Idols: Nietzsche's Qualified Nihilism

Closely allied with the action of revaluation is the destruction of ideals and "lies" which no longer serve to enhance and advance the superspecies. Such intellectual violence is neither immoral nor deplorable, but rather "natural":

> [E]very past, however, is worthy to be condemned—for that is the nature of human things: human violence and weakness have always played a mighty role

---

[25] *BG*, p. 97.

[26] Ibid., p. 126.

[27] *Z*, p. 285.

[28] *GM*, p. 98.

[29] Both Platonism and Christianity contributed to this abhorrent devaluation of the material world (*BG*, p. 32).

[30] *Z*, p. 206.

[31] *BG*, p. 53.

in them. It is not justice which here sits in judgment; it is even less mercy which pronounces the verdict: it is life alone, that dark, driving power that insatiably thirsts for itself.[32]

Nietzsche believed that in the life of every "high and select" kind of man, there comes a time of violent breaching with custom: "[T]he young soul is devastated, torn loose, torn out—it itself does not know what is happening. An urge, a pressure governs it, mastering the soul like a command: the will and wish awaken to go away, anywhere, at any cost … ."[33] However, he offered no short-term relief for a soul spasmed by existential "growth spurts": "The last thing *I* would promise would be to 'improve' mankind. I erect no new idols; let the old idols learn what it means to have legs of clay. *To overthrow idols* (my word for 'ideals')—that rather is my business."[34]

It would be easy to dismiss this inevitable "idol-smashing" as adolescent indulgence, the spiritual "vandalism" of someone who has been allowed to live "rent-free" in his parents' epistemological "basement." Nietzsche once exclaimed, "I know joy in *destruction* to a degree corresponding to my *strength* for *destruction*—in both I obey my dionysian nature, which does not know how to separate No-doing from Yes-saying. I am the first *immoralist*: I am therewith the *destroyer par excellence*."[35] However, he contended that destruction is essential to the natural order of life: the old forms of truth must be shredded like a "cocoon" in order for new metamorphoses to emerge:

[I]n hindsight, all *our* behavior and judgments will appear as inadequate and rash as the behavior and judgments of backward savage tribes now seem to us inadequate and rash. To understand all this can cause great pain, but afterwards there is consolation. These pains are birth pangs. The butterfly wants to break through his cocoon; he tears at it, he rends it: then he is blinded and confused by the unknown light, the realm of freedom. Men who are *capable* of that sorrow (how few they will be!) will make the first attempt to see if mankind *can transform itself* from *a moral* into a *wise* mankind.[36]

In response to accusations of existential immaturity, Nietzsche might have responded that his "youthful" prodigy has taken an epistemological "vow of

---

[32]   *UM*, p. 76.

[33]   *HA*, p. 6.

[34]   *EH*, pp. 3–4. I take this as a late sign of growing disillusionment that the race itself may be beyond improvement.

[35]   Ibid., p. 97.

[36]   *HA*, p. 75. In *Daybreak*, he wrote: "The snake which cannot shed its skin will perish. It is the same with minds which are prevented from changing their opinions: they cease to function as minds" (cited in Lou Salomé, *Nietzsche*, trans. and ed. Siegfried Mandel [Urbana and Chicago, 2001], p. 31).

poverty": "He is poor today, but not because one has taken everything away from him; he has thrown away everything. What is that to him? He is used to finding things. It is the poor who misunderstand his voluntary poverty."[37] From Nietzsche's perspective, a man must empty his hands in order to grasp even greater prizes. Within a closed universe in which there is neither Creator nor creation *ex nihilo*, power is a limited resource which can only be culled or carved from existing power structures. Hence, "In order for a shrine to be set up, *another shrine must be broken into pieces*: that is the law … ."[38]

Unsurprisingly, Christianity became the primary target of demolition on account of its hostility towards "natural" life, repression of the instincts, and the decaying, mediocrity-harboring façade of this once-formidable repository of moral and existential power which had dominated Europe.[39] Nietzsche was particularly incensed by its duplicitous pretence of unconditional love, which safeguards "an ecclesiastical order with priesthood, theology, cult, sacrament; in short, everything that Jesus of Nazareth had *combatted*."[40] Nevertheless, such demolition must be careful and selective, motivated by cool calculation rather than hatred and *réssentiment*. It took an able philosopher to wield "an ecstatic nihilism" masterfully "as a mighty pressure and hammer with which he breaks and removes degenerate and decaying races to make way for a new order of life, or to implant into that which is degenerate and desires to die a longing for the end."[41] In fact, the hammer became an emblem for the favorable form in which Nietzsche's philosophical activity was actualized—the short, swift strokes of his sledge-like aphorisms, patiently chipping away at society's monolithic idols of "truth."[42]

Nietzsche carefully qualified the use of nihilism, which he defined as "the radical repudiation of value, meaning, and desirability," as a means and never an end in itself.[43] There were at least four reasons why he could not condone rampant nihilism. First, he recognized that "idols" as such represent power sources which must be re-configured into more useful forms in the service of a "ruling thought" rather than wantonly destroyed. Second, nihilism must have remained ideologically repulsive to him on a deeper level, since he regarded it as the logical outcome of Christianity's will to truth which, having uncovered its own

---

[37] *GS*, p. 204.

[38] *GM*, p. 75.

[39] "But to attack the passions at their roots means to attack life at its roots: the practice of the Church is *hostile to life*…" (*TI*, p. 52). See also *GS*, p. 287; *BG*, p. 88; *GM*, pp. 118–19.

[40] *WP*, p. 116 [1887–88]. Nietzsche once quipped that this supreme historical irony could pass as evidence for the existence of "an ironical divinity" (*TI*, p. 160). See also *WP*, pp. 97–8 [1888].

[41] Ibid., p. 544 [1885].

[42] He was initially attracted to Sallust's epigrams, which were "[c]ompact, severe, with as much substance as possible" (*TI*, p. 116).

[43] *WP*, p. 7 [1885–86].

duplicity, lurches wildly from "'God is truth' to the fanatical faith 'All is false'"[44] Third, Nietzsche recognized a fundamental inconsistency and inherent lack of philosophical sophistication within nihilism:

> A nihilist is a man who judges of the world as it is that it ought *not* to be, and of the world as it ought to be that it does not exist. According to this view, our existence (action, suffering, willing, feeling) has no meaning: the pathos of "in vain" is the nihilists' pathos—at the same time, as pathos, an inconsistency on the part of nihilists.[45]

His point is a cogent one: if the world is truly meaningless, then why should nihilists even care? Finally, Nietzsche indiscriminately attacked any attempt to devalue the natural world, whether it be Christian, Buddhist, or nihilist. He insisted that humanity's attitude towards existence must be characterized by a radical exuberance—not the sour rejection, despair, and *réssentiment* personified by many nihilistic tendencies.

Embracing Suffering: Heroic Hermeneutics

A third essential exercise of power involves the conscious will to suffer. From his earliest writings the evolving self became a central motif in Nietzsche's unfolding theory of will to power: "Active, successful natures act, not according to the dictum 'know thyself', but as if there hovered before them the commandment: *will* a self and thou shalt *become* a self."[46] Although much human orientation is influenced by ancestry and the subconscious, one must strive to determine that core as much as humanly possible. "*What does your conscience say?*" Nietzsche asked. "You shall become the person you are."[47] Hence, an exceptional man does not merely will his actions—he wills himself to grow beyond and yet paradoxically "into" himself. Nietzsche became a champion for "the spectacle of that strength which employs genius *not for works* but for *itself as a work*; that is, for its own constraint, for the purification of its imagination, for the imposition of order and choice upon the influx of tasks and impressions."[48] The "refined" will to power constitutes, in effect, the will to self-determination despite the seemingly intractable constants of race, gender, and class.

But Nietzsche knew that this would be no easy task. Perhaps the most heroic tenet of Nietzsche's will to power lies in its response to one's own human frailties, ill health, and suffering. In his 1886 second preface to *The Gay Science*, Nietzsche observed that the book was saturated with "the gratitude of a convalescent": "'Gay

---

[44] Ibid.

[45] Ibid., p. 318 [1887, 88].

[46] *NR*, p. 232.

[47] *GS*, p. 219. Nietzsche traced this doctrine to Pindar (*HA*, p. 161).

[48] *NR*, p. 234.

Science': that signifies the saturnalia of a spirit who has patiently resisted a terrible, long pressure—patiently, severely, coldly, without submitting, but also without hope—and who is now all at once attacked by hope, the hope for health, and the *intoxication* of convalescence."[49] The sheer authenticity which punctuates his writings with the exclamation marks of *joie de vive* and the ellipses of anguish stems partly from the remarkable effort by which Nietzsche's personal optimism was birthed through the contractions of unmitigated pain.[50] Early in his writing career, he lauded the benefits of possessing "the Gorgon gaze that instantaneously petrifies everything into a work of art: that gaze from a realm without pain."[51] Throughout his life, Nietzsche refused to surrender to his suffering. His imagination sought an interpretative framework with which to snatch victory from the ever-present abyss of defeatism.[52]

Nietzsche also identified a dialectical relation between his genius and his illness: "I have a subtler sense for signs of ascent and decline than any man has ever had, I am the teacher *par excellence* in this matter—I know both, I am both."[53] Furthermore, the potentiality of losing life at any moment increased his ardour for living.[54] Nietzsche maintained that, by gouging its glacial girth across the bedrock of the "higher" soul, suffering deepens the human spirit:

> Only great pain, the long, slow pain that takes its time—on which we are burned, as it were, with green wood—compels us philosophers to descend into our ultimate depths and to put aside all trust, everything good-natured, everything that would interpose a veil, that is mild, that is medium—things in which

---

[49]   *GS*, p. 32. Salomé, p. 12, states, "Suffering and loneliness then are the two great lines of fate in Nietzsche's biography … . And they bear the strange double-face of an *exteriorly fated life* and at the same time a purely psychologically determined, *willed inner necessity*." Safranski argues that Nietzsche "pharmaceutically" tested concepts by the strength of their relief from his physical afflictions (*Nietzsche: A Philosophical Biography*, trans. Shelly Frisch [New York, 2003], p. 55). In January 1880, he wrote to his doctor, "My existence is an *awful burden*—I would have dispensed with it long ago, were it not for the most illuminating tests and experiments I have been conducting in matters of mind and morality …" (ibid., p. 178).

[50]   As his syphilitic symptoms worsened, resulting in severe migraines and failing vision, he resigned his professorship at Basel by the time he was 36, unable to see "three paces in front of me" (*EH*, p. 8).

[51]   Cited in Safranski, p. 27.

[52]   For example, he later credited his physical inability to read as "the *greatest* favour I have ever done myself" (*EH*, p. 62).

[53]   Ibid., p. 8. Hence, during the writing of *Daybreak* in 1880, he discovered that, after "an uninterrupted three-day headache accompanied by the laborious vomiting of phlegm … I possessed a dialectical clarity *par excellence* and thought my way very cold-bloodedly through things for which when I am in better health I am not enough of a climber, not refined, not *cold* enough" (ibid., p. 9).

[54]   *GS*, pp. 243–4.

formerly we may have found our humanity. I doubt that such pain makes us "better"; but I know that it makes us more *profound*.[55]

However, Nietzsche was selective in his application of the benefits of this interpretative *coup d'état*; for, suffering in and of itself is not sufficient to endow one's life with profundity. Rather, one has to seize the opportunity voraciously, tenaciously, hermeneutically— one has to wrestle life's difficulties and setbacks into the narrative framework of the will.[56] Contrary to the modern person who transforms suffering into "the foremost argument *against* existence,"[57] "higher" individuals liberate themselves from such slavish hatred by refusing to be defeated by time.[58] As Zarathustra jubilantly espoused, "To redeem the past and to transform every 'It was' into an 'I wanted it thus!'—that alone do I call redemption!"[59] Hence, a strong person is able to rise above the vicissitudes and petty pains of life, and embracing suffering is pivotal for this ascension: "[F]or life must be harder and harder for you. Only thus, only thus does man grow to the height where the lightning can strike and shatter him: high enough for the lightning!"[60]

To summarize, suffering is not merely beneficial to the "higher" man—it is essential. In opposition to the peddlers and meddlers of mediocrity, who seek to avoid discomfort at all costs, Nietzsche proclaimed,

> [W]e think that severity, force, slavery, peril in the street and in the heart, concealment, stoicism, the art of experiment and devilry of every kind, that everything evil, dreadful, tyrannical, beast of prey and serpent in man serves to enhance the species "man" just as much as does its opposite—we do not say enough when we say even that much … .[61]

It would, therefore, be counter-productive for a true proponent of the superspecies to eliminate the catalyst for all that is great, noble, and upright in humankind, "the discipline of great suffering":

---

[55] Ibid., p. 36.

[56] Nietzsche traced this hermeneutical tactic to both "early man" and Christianity, which staves off despair by assigning meaning to suffering because "[t]he aspect of suffering which actually causes outrage is not suffering itself, but the meaninglessness of suffering …" (*GM*, p. 49).

[57] Ibid.

[58] *UM*, p. 106. Zarathustra attributed all thirst for vengeance to "the will's antipathy towards time and time's 'It was'" (*Z*, p. 162).

[59] Ibid., p. 161.

[60] Ibid., p. 299.

[61] *BG*, p. 72. See also *WP*, p. 206 [1887, 88]: "I assess the *power* of a *will* by how much resistance, pain, torture it endures and knows how to turn to its advantage; I do not account the evil and painful character of existence a reproach to it, but hope rather that it will one day be more evil and painful than hitherto—."

> That tension of the soul in misfortune which cultivates its strength, its terror
> at the sight of great destruction, its inventiveness and bravery in undergoing,
> enduring, interpreting, exploiting misfortune, and whatever of depth, mystery,
> mask, spirit, cunning and greatness has been bestowed upon it—has it not been
> bestowed through suffering, through the discipline of great suffering?[62]

Like "sin" and "redemption," pain becomes a value judgment existing primarily
in the mind, to be re-evaluated within a more promising narrative;[63] for, mighty
spirits only emerge from the "smithies" of unrelenting anguish and adversity.[64]

Employing "Cruelty"

It becomes unnervingly evident that Nietzsche's attitude towards suffering
may easily elide into the subject of domination and the necessity of "cruelty."
Suffering becomes, for Nietzsche, an integral distinction in the widening rift
between higher and lower types of men, an elitist means of advancement over the
shallow masses:

> The spiritual haughtiness and disgust of every human being who has suffered
> deeply—*how* deeply human beings can suffer almost determines their order of
> rank—the harrowing certainty, with which he is wholly permeated and colored,
> that by virtue of his suffering he *knows more* than even the cleverest and wisest can
> know, that he is familiar with, and was once "at home" in, many distant, terrible
> worlds of which "*you* know nothing!" ... [T]his spiritual, silent haughtiness of
> the sufferer, this pride of the elect of knowledge, of the "initiated," of the almost
> sacrificed, finds all forms of disguise necessary to protect itself against contact
> with importunate and pitying hands and in general against everything which is
> not its equal in suffering. Profound suffering ennobles; it separates.[65]

Rather than denigrating existence on account of suffering, Nietzsche insisted,
"[W]e would do well to remember the times when exactly the opposite conclusion
was drawn, because mankind did not want to forgo the *infliction* of suffering, seeing
in it an enchantment of the first rank, an actual seduction and lure *in favour of*

---

[62] *BG*, p. 155.

[63] *HA*, p. 77: "When a misfortune strikes us, we can overcome it either by removing
its cause or else by changing the effect it has on our feelings, that is, by reinterpreting the
misfortune as a good, whose benefit may only later become clear." In a notebook entry,
Nietzsche even denied ontological reality to "pain," which he considered "an *intellectual*
occurrence in which a definite judgment is expressed—the judgment '*harmful*' in which a
long experience is summarized. There is no pain as such" (*WP*, p. 371 [1888]).

[64] Ibid., p. 465 [1887–88]: "[O]ne must be faced with the choice of perishing or
prevailing. A dominating race can grow up only out of terrible and violent beginnings."

[65] *BG*, p. 209.

life."[66] Because adversity is so essential to the formation of an exceptional person, Nietzsche wished "suffering, desolation, sickness, ill-treatment, indignities, ... profound self-contempt, the torture of self-mistrust, the wretchedness of the vanquished" on those he showed "concern" for.[67]

Once suffering is necessary, it takes an alarmingly small step to conclude that the instigation of suffering and/or refusal to alleviate suffering helps to engender hardier specimens. Moreover, by interpreting all human actions, regardless of their altruistic appearances, as attempts to gain power over the other,[68] cruelty in action and intent appears both ubiquitous and unavoidable. Nietzsche averred that, without "the spiritualization and intensification of *cruelty*" towards former ideals and "truths," higher culture cannot progress or even exist:

> What the Roman in the arena, the Christian in the ecstasies of the Cross, the Spaniard watching burnings or bullfights, the Japanese of today crowding in to the tragedy, the Parisian suburban workman who has a nostalgia for bloody revolutions, the Wagnerienne who, with will suspended, "experiences" *Tristan und Isolde*—what all of these enjoy and look with secret ardour to imbibe is the spicy portion of the great Circe "cruelty."[69]

From works of art like *Don Quixote* to the penal system, Nietzsche observed the inevitable welding of civilization and barbarity, cruelty and culture, the promulgation of toughness for the promise of longevity: "To witness suffering does one good, to inflict it even more so—that is a harsh proposition, but a fundamental one, an old, powerful, human all-too-human proposition, one to which perhaps even the apes would subscribe ... ."[70]

Such tolerable cruelty does not entail the wanton use of physical force, however, since such an unsophisticated deployment of power constitutes "a sign that we are still lacking power, or it shows a sense of frustration in the face of this poverty ... ."[71] In *Daybreak* Nietzsche pondered how to make a virtue of "refined cruelty,"[72] while Zarathustra advocated the Jacob-ian art of creative combat: "I wrestled long and was a wrestler, so that I might one day have my hands free

---

[66]   *GM*, p. 49.

[67]   *WP*, p. 481 [1887]. Tanner, p. 43, correctly warns not to misinterpret his condemnation of "pity" as condoning "neglect of others' basic requirements": "His attack is concerned with pity as a full-time occupation of sorting out people's lives, with a noble neglect, as we are taught, of one's own interests." For "pity" as a sign of contempt, see *GS*, p. 176; *NR*, p. 155.

[68]   *GS*, p. 86.

[69]   *BG*, p. 159.

[70]   *GM*, p. 48.

[71]   *GS*, p. 87.

[72]   Safranski, p. 187.

for blessing."[73] Furthermore, Nietzsche warned of the dangers of self-dissolution from constant conflict: "He who fights with monsters should look to it that he himself does not become a monster."[74] However, such caution was ill-suited for those who sought the arrival of the *Übermensch*. As he instructed all "preparatory human beings,"

> [T]he secret for harvesting from existence the greatest fruitfulness and the greatest enjoyment is—to *live dangerously*! Build your cities on the slopes of Vesuvius! Send your ships into uncharted seas! Live at war with your peers and yourselves! Be robbers and conquerors as long as you cannot be rulers and possessors, you seekers of knowledge![75]

If challenged, Nietzsche might have offered the following defence for the necessitation of cruelty within his philosophical project. First, "cruelty" is a hermeneutical rather than ontological reality and, as such, a highly relative valuation reflecting the self-interests of the interpreter. Hence, in contrast to the "slave morality" of Christianity, which condemned the liberties of the aristocratic "predators" to safeguard bovine security, Nietzsche asserted that "the healthier, stronger, richer, more fruitful, more enterprising a man feels, the more 'immoral' he will be, too."[76]

Second, Nietzsche would argue that cruelty is ubiquitously embodied within the material universe and is a "natural," unavoidable means by which power is consolidated.[77]

---

[73]   *Z*, p. 186. See Gen. 32:24–30.

[74]   *BG*, p. 102.

[75]   *GS*, p. 228. Similarly, Zarathustra exclaimed: "Thus commands my great love for the most distant men: *Do not spare your neighbour*! Man is something that must be overcome … . Overcome yourself even in your neighbour: and a right that you can seize for yourself you should not accept as a gift!" (*Z*, pp. 216–17).

[76]   *WP*, p. 213 [1887–88]. He also maintained that "[f]rightful energies—that which is called evil—are the Cyclopean architects and pathmakers of humanity" (*HA*, p. 151). Thus, Nietzsche fiercely opposed Christianity's "perverse" attempts to "emasculate" the species rather than "taking into service the great sources of strength, those impetuous torrents of the soul that are so often dangerous and overwhelming, and economizing them" (*WP*, p. 207 [1888]).

[77]   See *HA*, p. 9: "You ['the free spirit'] had to learn to grasp the *necessary* injustice in every For and Against; to grasp that injustice is inseparable from life, that life itself is *determined* by perspective and its injustice." The universality of self-cruelty within human culture alone encompasses all areas "wherever man allows himself to be persuaded to self-denial in the *religious* sense, or to self-mutilation, as among Phoenicians and ascetics, or in general to desensualization, decarnalization, contrition, to Puritanical spasms of repentance, to conscience-vivisection and to a Pascalian *sacrificial dell'intelletto*" (*BG*, pp. 159–60). Nietzsche regarded the hyperbolic ethic in the Sermon on the Mount as an instance of man taking "a voluptuous pleasure in violating himself by exaggerated demands and then deifying this something in his soul that is so tyrannically taxing" (*HA*, p. 95).

The whole past of the old culture is built on violence, slavery, deception, error; but we, the heirs of all these conditions, indeed the convergence of that whole past, cannot decree ourselves away, and cannot want to remove one particular part. The unjust frame of mind lies in the souls of the "have-nots," too; they are no better than the "haves," and have no special moral privilege, for at some point their forefathers were "haves," too.[78]

Nietzsche maintained that sociological cruelties such as class injustice and oppression play a pivotal role in the development of psychological distinctions:

Without the *pathos of distance* such as develops from the incarnate differences of classes, from the ruling caste's constant looking out and looking down on subjects and instruments and from its equally constant exercise of obedience and command, its holding down and holding at a distance, that other, more mysterious pathos could not have developed either, that longing for an ever-increasing widening of distance within the soul itself, the formation of ever higher, rarer, more remote, tenser, more comprehensive states, in short precisely the elevation of the type "man," the continual "self-overcoming of man," to take a moral formula in a supramoral sense.[79]

He argued that the impact of Christianity in demonizing suffering ("the *will* to misunderstand suffering"), promoting existential smugness, and binding crucial life-promoting instincts in a "strait-jacket" of endless guilt, constitutes genuine cruelty towards nature and humankind. Cruelty to particular individuals and classes is, therefore, permissible if it constitutes a greater kindness to the species as a whole.[80]

Third, to defend the role of cruelty in his project, Nietzsche may have insisted that he is not advocating wanton violence or anarchical instability, but a selective and highly sophisticated, controlled "cruelty" directed at outmoded institutions and fabricated "truths" which are, in actuality, cruelly obstructing the species from higher development and preserving society's "miscarriages."[81] Moreover, such will to cruelty is restricted to a minority of elite and well-cultivated individuals in

---

[78] Ibid., p. 216.

[79] *BG*, p. 192.

[80] *GM*, pp. 118–19. Nietzsche once suggested, "[*W*]hen one makes men more evil, one makes them better—and ... one cannot be one without being the other" (*WP*, p. 416 [1887]). There can be no "superhuman" without the "superbeast" (ibid., p. 531 [1887]).

[81] Ibid., p. 389 [1888]: "Society, as the great trustee of life, is responsible to life itself for every miscarried life—it also has to pay for such lives: consequently it ought to prevent them ... . Life itself recognizes no solidarity, no 'equal rights,' between the healthy and the degenerate parts of an organism: one must excise the latter—or the whole will perish." In *GS*, p. 129, a "holy man" advised a father to kill a severely handicapped newborn arguing, "But is it not crueler to let it live?"

any given society. After the common men, the "farmers of the spirit," have settled and "exploited" all available land, "the ploughshare of evil must come again and again" to break up the over-packed soils.[82]

Fourth, Nietzsche did not endorse any outward cruelty which was not first and foremost directed inwards by the higher individual himself.[83] He adamantly emphasized that the key to higher humankind consists of "*mature* freedom of the spirit which is fully as much self-mastery and discipline of the heart, and which permits paths to many opposing rays of thought."[84] Nietzsche once distinguished the category of genius by its exceptional self-severity, which is crucial for all remarkable achievements: "The genius—in his works, in his deeds—is necessarily a prodigal: his greatness lies in the fact that *he expends himself* ... . The instinct of self-preservation is as it were suspended; the overwhelming pressure of the energies which emanate from him forbids him any such care and prudence."[85]

The will to self-cruelty takes several forms in Nietzsche's writings. First, it manifests itself in relentless self-scrutiny. Since life in its entirety has become "a means of knowledge,"[86] the "scientific" explorer subjects himself to rigorous testing and self-vivisection: "Our attitude towards ourselves is one of hubris, for we experiment with ourselves in a way which we would never allow ourselves to experiment with any animal, we derive pleasure from our curious dissection of the soul of a living body."[87] However, this spiritual experimentation, unfettered by conventional morality and driven by "genius *not for works* but for *itself as a work*"[88]—opens the door to explorations of human brutality beyond the self:

> Who will attain anything great if he does not find in himself the strength and the will to *inflict* great suffering? Being able to suffer is the least thing; weak women and even slaves often achieve virtuosity in that. But not to perish of internal distress and uncertainty when one inflicts great suffering and hears the cry of this suffering—that is great, that belongs to greatness.[89]

Second, self-cruelty is incarnated in all "ascetic" tendencies which, according to Nietzsche, originate in men whose efforts at external mastery have failed: "[I]t finally occurs to them to tyrannize certain parts of their own being, as if they were

---

[82]   Ibid., p. 79.

[83]   See *UM*, p. 119, where he advocated that "each one of this generation must overcome himself"; that is, "the nature already educated into one."

[84]   *HA*, p. 7.

[85]   *TI*, p. 109.

[86]   *GS*, p. 255.

[87]   *GM*, p. 92. See also *GS*, p. 253.

[88]   *NR*, p. 234.

[89]   *GS*, p. 255. Kaufmann tempers this section by interpreting this inflicted suffering as the grief which Nietzsche's radical views caused his family and friends (ibid., n. 52).

sections or stages of their selves."[90] Third, self-cruelty is also championed as a means for actualizing the commanding idea which benefits the race—the sacrifice of both the one and the many for the greater accomplishment of the superspecies.[91] Regardless of whether it was directed towards the self or others, the refinement of spiritual raw materials clearly necessitates an unwavering acceptance of cruelty.

Aestheticizing the World

Throughout Nietzsche's writings, there is a tendency for the "in-itselfness" of the world to be supplanted by a hermeneutical *tabula rasa* of becomings and limitless potentialities: the aestheticization of the humanly perceived "world." In *The Birth of Tragedy*, he contested Schopenhauer's belief that the efficacy of music pertains to the interaction between the "subjective" listener and the "objective" purity of the acoustic stimuli. Instead, Nietzsche argued that the distinctions between art and artist, "subjective" and "objective" realities break down:

> [B]ut we can indeed assume for our own part that we are images and artistic projections for the true creator of that world, and that our highest dignity lies in the meaning of works of art—for it is only as *an aesthetic phenomenon* that existence and the world are eternally *justified*—while of course our awareness of our meaning differs hardly at all from the awareness that warriors painted on canvas have of the battle portrayed.[92]

If the natural universe is, in fact, overlaid with an aesthetic veneer to become "the world as we know it," the world can be embraced for its beauty,[93] the standards of

---

⁹⁰   *HA*, p. 95. See also *UM*, p. 163.

⁹¹   *WP*, p. 380 [1888]: "[M]ankind is merely the experimental material, the tremendous surplus of failures: a field of ruins." See also ibid., p. 360 [1883–88]: "The basic phenomenon: countless individuals sacrificed for the sake of a few, to make them possible.—One must not let oneself be deceived; it is just the same with peoples and races: they constitute the 'body' for the production of isolated valuable individuals, who carry on the great process."

⁹²   *BT*, p. 32. However, Nietzsche somewhat inconsistently still maintained that this aesthetic reality can be distinguished from the foundations of nature upon which it was based: "[A]rt is not only an imitation of the truth of nature but a metaphysical supplement to that truth of nature, coexisting with it in order to overcome it" (ibid., p. 114). Alexander Nehamas creatively endeavors to reconcile Nietzsche's perspectivism with his many apparent truth-claims by arguing that Nietzsche resolved this paradox by "creating an artwork out of himself, a literary character who is a philosopher" (*Nietzsche: Life as Literature* [London and Cambridge, 1985], p. 8).

⁹³   In a notebook entry, Nietzsche once ascribed "the highest sign of power" to beauty "because in beauty opposites are tamed; the highest sign of power, namely power over opposites; moreover, without tension:— that violence is no longer needed" (*WP*, p. 422 [1883–88]).

which are open to a rich variety of interpretations which are not predetermined to be "good" or "evil" in and of themselves.[94] In *The Gay Science*, he observed that the higher individual needs assistance to dispel the illusion of "external" truth:

> The higher human being always becomes at the same time happier and unhappier. But he can never shake off a *delusion*: He fancies that he is a *spectator* and *listener* who has been placed before the great visual and acoustic spectacle that is life; he calls his own nature *contemplative* and overlooks that he himself is really the poet who keeps creating this life.[95]

This accorded Nietzsche a great deal of optimism:[96] if human beings are self-generated/self-generating works of art, then the species can theoretically be shaped within the hands of a capable philosophical "potter," so long as he receives pristine materials with which to work.[97] Furthermore, an "aestheticized" world allows previously "transcendent" and "God-given" mores to be subverted, with "*taste* as the sole means of arbitrating between values."[98] It also counters the sting of reality's most biting tragedies by injecting an "artistic distance":

> As an aesthetic phenomenon existence is still *bearable* for us, and art furnishes us with eyes and hands and above all the good conscience to be *able* to turn ourselves into such a phenomenon. At times we need a rest from ourselves ... and, from an artistic distance, laughing *over* ourselves or weeping *over* ourselves.[99]

Furthermore, the "aesthetic" epistemology may foster a structure conducive to elitism and hierarchy by generating a "canon" of men whose evaluation may be determined exclusively by "experts" and who, subsequently, merit the highest pedestals of privilege and freedom.

---

[94] The aesthetizing of the world provides a useful corollary in suspending the importance of historical effect. Like a "work of art," it is no longer fair to "appraise the value of a man according to how useful he is to men, or how much he costs, or what harm he does to them" (Ibid., p. 469 [1887]).

[95] *GS*, p. 241.

[96] On art as "the only superior counterforce to all will to denial of life, as that which is anti-Christian, anti-Buddhist, antinihilist *par excellence*," see *WP*, pp. 452–3 [1886].

[97] Some commentators suggest that Nietzsche's writing is itself an exercise in self-creation. Thomas Mann exclaims: "[D]own to his self-mythologizing in his last moment, down to madness, this life was an artistic production ... a lyric, tragic spectacle, and one of utmost fascination ..." (cited in Safranski, pp. 324–5).

[98] Irving Zeitlin, *Nietzsche: A Re-Examination* (Cambridge, 1994), p. 171. Nietzsche would also apply his universal standard of "life-enhancement" to gauge the relative worth of values.

[99] *GS*, pp. 163–4.

Nietzsche's aesthetic emphasis encompassed many of his predominant themes: the heightened role of instincts over reason, the celebration of the sensual, corporeal world, the superabundance of the "higher" man, the privileged status of genius, the supplanting of ontology by hermeneutics, and also the necessity of conflict. From *The Birth of Tragedy* onwards, Nietzsche esteemed the Dionysian aesthetic based upon "the desire for destruction, for change, for *becoming*" over the Apolline aesthetic based upon "the desire for rigidity, eternity, *being*" which, driven by a profound disdain for materiality, resulted in an art of "impoverishment" instead of the Dionysian "overfull power pregnant with the future."[100] He contended that, "[f]or art to exist, for any sort of aesthetic activity or perception to exist, a certain physiological precondition is indispensable: *intoxication*,"[101] a condition which resonates with the superabundant power of the "higher" man: "The essence of intoxication is the feeling of plentitude and increased energy. From out of this feeling one gives to things, one *compels* them to take, one rapes them—one calls this procedure *idealizing*."[102] The self-styled philosopher-poet had no patience for any alleged passivity of art: "[W]hat does all art do? Does it not praise? ... By doing all this it *strengthens* or *weakens* certain valuations."[103] The image of artist and *Übermensch* apparently merge as Nietzsche elucidated the notion of intoxication:

> In this condition one enriches everything out of one's own abundance: what one sees, what one desires, one sees swollen, pressing, strong, overladen with energy. The man in this condition transforms things until they mirror his power—until they are reflections of his perfection. This *compulsion* to transform into the perfect is—art.[104]

The will to art would resonate in its most ambitious manifestation within the philosophical vision of the *Überkünstler* [over-artist] himself—the drafting of a destiny, the sculpting of the species.

Breeding the Species

In an 1884 notebook entry, Nietzsche equated the artist with an unrelenting desire for dominance:

---

[100]   *WP*, pp. 445–6 [1885–86].

[101]   *TI*, p. 82. Intoxication encompasses sexual excitement, military vanquishing, cruelty, destruction, celebration, indulgence in narcotics, the change of seasons, and "the intoxication of an overloaded and distended will" (Ibid., pp. 82–3).

[102]   Ibid., p. 83.

[103]   Ibid., p. 92.

[104]   Ibid., p. 83. The phallic overtones of a patriarchal vision of creativity penetrate this passage.

Misunderstanding of egoism—on the part of *common* natures who know nothing whatever of the pleasure of conquest and the insatiability of great love, nor of the overflowing feeling of strength that desires to overpower, to compel to itself, to lay to its heart—the drive of the artist in relation to his material.[105]

Nietzsche had no qualms over couching this drive for mastery within metaphysical motifs. Hence, he once abrogated the powers of the "Creator" within the creative potential of certain men:

There is a slavish love that submits and gives itself; that idealizes, and deceives itself—there is a divine love that despises and loves, and reshapes and elevates the beloved. To gain that tremendous energy of greatness in order to shape the men of the future through breeding and, on the other hand, the annihilation of millions of failures, and not to perish of the suffering one creates, though nothing like it has ever existed![106]

Much of his model for crafting the species was derived from the personal impact which Schopenhauer had upon him. He once described Schopenhauer's legacy as the knowledge that

[n]either riches nor honours nor erudition can lift the individual out of the profound depression he feels at the valuelessness of his existence, and how the striving after these valued things acquires meaning only through an exalted and transfiguring overall goal: to acquire power so as to aid the evolution of the *physis* and to be for a while the corrector of its follies and ineptitudes.[107]

Wagner was another methodological influence, whose music "transmits the fundamental impulses in the depths of the persons represented in the drama directly to the soul of the listeners" with greater impact than the gestures and

---

[105] *WP*, p. 467 [1884].

[106] Ibid., p. 506 [1884]. Tracy Strong highlights the significance of breeding in Nietzsche's thought as well as the "facile" manoeuvres by which commentators attempt to avoid this political minefield (*Friedrich Nietzsche and the Politics of Transfiguration* [Berkeley, Los Angeles and London, 1975], p. 274). Jacob Golomb argues, "The transfiguration of our nature and the sublimation of our desires and psychological makeup, which provide the necessary and sufficient conditions of the morality of positive power, distance Nietzsche from Nazi eugenics or racism based on a given or preferred set of biological traits" ("How to De-Nazify Nietzsche's Philosophical Anthropology?" in Jacob Golomb and Robert Wistrich [eds], *Nietzsche, Godfather of Fascism? On the Uses and Abuses of a Philosophy* [Princeton, 2002], p. 40).

[107] *UM*, p. 142.

words of his characters.[108] Further development ensued while Nietzsche ruminated over the inadequacies of Darwin's theory of species, begging the question of how one might strengthen the race.[109]

In a letter dated July 1883, Nietzsche wrote, "We should persevere in realizing our idea of man; we ought to be adamant about enforcing it on others as well as on ourselves, and thus exert a creative impact!"[110] Nietzsche's project of shaping the species represents a nexus of several key emphases in his thought: the primacy of the "natural," physical world, the revaluation of human "good" and human "evil," the attempt to control nature through cultural institutions, the creative mastery of the artist, the universal *telos* of constructing larger power units, and the predominance of a "commanding idea" which endeavors to "implant a need" in the human breast so that "out of a vigorous need there will one day arise a vigorous deed."[111] Even his aphoristic style, Tanner notes, was calculated towards "transforming the reader's consciousness."[112]

In his role as philosophical breeder, Nietzsche considered himself to be a veritable "blood" hound: "I have in this sensitivity psychological antennae with which I touch and take hold of every secret: all the *concealed* dirt at the bottom of many a nature, perhaps conditioned by bad blood but whitewashed by education, is known to me almost on first contact."[113] Meanwhile, he simultaneously sought to heat up the cultural and philosophical climate of his era in order to bolster the emergence of his delicate, "tropical" superspecies. The fostering of "a more virile, warlike age" is instrumental for the evolution of an even higher age: "To this end we now need many preparatory courageous human beings who cannot very well leap out of nothing, any more than out of the sand and slime of present-day civilization and metropolitanism ... ."[114] Inspired by the measured upspringing and upbringing of the aristocracy, Nietzsche believed that the discovery and conquest of brave new worlds—philosophical or otherwise—rely solely upon those who are "born or, expressed more clearly, *bred* for it."[115]

Rejecting the "shrunken, almost ludicrous species, a herd animal, something full of good will, sickly and mediocre [which] has been bred, the European of

---

[108]   Ibid., p. 239. Nietzsche's writings strongly parallel his own analysis of Wagner's self-commentaries: "They are attempts to comprehend the instinct which impelled him to create his works, and as it were to set himself before his own eyes; if he can only manage to transform his instinct into knowledge, he hopes the reverse process will take place within the souls of his readers: it is with this objective that he writes" (ibid., p. 248).

[109]   *HA*, p. 139.

[110]   Cited in Safranski, p. 167.

[111]   *UM*, p. 82. On implanting habits, see also *HA*, p. 76.

[112]   Tanner, p. 23.

[113]   *EH*, p. 18.

[114]   *GS*, p. 228.

[115]   *BG*, p. 145.

today,"[116] Nietzsche sought "forefathers and ancestors of the *Übermensch*,"[117] those who strive "[n]ot to bear their race to the grave, but to found a new generation of this race … ."[118] This artistic "medium" demonstrates biological as well as cultural superiority, boasting a psychological "genome" which can—to a certain degree—be philosophically engineered. As early as 1884, he contended, "A doctrine is needed powerful enough to work as a breeding agent: strengthening the strong; paralysing and destructive for the world-weary."[119] The extent to which a judgment is " life-advancing, life-preserving, species-preserving, perhaps even species-breeding" formed the basis of his philosophical and moral assessments.[120] This "commanding thought" would remain with him throughout his writing career. Hence, even as he grew demoralized by the rampant dissemination of "slave" culture across Europe, he mused, "The increasing dwarfing of man is precisely the driving force that brings to mind the breeding of a stronger race—a race that would be excessive precisely where the dwarfed species was weak and growing weaker (in will, responsibility, self-assurance, ability to posit goals for oneself)."[121]

To recapitulate, Nietzsche was able to consolidate his validated exercises of power—moral revaluation, the destruction of deleterious "truths," the brave acceptance and volitional approval of suffering, the deployment of cruelty to self and to others, and the aestheticization of the material world—within the role of "philosophical breeder," whose job description entails the grandiose and "god-like" project of "strengthening and enhancement for the human type."[122] While humankind supplies the "raw materials" for this illustrious program of "philosophical eugenics" engineered by "we free spirits," the philosopher remains "the man of the most comprehensive responsibility who has the conscience for the collective evolution of mankind," who alone is capable of selecting and rejecting diverse cultural components—religious, political, economic, etc.—"for his work of education and breeding."[123]

Conclusion

Throughout Nietzsche's exploration of the will to power, there is a glowing thread of intentionality and purpose leading humankind through the reticular recurrences of nature's magisterially indifferent "labyrinth." All of the natural universe blindly surges towards the formation of larger power units, and human beings must accept

---

[116]   Ibid., p. 89.
[117]   *Z*, p. 110.
[118]   *UM*, p. 106.
[119]   *WP*, p. 458 [1884].
[120]   *BG*, p. 35.
[121]   *WP*, pp. 477–8 [1888].
[122]   *GS*, p. 338.
[123]   *BG*, p. 86.

their deprivileged positions within this cosmic dynamo. According to Nietzsche, humankind's primary purpose is to better itself to the point of species self-sacrifice, self-overcoming in order to actualize the advent of the superspecies. As such, he did not endeavor to establish specific societal reforms or found new institutes or hierarchies which differ significantly from the time-tested formulae of ancient Rome and Greece.[124] In a moment of self-reverie, Nietzsche once explained,

> I am not a man, I am dynamite.—And with all that there is nothing in me of a founder of religion—religions are affairs of the rabble. I have need of washing my hands after contact with religious people … I do not *want* "believers," I think I am too malicious to believe in myself, I never speak to masses … I have a terrible fear I shall one day be pronounced *holy* … . I do not want to be a saint, rather even a buffoon … Perhaps I am a buffoon … And none the less, or rather *not* none the less—for there has hitherto been nothing more mendacious than saints—the truth speaks out of me.—But my truth is *dreadful*: for hitherto the *lie* has been called truth.—*Revaluation of all values*: this is my formula for an act of supreme coming-to-oneself on the part of mankind which in me has become flesh and genius.[125]

Given his almost feverish exuberance to embrace all of the material universe, Nietzsche would not waste one iota of fact or fiction. In its ideal form, even Christianity can be transformed into something life-enhancing, both by promulgating peace and prosperity among a pacified populace, as well as by training exceptional individuals in honor and ascetic self-strengthening. In its more virulent forms, Christianity becomes a menace to materiality, demolishing the barriers of rank and social privilege and inundating all of Europe with its "slave values." While the Christian faith represented, for Nietzsche, a refuge and bastion of mediocrity for the motley masses who live in collective fear and hatred of exceptionality, it ironically comprised the sole sanctum for the safety and sanctity of exceptionality for another brilliant nineteenth-century thinker who also went to great lengths to keep his distance from the masses of Christendom.

---

[124] Nehamas, pp. 221–2.

[125] *EH*, p. 96. Safranski, p. 200, posits that Nietzsche periodically toyed with the notion of a bicameral system of culture which balances scientific knowledge with passion/aestheticized "truth": "If he had held to it, he might well have spared himself some of his mad visions of grand politics and the will to power."

Chapter 4

To Have and Uphold:
Kierkegaard's View of the Universe

The Cosmological Tier

Because of the anti-systematic nature of Kierkegaard's corpus, deliberately designed to thwart philosophical assimilation, it is difficult to extract a particular theme—such as power—which is diffused throughout the authorship. Based on Kierkegaard's theological convictions, the Christian's relationship to power stems from her identification with Christ, the paradigm for all human experience. However, the Incarnation is inextricably embedded within the all-encompassing goodness of divine Providence. Thus, in order to comprehend his concept of power on an individual level, it is necessary to examine the over-arching principles of cosmology, divine and human identity, and authority which permeate his writings. The following two chapters will adopt the same three-tier approach taken in the analysis of Nietzsche's thought. However, Kierkegaard's model contains the added dimension of a supernatural or eternal reality in addition to "created" reality. Subsequently, each tier incorporates a dichotomy: the cosmological tier explicates the relationship between the temporal and the eternal; the anthropological tier examines the relation between the crowd and the individual; the tier of authority explores the relation between the sensate and the spiritual.

Outlining the Divisions

The main reason for emphasizing the bifurcation of the eternal from the temporal is to underscore the centrality of Kierkegaard's insistence on the incommensurability between the "quantitative" sphere of the created order and the "qualitative" sphere of the eternal.[1] This "Athanasian" *chorismos*[2] was particularly crucial for Kierkegaard due to the prevalent cultural and intellectual assimilation of the religious by the aesthetic sphere.[3] On the surface, this stark dichotomy might

---

[1] *BA*, p. 38; *CUP*, vol. 1, pp. 213–14.

[2] A qualitative barrier which expressed the "chasm" of heterogeneity between God and creation, as insisted upon by Athanasius during his debates against the Arians ("Orations Against the Arians, Book 1," in William Rusch [ed.], *Sources of Early Christian Thought: The Trinitarian Controversy* [Philadelphia, 1980], p. 121).

[3] *CUP*, vol. 1, p. 432. The aesthetic sphere represents existence at a basic level of immediacy, which focuses primarily on external appearances and surfaces to the neglect of

suggest either a denigration of the created order in favour of the eternal—justifying Nietzsche's abhorrence of transcendental escapism—or a spectacularly remote God, safely sterilized in an inaccessible, "shrink-wrapped" seal of omnipotent insouciance. However, both would be gross misrepresentations of Kierkegaard's beliefs, particularly in light of his scathing critique of Hegelianism for obliterating the contingent via the ideal.[4]

There are at least three central nexuses in Kierkegaard's thought which crucially connect the temporal and the eternal, exposing the inadequacy of a sheer dichotomy. First, the created order is entirely dependent for its existence upon God's ongoing participation in history,[5] a relationship which is intrinsically grounded in divine freedom and love: "What is it that really binds the temporal and the eternal? What is it other than love, which therefore is before everything else and remains when all else is past."[6] Because God has brought everything into being, humans are responsible for maintaining an attitude of love and gratitude towards the world and everything in it; hence, for Kierkegaard, transcendental escapism is not an option, for it betrays a fundamental mistrust in Providence.[7] Second, temporality and eternity are forever wedded in the quintessential paradox and central truth claim of Christianity, the Incarnation: "that the eternal once came into existence in time."[8] Moreover, when individuals enter a moment of decision before God, that "moment" entails a "meeting" of time and eternity.[9] Third, every human being represents a bond of created matter and spirit:[10] "A human being is a synthesis of the infinite and the finite, of the temporal and the eternal, of freedom and necessity."[11] Hence, in "Two 'Notes' Concerning My Work as an Author,"

---

internal and eternal realities. See *BA*, p. 13; *SW*, p. 476.

[4]   For example, *BA*, p. 212 [4 July 1840]. Contrary to Hegel's epistemological tyranny of the ideal, Kierkegaard maintained, "But actuality (historical actuality) stands in a two-fold relation to the subject: partly as a gift that refuses to be rejected, partly as a task that wants to be fulfilled" (*CI*, p. 276). In response to Lessing's contention that "accidental truths" are incommensurable with "essential truths," Climacus observed: "The basis of the paradox of Christianity is that it continually uses time and the historical in relation to the eternal" (*CUP*, vol. 1, p. 95).

[5]   *JP*, vol. 3, p. 321 [1850].

[6]   *WL*, p. 24.

[7]   *JP*, vol. 4, pp. 49–52 [1840–41]. In *EUD*, p. 259, he denounced existential escapism as "not the expectancy of the eternal but a superstitious belief in the future."

[8]   *BA*, p. 38.

[9]   *TM*, p. 630, n. 1. Climacus explicitly connected the "moment" and Christ by referring to Galatians 4:4: "Let us call it: *the fullness of time*" (*PF*, p. 18).

[10]   *JP*, vol. 3, p. 338 [1854]; *CD*, p. 141; *WL*, p. 12; *UD*, p. 195; *CA*, p. 85; *EUD*, p. 163.

[11]   *SD*, p. 43. Kierkegaard attributed the human consciousness of time to "the eternal within him," lest a man live "*totally*" in the purely momentary" (*CD*, pp. 77–8; *EUD*, p. 17), and regarded the unity between one's "divine necessity" and "accidental finitude" as "implicit in consciousness, which is the point of departure for personality" (*BA*, p. 212 [4 July 1840]).

Kierkegaard stated, "[T]o be a human being is to have kinship with the divine."[12] Moreover, the central paradox of the Incarnation supremely grounds and upholds the temporal universe in the unwavering love of God whereby "every Christian is Christian only by being nailed to the paradox of having based his eternal happiness on the relation to something historical."[13] Thus, according to Kierkegaard, genuine faith validates temporality—it does not vitiate it.[14]

The limitations of this dichotomous structure also apply to the division between "sensate" and "spiritual" authority in the following chapter. I have chosen the term "sensate" to denote any human authority—whether intellectual, theological, moral, or political—which is not self-consciously submissive to God for several reasons: it is not an over-used term, it is found in translations of Kierkegaard's writings,[15] and it largely avoids certain problematic or pejorative connotations of words such as "natural," "material," "classical," "contingent," "worldly," "sensual," "transitory," "accidental," or "secular."[16] As with every element of temporality for Kierkegaard, sensate authority possesses the potential for transformational "renewal" through a restored relationship with God. An obvious limitation of the word is that it may seem to suggest an authority which is merely physical in nature. However, "sensate" is intended to include intellectual and emotional spheres as well. As long as this qualification is kept in mind, the term will hopefully provide more clarification than consternation. In light of these considerations, I will begin by articulating Kierkegaard's understanding of the eternal before examining his views on the created realm of temporality.

Kierkegaard's Comprehension of the Eternal: The Attributes of God

God's transcendental otherness

Kierkegaard outlined one of his fundamental theological premises in a journal entry written in 1851: "I have often pointed out that Christianity can be presented in two ways: either in man's interest (mitigating accommodation) or in God's interest (true Christianity) ... ."[17] Because of the overwhelming "compromises" of Danish Lutheranism, Kierkegaard sought to remain true to Christianity by retaining a theocentric focus. Within his writings, God is not reduced to the sum of several self-contained properties; rather, attributes such as God's goodness, omnibenevolence, and omnipotence remain interconnected and almost "perichoretic" in relation to

---

Although the human spirit can be "finitized" when lacking inwardness, Vigilius contended, "Inwardness is therefore eternity or the constituent of the eternal in man" (*CA*, p. 151).

[12] *PV*, p. 106.

[13] *CUP*, vol. 1, p. 578.

[14] *EUD*, p. 260.

[15] For example, *TM*, p. 460 [1854]; *PV*, p. 48; *PC*, p. 158; *EUD*, pp. 379, 382.

[16] I am particularly indebted to Dr. Michael Partridge for highlighting the terminological difficulties and providing helpful suggestions.

[17] *JP*, vol. 3, p. 457 [1851].

one another. In *Upbuilding Discourses in Various Spirits*, he wrote: "Everything that a human being knows about the eternal is contained primarily in this: it is God who rules, because whatever more a person comes to know pertains to *how* God has ruled or rules or will rule."[18] He later described this divine governing as "the rule of God's love," which human beings are not expected to understand although "we certainly are required to be able to believe and, believing, to understand that he is love."[19] The unfolding of God's communicated identity and expectations for human beings, which culminate in the Incarnation, is an essential manifestation of God's rulership: "Christianity is an *existence-communication*, brought into the world by the use of *authority*."[20]

If Kierkegaard's theological foundation could be encapsulated in a single phrase, a likely candidate would be Athanasius' pithy response to Arianism—"God is not as man."[21] Climacus echoed this sentiment by contending, "[I]f a human being is to come truly to know something about the unknown (the god), he must first come to know that it is different from him, absolutely different from him."[22] It is fallacious to extend human concepts of existence to God for, as Climacus contended, "God does not exist, he is eternal."[23] Without God's expressed self-communication, God would remain forever incomprehensible to human reason; therefore, Kierkegaard insisted that revelation must be approached on its own terms. While criticizing "aesthetic" and "ethical" approaches to Christianity, which inevitably dismiss the revelatory aspect, he declared, "A revelation-fact is, in qualitative dialectic, essentially different from everything else and in a qualitative dialectical sense essentially belongs in the essentially religious sphere, the paradoxical-religious."[24]

If God were merely a "passive," incomprehensible object for human knowledge, agnosticism would be legitimated; however, Kierkegaard believed that humankind is facing a God who is "pure subjectivity,"[25] who personally ensures that an accurate self-portrayal is transmitted.[26] Human subjectivity is, therefore, not an isolated phenomenon for Kierkegaard, but a participation in the ultimate subjectivity of God: "It is perfectly true, isolated subjectivity is, in the opinion of the ages, evil;

---

[18]   *UD*, p. 258.

[19]   Ibid., p. 268.

[20]   *JP*, vol. 1, p. 75 [1849].

[21]   Athanasius, p. 90.

[22]   *PF*, p. 46.

[23]   *CUP*, vol. 1, p. 332. In *PF*, p. 74, Climacus argued that God is "necessary" and, therefore, cannot come into being because he simply is.

[24]   *BA*, p. 20. The ethical sphere represents an intermediate life mode which ventures beyond the shallow egotism of the aesthetic sphere in pursuit of justice and ordered society. However, it is incapable of acknowledging the inevitability of human failings in the absence of divine grace. See *SW*, pp. 435, 476.

[25]   *JP*, vol. 3, p. 345 [1854].

[26]   *PF*, p. 42.

but 'objectivity' as a cure is not one whit better. The only salvation is subjectivity, *i.e.*, God, as infinite compelling subjectivity."[27] Thus, to present Christianity as "a sum of doctrines" which has no direct bearing on the lives of the listeners is, for Kierkegaard, tantamount to paganism.[28] Nevertheless, humankind is without excuse, and Kierkegaard once maintained that genuine atheism within Christendom does not exist due to the efficaciousness of divine revelation.[29] God's power remains inexplicable and largely unnoticed according to human standards of power; hence, Kierkegaard identified "inferior externality and interior divine power as the characteristic mark of the divine, whereas paganism is interior emptiness supported by external ostentation."[30] On account of human sinfulness and the contemporary prevalence of the "aesthetic fallacy," which measures internal realities based on external appearances,[31] Kierkegaard asserted, "This is Christianity's view: what is eternal, what is true, cannot possibly win the approval of the moment, must inevitably win its disapproval."[32]

God's utter incontestability
God's transcendental otherness, which remains incomprehensible to human reason apart from faith, is conjoined with the utter incontestability of God's rulership. On account of God's uniqueness, there are no equals to either rival or assist God. Because the power of God cannot be contested, Kierkegaard believed that there is no need for God to respond immediately to human rebellion. Rather, God waits, having all of the time in the world at God's disposal.[33] In an upbuilding discourse, Kierkegaard carefully explained that speaking of God's "victory" over anything is misleading, since nothing is even capable of challenging or threatening God:

---

[27] *JK*, p. 184 [1850]. It is important to emphasize that Kierkegaard is not questioning the "objective" veracity of the Christian faith with the concept of "subjectivity." The former is taken on trust rather than human rationalization: "It is Christ's personal authority, attested by his heterogeneity with fallen human nature, and manifested in his maieutic method of communication, that certifies (even if it does not demonstrate with rational certainty) the objective validity of the Christian world-and-life-view ..." (David Aiken, "The Decline from Authority: Kierkegaard on Intellectual Sin," *International Philosophical Quarterly*, 33/1 [1993]: 25). Aiken helpfully suggests that "objective truth, subjectively appropriated" is a better understanding than the "potentially misleading Climacan maxim 'Truth is subjectivity'" (ibid., p. 28).

[28] *CD*, pp. 214–15; *PV*, p. 228.

[29] *JP*, vol. 3, p. 662 [1844]: "[J]ust as no one has ever proved it [God's existence], so has there never been an atheist, even though there certainly have been many who have been unwilling to let what they knew (that the God exists) get control of their minds."

[30] Ibid., vol. 4, p. 458 [1851].

[31] *WL*, p. 305. Climacus stated that only God "possesses the medium that is the commensurability of the outer and the inner. But the human mind cannot see world history in this way" (*CUP*, vol. 1, p. 141).

[32] *CD*, p. 227.

[33] *TM*, p. 274.

"God's omnipotence and holiness do not mean that he can be victorious over everyone, that he is the strongest, for this is still a comparison; but it means, and this bars any comparison, that no one can manage to fight with him."[34] God can never fight fair—God is simply too big!

According to Kierkegaard, this divine unthwartability encompasses everything that transpires in the cosmos. The problem with "the problem of evil" challenges is that they fail to recognize "the differentiation that God accomplishes the good and merely permits the evil."[35] He contended that divine providence is able to incorporate the gravest misfortunes within its incontrovertible scope of love. Subsequently, Kierkegaard once proclaimed, "[U]ltimately everything must be ascribed to God if there is to be a God and a godly view of life."[36] This conviction remains consistent throughout the journal entries in which he comes to terms with personal suffering and tragedy.[37] Reflecting upon a certain error, he once wrote: "[I]t was still your governance which permitted it to happen and promptly and lovingly lifted it up into your fatherly purpose for me, lovingly disposing of the millions of possibilities so that even the mistake would become truly useful to me."[38]

God's omnibenevolence

If God is characterized only by sheer otherness and utter incontestability, the universe would be little more than one tyrannical system in which human free will is a mere illusion. At times, Kierkegaard leans toward such a view. For example, in his interpretation of Matthew 6:24, "No one can serve two masters ...," he concluded that a person serves God no matter which choice one makes, so one might as well serve God willingly.[39] A similar strand of "Christian fatalism" occurs in *Without Authority*: "God's will is still done anyhow; so strive to make a virtue of necessity by unconditionally obediently doing God's will."[40] However, Kierkegaard believed that God's rule, incontestable and beyond the grasp of human rationality

---

[34]   *UD*, p. 286. Klaus-M. Kodalle posits, "The new Kierkegaardian way of thinking and the freedom that comes with it leave the traditional view of God behind, that is, God as an omnipotent being ruling in the mode of domination" ("The Utilitarian Self and the 'Useless' Passion of Faith," in Alastair Hannay and Gordon Marino (eds), *The Cambridge Companion to Kierkegaard* (Cambridge, 1998), p. 400).

[35]   *TM*, p. 390 [1846].

[36]   *EUD*, p. 386.

[37]   "Governance" employed depression and "a troubled conscience" to "hold me in rein" (*CD*, p. 421 [1848]), in addition to expanding biographical incidentals into significant principles such as "that single individual"—originally a reference to Regine Olsen (*WA*, p. xviii). Publication pressures, anxiety over authorship, and the death of Regine's father were regarded as "hints from Governance" (*PV*, p. 226 [1849]).

[38]   *JP*, vol. 3, p. 575 [1850].

[39]   *CD*, p. 83. See also *WA*, p. 197 [1847].

[40]   Ibid., p. 30.

or manipulation, is simultaneously characterized by omnibenevolence: "God is pure subjectivity and in love it pleases God to be concerned about man."[41] Because God is transcendent and omnipotent, God lacks nothing. Climacus concluded, "But if he moves himself and is not moved by need, what moves him then but love, for love does not have the satisfaction of need outside itself but within."[42] Anti-Climacus defined this "divine compassion" as radical intervention, "the unlimited *recklessness* in concerning oneself only with the suffering, not in the least with oneself, and of unconditionally recklessly concerning oneself with *each* sufferer."[43] God's compassion is itself indefatigable, based upon "the omnipotence with which God the omnipotent One bears all your sorrow lightly as nothing."[44]

The doctrine that God is love was indispensable to Kierkegaard, who once declared that, should anyone observe a single event "that is incompatible with the idea that God is love,"[45] it would disprove God's existence, "for if God is not love, and if he is not love in everything, then God does not exist at all."[46] God's love is not only evident in the universe he has created, but also in the fact that he remains a self-giving God. This applies to the Incarnation, as well as to the ongoing work of the Holy Spirit, whose promptings constitute "God's gifts in a far deeper sense than food and clothing, not only because it is God who gives them but because God gives himself in these gifts!"[47]

God's constancy

The final attribute of God which is prominent in Kierkegaard's writings forms the crux of his favorite passage of scripture, James 1:17–21: God never changes.[48] Despite the suffering which God brings upon Godself through intimate involvement with a "fallen" creation characterized by misused freedom, Kierkegaard comforted those who suffered for the truth: "[B]e assured that in love God suffers more than you are suffering, but he cannot be changed by that."[49] Accordingly, he once described "divine fatherly love" as "the one single unshakable thing in life, the true Archimedean point."[50] Because of the attributes of extreme otherness, utter incontestability, unshakable love, and acute immutability, God's ability to will and accomplish the good for temporality is ultimately unthwartable.

---

[41]   *JP*, vol. 3, p. 345 [1854].

[42]   *PF*, p. 24.

[43]   *PC*, p. 58.

[44]   *WA*, p. 43.

[45]   *UD*, p. 270.

[46]   Ibid., p. 267. He added: "But no human being would be able to endure this horror …" (ibid., p. 270).

[47]   *CD*, p. 253.

[48]   *TM*, p. 268; *CI*, p. 476, n. 70.

[49]   *TM*, p. 295.

[50]   Ibid., p. xii.

Kierkegaard's Comprehension of the Temporal: Limitations of Actuality

Contingent knowledge of God

In contrast to the otherness, incontestability, omnibenevolence, and immutability of God, the temporal universe—everything that exists, that is, was created by God—is characterized by contingency and limitation. Humans are particularly limited in acquiring true and complete knowledge of who God is. Kierkegaard adamantly maintained that God is clearly beyond the ordinary purview of human rationality and thinkability.[51] Without God's personal self-disclosure, humankind would remain trapped within mythical constructions and projections. According to the Danish thinker, erroneous interpretations of God's transcendence take two contrary forms: either, God is held "too close" by a religiousness of immanence and thereby encased within the temporal order of creation and made subject to its laws and limitations;[52] or, God is held "too distant," whereby people fail to recognize God's intimate interactions with creation. By contrast, he maintained, "[T]he eternal is the dominant, which does not want to have its time but wants to make time *its own* and then permits the temporal also to have its time."[53]

It is tempting to conjecture on Kierkegaard's attitude towards natural revelation. He clearly believed that creation displays the beauty and handiwork of God. While explaining the *imago Dei*, he stated: "The upright gait is the sign of distinction, but to be able to prostrate oneself in adoration and worship is even more glorious; and all nature is like the great staff of servants who remind the human being, the ruler, about worshiping God."[54] However, such praise likely arises after reconciliation through God's primary revelation—the life and person of Jesus Christ. Kierkegaard showed little tolerance for religions of immanence: "Temporality, as it is knowable, cannot be the transparency of the eternal; in its given actuality, it is the *refraction* of the eternal."[55] According to Kierkegaard, the pagan mistakenly strove to emulate the divine by ruling rather than by humble adoration: "To worship is not to rule, and yet worship is what makes the human being resemble God, and to be able truly to worship is the excellence of the invisible glory above all creation. The pagan was not aware of God and therefore sought likeness in ruling."[56]

Because of his aversion to Hegelian "quantification"—the assimilation of the eternal by human formulations and standards—Kierkegaard adamantly attacked

---

[51]   The natural outcome of the encounter between unregenerate humanity and God is, therefore, offence. See *PC*, pp. 75–144.

[52]   Climacus calls this "Religiousness A" in contrast to "Religiousness B," the religion of transcendence. See *CUP*, vol. 1, pp. 555–74.

[53]   *UD*, p. 11.

[54]   Ibid., p. 193. Kierkegaard also believed that God's will is explicitly revealed "in Holy Scripture and in my conscience" (*JK*, p. 203 [1850]).

[55]   *UD*, p. 90.

[56]   Ibid., p. 193.

the view that Christian faith is merely one stage in the unfolding evolution of humankind which must be superseded by a higher stage of development.[57] Instead, Christian faith entails a "collision" whereby the temporal encounters the eternal on its own terms. He denied the efficacy of any human-made artifice—whether physical or intellectual—to communicate God directly to any individual.[58] Climacus ironically observed,

> No anonymous author can more slyly hide himself, and no maieutic can more carefully recede from a direct relation than God can. He is in the creation, everywhere in the creation, but he is not there directly, and only when the single individual turns inwards into himself … does he become aware and capable of seeing God.[59]

Redeeming the fallen realm

In stark contrast to the immutability of the eternal, temporality is characterized by its intrinsic changeability and susceptibility to corruption.[60] Subsequently, Kierkegaard believed that clinging earnestly to the uncertain is tantamount to insanity,[61] for *"only the eternal can be gained eternally."*[62] At the same time, however, temporality is bound to God's loving purposes and "God's plan of existence— that time is purely and simply development, prior complication, and eternity the solution."[63] Even political events, such as war and revolution, are incorporated within God's indefatigable plan for temporality. Hence, while reflecting upon the upheavals of 1848, he once contended, "And when the preliminary, the convulsive seizure, has run its course, the human race will be so exhausted from sufferings and loss of blood that this matter of eternity might at least be allowed to receive consideration."[64] Although Vigilius wrote that it is the nature of "the demonic" to fear the irrevocable annihilation of the temporal by the eternal, he insisted: "In eternity … all contradiction is cancelled, the temporal is permeated by and preserved in the eternal … ."[65] Just as the "lower" spheres of existence—the aesthetic, ethical,

---

[57] *CUP*, vol. 1, pp. 291–4. The incommensurability of Christianity with human development is based on the paradoxical nature of the eternal entering the temporal in the Incarnation.

[58] *WL* [revised], p. 409 [January 1847].

[59] *CUP*, vol. 1, p. 243.

[60] *WA*, p. 40. Kierkegaard's famous image of "floating out upon the depths of 7,000 fathoms of water" expressed "how uncertain everything is" (*CD*, p. 255).

[61] Ibid., p. 256.

[62] Ibid., p. 137.

[63] *WL*, p. 236.

[64] *BA*, p. 232 [October 1848].

[65] *CA*, p. 154.

and Religiousness A—are not negated as in Hegelian "mediation,"[66] but swept up in an "Elijan" whirlwind of fire and transfigured into something higher within Religiousness B,[67] likewise the temporal is not discarded but transformed into perfection.[68] In order to investigate the implications of sin and redemption more closely, we will now focus on Kierkegaard's understanding of humanity.

The Anthropological Tier

The Universal: Abortion of Selfhood through Collectivity

The gift of free will
Within the glorious cosmos which God has freely created, humankind occupies a unique and privileged position. For Kierkegaard, one of the greatest expressions of God's love—and equally expressive of God's supreme otherness and utter incontestability—is human freedom: "The greatest good, after all, that can be done for a being … is to make it free. In order to do just that, omnipotence is required."[69] Contrary to many philosophical and theological disputations of the inherent contradictions between divine and human freedom, Kierkegaard believed that the existence of human free will is a miracle created and perpetually sustained by the omnipotent love and creative liberty of God:

---

[66]   *EO*, vol. 1, p. 478 [1837]: "Hegel's subsequent position swallows up the previous one, not as one stage of life swallows another, with each still retaining its validity, but as a higher title or rank swallows up a lower title."

[67]   See Patrick Gardiner, *Kierkegaard: A Very Short Introduction* (Oxford, 2002), p. 67: "While the importance of moral requirements is not as such denied, the absolute sovereignty of the ethical can no longer be assumed …." Walter Hong shares this interpretation in *WL* [revised], p. 316, n. 40: "The becoming of the person, or 'stages *on life's way*,' thereby involves 'cutting the tap roots' of the esthetic, the ethical, and the immanental religious, but not abrogating them, and in the life of faith catching them up in 'spontaneity after reflection.'" "Religiousness A" refers to a humanly constructed religion of immanence, while "Religiousness B" is a religion featuring transcendental components.

[68]   See, for example, *BA*, p. 21, where Kierkegaard contended that the ethical requirement defends the religious sphere against the aesthetic sphere's attempts to reduce it to "art": "The religious sphere includes or ought to include the ethical … ." In speaking of love versus faith and hope, he wrote: "[T]he greatest must be able to undertake the business of the lesser ones (if I may put it this way) and makes them more perfect" (*WL*, p. 213). See also *FT*, p. 70, where the ethical is not nullified but "receives a completely different expression," and *EO*, vol. 1, p. 205, where Faust is described as a later "reproduction" or "stage" of Don Juan: "[T]o reproduce another stage does not mean only to become that but to become that with all the elements of the preceding stage in it."

[69]   *TM*, p. 390 [1846].

[I]f a human being had the slightest independent existence over against God (with regard to *materia*), then God could not make him free. Creation out of nothing is once again the Omnipotent One's expression for being able to make [a being] independent. He to whom I owe absolutely everything, although he still absolutely controls everything, has in fact made me independent.[70]

He contended that true independence can only be given by one who can completely remove all vestiges of obligation and dependency from the recipient.[71] Subsequently, the gift of liberty cannot represent a loss of liberty on the part of the giver, otherwise, Kierkegaard argued, the recipient will be bound by the gift and not truly liberated: "If in creating man God himself lost a little of his power, then precisely what he could not do would be to make a human being independent."[72] Creation *ex nihilo* becomes a vital doctrine for Kierkegaard, underscoring the qualitative difference between temporal and divine power and creativity:

A human being cannot bear to have his "creations" be something in relation to himself; they are supposed to be nothing; and therefore he calls them, and with disdain, "creations." But God, who creates from nothing, omnipotently takes from nothing and says, "Become"; he lovingly adds, "Become something even in relation to me." What wonderful love; even his omnipotence is in the power of love.[73]

The gift of true independence requires great subtlety. In *Works of Love*, Kierkegaard claimed, "[T]he greatest benefaction cannot be accomplished in any way whereby the recipient gets to know that he is indebted."[74] If someone argued that humankind has nevertheless become "indebted" to God for their freedom, Kierkegaard might respond that God has not lost or gained anything from his gift and, therefore, there is neither a genuine debt nor a "contractual" obligation for repaying it. On account of God's utter incontestability and limitless power, only God can truly liberate a living being:

All finite power makes dependent; only omnipotence can make independent, can form from nothing something that has its continuity in itself through the continuous withdrawing of omnipotence. Omnipotence is not ensconced in a

---

[70]   Ibid., pp. 391–2 [1846]. See also *WL* [revised], p. 405 [1846]: "It is incomprehensible that omnipotence is able not only to create the most impressive of all things—the whole visible world—but is able to create the most frail of all things—a being independent of that very omnipotence."

[71]   *TM*, p. 391 [1846]: "God's omnipotence is therefore his goodness. For goodness is to give oneself away completely, but in such a way that by omnipotently taking oneself back one makes the recipient independent."

[72]   Ibid., pp. 392 [1846].

[73]   *CD*, p. 127.

[74]   *WL*, p. 256.

relationship to another, for there is no other to which it is comparable—no, it can give without giving up the least of its power, that is, it can make independent.[75]

This suggests that, for Kierkegaard, true power is represented by the ability to empower another without enslaving that person to either the giver or to the gift—a task accomplishable only by omnipotence.

Complying with gospel tradition,[76] Kierkegaard contended that it is only through willingly relinquishing the temporal that a person truly gains both the temporal and the eternal,[77] an act made possible only by grace: "Only with the help of the eternal is a person able to let go of the lost temporal thing in such a way that he loses it only temporally. If the eternal does not help, then he loses much more than the temporal."[78] Michael Matthis lucidly explains that the Christian attains true selfhood before God, which is unavailable to the aesthetic or ethical "self," each of which,

> seeks to simplify the complexity of selfhood and find a solution within immanence to the problem of selfhood that the religious self faces in going beyond the immanent, i.e., beyond the control of its own powers, that problem being the reconciliation of the total freedom that selfhood demands and the fact of otherness without which that freedom becomes a mirage, a mere play of fantasy.[79]

Subsequently, before a truly omnipotent God, the individual's freedom is recognized and ratified by an Other who can neither threaten nor be threatened by this freedom.

God's loving omnipotence is not only necessary to create "independent" humanity *ex nihilo*. Kierkegaard believed that God's omnipotence is constantly required to prevent creation from being overwhelmed by God's abundance.[80]

---

[75] *TM*, p. 391 [1846]. See also *CUP*, vol. 1, p. 260, where Climacus stated, "[N]o one is as resigned as God, because he communicates creatively in such a way that in creating he *gives* independence vis à vis himself."

[76] Mt. 16:24–6; Mk 8:35.

[77] *CD*, pp. 134, 43.

[78] Ibid., p. 142.

[79] Michael Matthis, "Kierkegaard and the Problem of the Social Other," *Philosophy Today*, 38/4 (1994): 422.

[80] Jürgen Moltmann develops a similar view of divine self-limitation, building upon Isaac Luria's doctrine of *zimzum*. See *God in Creation: An Ecological Doctrine of Creation*, trans. Margaret Kohl (London, 1985), pp. 86–8, and *The Trinity and the Kingdom of God: The Doctrine of God*, trans. Margaret Kohl (London, 1981), pp. 108–11.

Divine power is as much a "holding back"[81] as a holding forth,[82] since true power need not be "conspicuous" in its deportment. As Judge William explained,

> [T]here are different ways of measuring strength. When Holger Danske squeezes sweat out of an iron glove, that is strength, but if he were handed a butterfly, I am afraid that he would not have sufficient strength to take it properly. To mention the sublime example, God's omnipotence appears great in having created everything, but does it not appear equally great in the omnipotent moderation that can permit a blade of grass to grow its season.[83]

Hence, in God's continuous interaction with humanity, God's compassion is expressed by the refusal to impede the freedom of God's creations through either the blatant use of power,[84] or an oppressive—because overwhelming—divine disclosure. Thus, Kierkegaard exclaimed, "[I]n your goodness you conceal yourself from him [mankind], and your omnipotence makes it impossible for him to see you, since in that case he himself would become nothing!"[85]

It would be somewhat misleading to label Kierkegaard's view of divine power as "kenotic" or self-emptying, given that God's "holding back" is, paradoxically, an invisible display of his unwavering omnipotence.[86] What then seems "powerless" from the perspective of temporality is, in fact, the full and radical entrance of God in time. In addition to the gift of liberty itself, lovingly bestowed from freedom for freedom, Kierkegaard believed that human free will receives a second inestimable honor—God renders Godself an object of human choice: "Do you know any more overwhelming and humbling manifestation of God's complaisance and indulgence toward human beings than that in a sense he places himself on the straight line of choice with the world just in order that the human being can choose ... ."[87]

---

[81]   Kodalle, p. 400.

[82]   Matthis, p. 431, argues that this is not a violation of the principle of contradiction, "since it occurs at the level of the transcendent."

[83]   *SW*, p. 144. See also *WA*, p. 42: "God the Omnipotent One carries the whole world and all its sorrow ... with extreme lightness."

[84]   *UD*, p. 62.

[85]   *EUD*, p. 310. See also *PF*, pp. 26–30.

[86]   The impression of God's literally having to "shove over" to make room for human freedom seemingly implies a commensurability between divine power/freedom and human power/freedom, which would be untenable from a Kierkegaardian perspective. Hence, I believe Kierkegaard would have agreed with Bonhoeffer's assessment: "[T]he doctrine of kenosis tried to reduce the claims of the divine nature until ultimately divine and human nature would fit together" (*Christology*, trans. Edwin Robertson [London, 1981], p. 97). God's otherness must be an "other" otherness from human "otherness."

[87]   *UD*, p. 206. This accounts for the eternal peril of choosing not to choose God or avoiding the choice altogether (ibid., p. 207).

For Kierkegaard, the major implications of this divine "self-restraint" in light of human independence are two-fold. First, in permitting creations to choose to reject God, God is vulnerable to suffering. This vicissitude is eloquently illustrated in Climacus' parable of the love-struck king who seeks to woo a peasant maiden without overwhelming her by his grandeur: "Who grasps the contradiction of this sorrow: not to disclose itself is the death of love; to disclose itself is the death of the beloved."[88] Climacus then pressed his point concerning human illusions of power: "The human mind so often aspires to might and power, and in its constant preoccupation with this thought, as if achieving it would transfigure everything, it does not suspect that there is not only joy in heaven but sorrow also ... ."[89] Second, there is a dialectic at work between human and divine freedom. In *Works of Love*, the author observed that *"everything which shall be kept alive must be kept in its element. But love's element is infinitude ... ."*[90] In order for human love to be sustained, it must exist within the bounds of divine love. Similarly, one might argue that, for human freedom to be sustained, it must flourish within the confluence and effluence of God's freedom.

"Crowding out" God: sin as revaluation

Tragically, humankind chose to misuse its freedom in order to pursue a sinful autonomy from God, a travesty of truth which persists, with ever evolving cunning, to the present. Commenting on the widespread indolence inherent in a cost-free "grace," Kierkegaard wrote: "Man thinks he will have the easiest time of all when there is no God at all—then man can play the lord. After that God becomes at most a handsome ornament, a luxury item—for there is no duty toward God."[91] One of the most important ramifications of human rebellion for Kierkegaard is the intentional loss of individual identity before God by conglomeration *en masse*, fostered by fear of "the risky odyssey of becoming a self."[92] He maintained, "The same people, who as individuals are able to will the good in truth, are immediately corrupted as soon as they unite and become many ... ."[93] When humans "band" together, rebellion rises, God is forgotten,[94] and a Babel-like assault upon the "heavens" is inevitable.[95] Anti-Climacus stated,

---

88   *PF*, p. 30.

89   Ibid.

90   *WL*, p. 176.

91   Cited in Merold Westphal, "Kierkegaard's Sociology," in George Connell and C. Stephen Evans (eds), *Foundations of Kierkegaard's Vision of Community: Religion, Ethics, and Politics in Kierkegaard* (New Jersey and London, 1992), p. 145.

92   Kodalle, p. 405.

93   *UD*, p. 96. See also *WA*, p. 76; *WL* [revised], p. 404 [1846]; *EO*, vol. 1, p. 31.

94   *WA*, p. 17.

95   Gen. 11:4–9.

Once people are allowed to merge in what Aristotle terms the animal category—
the crowd, then this abstraction (instead of being less than nothing, less than the
least significant individual human being) becomes regarded as some thing. And
then it isn't long before this abstraction becomes God.[96]

In Kierkegaard's writings, the crowd represents both the epitome of conformity
and the demise of the particular, the "degradation to copies."[97] He did not, however,
condemn all forms of congregation,[98] but merely those associations which elevate
the worth of the crowd over the worth of the individual, a reversion to "the old
paganism" wherein the particular is reduced to mere specimens of the general race
or species.[99] Hence, the danger of the crowd lies specifically in its ability to thwart
individual selfhood. Within this context, Merold Westphal explains, *"Kierkegaard
seeks to un-socialize the individual in order to un-deify society."*[100]

According to Anti-Climacus, the human being is a synthesis of the finite
(which "combines") and the infinite (which "expands"). If the infinite is allowed
to expand without being called back to itself, the individual becomes "fantastic":

When emotion becomes fantastic in this way, the self is simply more and more
volatilized and eventually becomes a kind of abstract sensitivity which inhumanly
belongs to no human, but which inhumanly participates sensitively, so to speak,
in the fate of some abstraction, for example, humanity *in abstracto*.[101]

As a result, the individual loses all particularity and becomes "a cipher, one more
person, one more repetition of this perpetual *Einerlei* [one-and-the-same]."[102] This
constitutes the worst sort of despair: when a person denies her responsibility of
having to become a self—a possibility which is actualized only by intentional
living in the presence of God.[103] Kierkegaard contended that only the individual
can thwart one's own selfhood:

People continually think that it is the world, the environment, the circumstances,
the situations that stand in one's way, in the way of one's fortune and peace and
joy. Basically it is always the person himself who stands in his way, the person

---

[96]   *SD*, p. 151.

[97]   *JP*, vol. 3, p. 333 [1854].

[98]   In fact, he argued that individuals cannot truly unite without particularity (*TA*,
p. 91). See also *JP*, vol. 1, p. 155 [1848]: "[T]he defect in the life of Christendom ... is that
people ... live too remote from each other."

[99]   *PV*, p. 107.

[100]   "Kierkegaard's Politics," *Thought*, 55/218 (1980): p. 325.

[101]   *SD*, p. 61. While the idealist "dissipates" the self into abstraction, the determinist
"suffocates" the self because "it is impossible to breathe necessity alone ..." (ibid., p. 70).

[102]   Ibid., p. 63.

[103]   Ibid., p. 64.

himself who is bound up too closely with the world ... so that he is unable to come to himself, to find rest, to hope.[104]

Contrary to Socrates' belief that truth resides within the immortal soul of man,[105] Kierkegaard posited that animosity "naturally" arises between humanity and truth. Climacus insisted that living in a state of "untruth" entails not being "merely outside the truth," but being fundamentally opposed to the truth.[106] Instead of preoccupation with truth, Anti-Climacus claimed, "The world really only interests itself in intellectual or aesthetic limitations, or in the indifferent ... ."[107] Sin, therefore, becomes the ultimate human revaluation, "For worldliness is precisely to ascribe infinite value to the indifferent."[108] Anti-Climacus insisted that any created being who attempts to attain autonomy independent of the eternal power which establishes it is consigned to failure and despair.[109] By attempting to replace God, temporality "becomes something by stealing the power of eternity from a person and then in return remains with him and makes him its slave."[110] Subsequently, sin precipitates a catastrophic revaluation whereby "death"—a separation from the source of life and freedom, God—is deemed "life" and "life"—a relationship of intentional submission before God—is regarded as "death."[111] If individuals are truly living out of a pseudo-self based on this value inversion, any attempt to strip them of this centre of existence will be met with stiff resistance and the generation of "offence": "[I]t is the New Testament's most definite statement—that Christianity and being a true Christian must to the highest degree be an offense to the natural man, that

---

[104]   *CD*, pp. 109–10.

[105]   Climacus critiqued the Socratic tenet of recollection in *PF*, pp. 9–11.

[106]   Ibid., p. 15.

[107]   *SD*, p. 63.

[108]   Ibid.

[109]   Ibid., p. 99. Anti-Climacus would take issue with interpreters who grant individuals the ability of willing the "leap" from one existence sphere to another. See, for example, Charlotte Cope, "Freedom, Responsibility, and the Concept of Anxiety," in *International Philosophical Quarterly*, 44/4 (2004): 557, who examines the difficulties of assigning responsibility to non-leapers if the leap is not volitional. M. Jamie Fereirra helpfully proposes the term "leap to faith" to depict more accurately that the leap is not initiated by the leaper's own faith. See "Faith and the Kierkegaardian Leap," in Alastair Hannay and Gordon D. Marino (eds), *The Cambridge Companion to Kierkegaard*, (Cambridge, 1998), p. 207.

[110]   *CD*, p. 99.

[111]   See, for example, *EUD*, p. 377—"There is a condition of the struggle that removes every doubt, consequently a condition of the struggle that makes the contender truly joyful and intrepid, and this is the condition: if he loses, then he is victorious."—and *UD* 181: "[T]o be dependent on God, completely dependent—that is independence." Due to the illusions of sin, Kierkegaard contended that, contrary to the claims of Ludwig Feuerbach and others, temporality—and not the eternal—serves as a crutch for the weak (*FS*, p. 114).

he must regard Christianity as the greatest treason and the true Christian as the meanest traitor to being a human being … ."[112]

"Particular" losses

Kierkegaard presented three major ramifications of the abortion of individual selfhood through "over-crowding." First, the individual loses the ability to consolidate the will and centre one's focus upon God,[113] seeking instead to hide from God beneath the foliage of abstract collective categories. As Climacus dourly observed, "Because of the jumbling together with the idea of the state, of sociality, of community, and of society, God can no longer catch hold of the single individual."[114] In a journal entry, Kierkegaard once compared the psychological anonymity of "herdism" to demonic possession:

> [T]his demonic lust, a lust to lose oneself in order to evaporate in a potentiation, so that a person is outside of himself, does not really know what he is doing or what he is saying or who it is or what it is speaking through him, while the blood rushes faster, the eyes glitter and stare fixedly, the passions boil, lusts seethe.[115]

Truly there is—or so the masses insist—safety in numbers from God's judicial scrutiny.

The second implication of losing one's self in the crowd is imprisonment within lateral comparisons wherein the true ideal and true community vanish. Instead of holding herself accountable to an unshakable standard, a person justifies her behavior based on both the underperformance of "the others,"[116] as well as the apparent futility of opposing the majority: "[H]ow could one individual be able to stand against the crowd, which has the power!"[117] Hence, Kierkegaard expounded, "[T]he crowd either produces impenitence and irresponsibility or at least weakens the individual's sense of responsibility by making it a fractional category."[118] He attributed this tendency to the rise of anthropocentred living: "The more that culture, education, and understanding get the upper hand, the more that people begin to live by way of comparison … ."[119]

The third impact of loss of selfhood through "over-crowding" is increased fear and subsequent thirst for power. Kierkegaard once wrote, "Deep within every man there lies the dread of being alone in the world, forgotten by God,

---

[112]   Ibid., p. 140. See also *PF*, pp. 49–50.

[113]   *UD*, p. 127.

[114]   *CUP*, vol. 1, p. 544.

[115]   *JP*, vol. 4, p. 167 [1850].

[116]   *WL*, p. 121; *SW*, p. 440.

[117]   *WL* [revised], p. 404 [1846].

[118]   *JP*, vol. 3, pp. 307–8 [1847–48].

[119]   *BA*, p. 109.

overlooked among the tremendous household of millions upon millions."[120] He maintained that every person especially fears the true means of gaining the self, the risk of interaction with truth: "[A]nd that is what is human, for truth is related to being 'spirit'—and that is very hard for flesh and blood and the physical lust for knowledge to bear. Between man and truth lies mortification—you see why we are all more or less afraid."[121] The power craved by the masses, however, is transient, depersonalized, and "cannot be defined humanly but can be more accurately defined as the power of a machine, ... the power of the crowd is always horse-power."[122] Ironically, like Nietzsche, Kierkegaard believed that past abuse of power by the nobility has greatly contributed to the rise of populist power: "This, you see, is the result of centuries of fighting against popes and kings and the powers that be, and, on the other hand, regarding the people and the crowd as holy."[123] Kierkegaard thought that populist movements represent the greatest kind of tyranny, "for how is it possible to get hold of the crowd[?]."[124] In the wake of the deleterious impact of human sinful collectivity, it is necessary to examine the divine solution as Kierkegaard perceived it.

The Particular: The Salvation of the One

Despite his intense aversion to the false communitarianism which permeated nineteenth-century Europe, Kierkegaard remained hopeful that salvation is possible and provides effective "crowd control":

> And this is my faith, that however much confusion and evil and contemptibleness there can be in human beings as soon as they become the irresponsible and unrepentant "public," "crowd," etc.—there is just as much truth and goodness and lovableness in them when one can get them as single individuals.[125]

Anti-Climacus inextricably conjoined self-conscious, individual existence with true knowledge of God when he lamented over the man who

---

[120]   *JK*, p. 129 [1847].

[121]   Ibid., p. 202 [1850].

[122]   *WA*, p. 229 [October 1848].

[123]   *JP*, vol. 4, p. 141 [1847].

[124]   Ibid. Kierkegaard shared Martin Luther's disdain for the "masses": "[T]he world and the masses are and always will be unchristian, although they are all baptized and are nominally Christian" (*Selections from His Writings*, ed. John Dillenberger [New York, 1962], p. 371).

[125]   *PV*, pp. 10–11. For this reason, Kierkegaard opposed all "mass" programs of reform: "[T]he essentially Christian reformation means to turn against the mass, for the essentially Christian reformation means that each person must be reformed, and only then is the most ungodly of all unchristian categories overthrown: the crowd, the public" (*JP*, vol. 3, p. 307 [1847]).

never became decisively, eternally, conscious of himself as spirit, as self, or, what is the same, ... he never became aware—and gained in the deepest sense the impression—that there is a God there and that "he," himself, his self, exists before this God, which infinite gain is never come by except through despair.[126]

Contrary to Hegelian aspirations, Climacus emphasized that "the task is not to move from the individual to the race, but from the individual through the race (the universal) to reach the individual."[127] Kierkegaard's focus on "that individual" [*hiin Enkelte*],[128] however, "corresponds to the fact that the truth was in one person, in Christ, in opposition to the whole race."[129] This "singular" emphasis also reflects the nature of Christ's redemptive work: "The sacrifice he offered he did not offer for people in general— and it cannot be done that way either. No, he sacrificed himself in order to save each one individually ... ."[130] Authentic human identity, for Kierkegaard, is thus based upon a "relational individualism": "individual" because one stands and acts alone before God, but "relational" in both its foundation of "relating infinitely to the eternal,"[131] as well as its outworking in non-preferential love towards one's neighbours.[132]

Kierkegaard's understanding of conversion parallels orthodox Christian belief. Because of the "infinite, qualitative difference between man and God," God must "disrupt the learner" and radically reconfigure her: for Kierkegaard, there is literally no room for "improvement."[133] Instead, a complete transformation or *metanoia* is

---

[126]   *SD*, p. 57. Kierkegaard even went so far as to deny authentic "selfhood" to pagans: "The lowly pagan, he is without God in the world and therefore is never essentially himself (which one is only by being before God) ..." (*CD*, p. 44). He was, however, confident that God provides ample means of salvation for everyone: "That is, the need brings its nourishment along with it ..." (ibid., p. 244). On the prospects of living "truthfully" though one does not possess the truth, see *UD*, pp. 25, 35; *CUP*, vol. 1, p. 199; *TA*, p. 64.

[127]   *CUP*, vol. 1, p. 428.

[128]   Robert Perkins (ed.), *International Kierkegaard Commentary: Two Ages* (Macon, 1984), p. xiii.

[129]   *JP*, vol. 3, p. 341 [1854]. Kierkegaard's formulation is strongly influenced by Socrates who, he claimed, had used the category of "single individual" to "disintegrate paganism" (*PV*, p. 123) and practiced "closing himself in with himself in order to be expanded in the divine" (*CA*, p. 134).

[130]   *CD*, p. 272.

[131]   Murray Rae succinctly states, "There is really no such category as 'the individual' in Kierkegaard's work. It is rather 'the individual before God' who is the focus of Kierkegaard's concern" (*Kierkegaard's Vision of the Incarnation: By Faith Transformed* [Oxford, 1997], p. 145).

[132]   See Robert Perkins, "Envy as Personal Phenomenon and as Politics," in Robert Perkins (ed.), *International Kierkegaard Commentary: Two Ages* (Macon, 1984), p. 116. For a lucid examination of Kierkegaard's sociology, see Merold Westphal, "Kierkegaard's Sociology," pp. 133–54.

[133]   *TM*, p. 393 [1847].

necessary: "This life-giving in the Spirit is not a *direct* heightening of the natural life in a person in *immediate* continuation from and connection with it ... . [I]t is a new life."[134] Regarding the unregenerated self, Kierkegaard once wrote: "[T]o speak merely humanly, God is indeed a human being's most appalling enemy, your mortal enemy. Indeed he wants you to die, to die to the world; he hates specifically that in which you naturally have your life, to which you cling with all your zest for life."[135] Christian dogma demands that one must relinquish personal autonomy in lieu of a life of personal obedience to God, and acknowledge one's failure to meet divine expectations for human life, a "natural" impossibility since, "No human being is able to say, of his own and by himself, what sin is, for sin is the very thing he is in."[136] For this reason, a person cannot even perceive the need for renewal prior to receiving that renewal.[137] Climacus contended, "[T]he teacher, before beginning to teach, must transform, not reform, the learner. But no human being is capable of doing this; if it is to take place, it must be done by the god himself."[138] Any attempt at a human solution to sin is as futile as allowing the "disease" to prescribe its own remedy.[139]

Anti-Climacus stated that this transformation is only possible through "contemporaneous" interaction with Christ.[140] Because this crucial encounter based on the miraculous entrance of Christ into history can only take place in the present moment,[141] Kierkegaard criticized any idealistic annulment of human

---

[134]　*FS*, p. 76. N.H. Søe observes that Kierkegaard's view of the centrality of redemption, which "must come from God," was formulated by the time he was 22 ("Christ," in Niels Thulstrup and M. Mikulová Thulstrup [eds], *Bibliotheca Kierkegaardiana: Theological Concepts in Kierkegaard* [16 vols, Copenhagen, 1980], vol. 5, p. 55). Kierkegaard maintained this christological focus until his dying day. When Emil Boesen asked if he could die in peace, Kierkegaard responded affirmatively. When his friend asked if this was because of "the grace of God in Christ," he replied, "Yes, naturally, what else?" (ibid., p. 70).

[135]　*TM*, p. 177. See also *JP*, vol. 3, p. 733 [1851], and *FS*, p. 177, where he described Christ as the "ultimate threat" to "that in which we human beings have our lives." Unlike the religion of immanence which constitutes subtle self-reliance through "inward deepening" (*CUP*, vol. 1, p. 561), the religion of transcendence or "Religiousness B" insists that one "become something else" (*BA*, p. 113).

[136]　*SD*, p. 127. See also *CD*, p. 102; *UD*, p. 285; *CUP*, vol. 1, p. 585. Hence, Kierkegaard explained, "It is therefore very consistent for Luther to teach that a person must be taught by a revelation concerning how deeply he lies in sin, that the anguished conscience is not a natural consequence like being hungry" (*WL* [revised], p. 407 [1846]).

[137]　*CUP*, vol. 1, p. 156.

[138]　*PF*, pp. 14–15.

[139]　*CUP*, vol. 1, p. 112. This is why ethics must fail, according to Vigilius (*CA*, p. 16).

[140]　*PC*, p. 34. See also *PF*, pp. 67–9.

[141]　*PC*, p. 63; *PF*, p. 62.

history, as in Plato or Hegel, where the historical serves as a mere "vanishing point" for apprehending the truth of Ideal forms or *Geist*.[142]

Kierkegaard avoided salvific legalism by contending that divine command is always conjoined with divine promise—"Thou shalt" means not only that you will do a task but that you will be able to do it by the grace of God[143]—and by refusing to identify any prescribed "externalities" with Christian faith: "Now let these conditions be acts, specific conceptions, moods—who really knows himself so intimately that he would take the responsibility for guaranteeing that these conditions are present in him just as they ought to be and are not illegitimate children of doubtful parentage!"[144] By contrast, "The secular mind always needs to have decision externalized; otherwise it mistrustfully believes that the decision actually does not exist."[145] However, Kierkegaard's later emphasis on Christ as exemplar shows that he did not envision a purely idealistic faith with no external manifestations. Rather, he insisted that externalizations cannot serve as accurate gauges of inward passions or right relationship with God for either oneself or others.[146]

To summarize, Kierkegaard believed that humankind cannot "naturally" choose to respond positively to God prior to the divinely initiated "collision of the eternal and the temporal in the moment."[147] On account of Christ's sacrifice, every individual is given the choice to either embrace or reject God's initiative; however, only acceptance can transform the otherwise unspeakable horror of one's consciousness of personal sinfulness before a holy and righteous God into "sheer leniency, grace, love, mercy."[148] The refusal to accept God's grace on the grounds that one is "beyond redemption," according to Kierkegaard, constitutes supreme arrogance: "It would be presumptuous and blasphemous if someone would think that by his unfaithfulness he has the power to change him [Jesus], the power to make him less loving than he was ... ."[149] However, the Incarnation of the Second Person of the Trinity does not only provide a means for transforming the broken

---

[142]   Ibid., p. 13. Subsequently, Climacus identified this as the central paradox of the Christian faith: "That an eternal happiness is decided in time by the relation to something historical" (*CUP*, vol. 1, p. 369).

[143]   *WA*, pp. 32, 185.

[144]   *EUD*, p. 269. See also *BA*, p. 100: "[T]he greater the need for a striking outer manifestation of the decision, the less the inner certitude."

[145]   *WL*, p. 145.

[146]   See Stephen Dunning, "Who Sets the Task? Kierkegaard on Authority," in George B. Connell and C. Stephen Evans (eds), *Foundations of Kierkegaard's Vision of Community: Religion, Ethics, and Politics in Kierkegaard* (New Jersey and London, 1992), p. 31, n. 42; C. Stephen Evans, *Kierkegaard's "Fragments" and "Postscript": The Religious Philosophy of Johannes Climacus* (New Jersey, 1983), pp. 283–4.

[147]   *BA*, p. 167.

[148]   *PC*, p. 67.

[149]   *CD*, p. 285.

autonomy of individual sinful human beings into right relationship with God through his life and death; Jesus personally delivered a supreme judgment upon rebellious sensate authority.

Chapter 5
Abundant Power:
Kierkegaard's Concept of Power

The Tier of Authority

During the past few decades, many commentators have focused increasing attention upon the socio-political implications of Kierkegaard's thought.[1] In his magisterial book, *Kierkegaard in Golden Age Denmark*, Bruce Kirmmse writes,

> Kierkegaard's social and political views are often interpreted as being those which were shared by his Golden Age contemporaries, and he is thus depicted as having no politics at all, or, what amounts to the same thing, as having embraced a nostalgic, traditionalist, and irrational authoritarianism, a misty reverence for hierarchy and monarchy which was completely irrelevant to the emerging social and economic realities of his time.[2]

Several scholars trace an "exodus" from the conservative political views of the cultural and intellectual elite to which Kierkegaard was initially allied as a young man, to a more "liberal" acceptance of egalitarianism and democracy following the social and political tumult of 1848, which roused Kierkegaard from his political slumbers.[3] Kirmmse highlights Kierkegaard's growing acrimony towards the political and religious establishment of the day, which climaxed in his staggering attack upon Christendom, employing the "popular" media in his campaign.[4] The Danish thinker definitely disdained the "aristocratic" elitism with which the

---

[1]   See, for example, Merold Westphal, "Kierkegaard's Politics," *Thought*, 55/218 (1980): 320–32; Robert L. Perkins (ed.), *International Kierkegaard Commentary: Two Ages* (Macon, 1984); Mark Dooley, *The Politics of Exodus: Kierkegaard's Ethics of Responsibility* (New York, 2001), and Robert L. Perkins, "Habermas and Kierkegaard: Religious Subjectivity, Multiculturalism, and Historical Revisionism," *International Philosophical Quarterly*, 44/4 (2004): 481–96.

[2]   Bruce Kirmmse, *Kierkegaard in Golden Age Denmark* (Bloomington and Indianapolis, 1990), p. 3.

[3]   See ibid., pp. 65–73.

[4]   See ibid., pp. 451–81.

wealthy disregarded the lower classes, and cheerfully mingled with anyone he happened to meet.[5] As Kirmmse states,

> Precisely because of his otherworldly Christian moorings, Kierkegaard does not feel the need to cling to what is known and personally advantageous in worldly matters—namely, the aristocratic conservatism to which his peers and his social background would normally have led him.[6]

However, in keeping with his wariness of "human" politics eliding into religion, his aversion of "mass movements," and his Christian sensibility towards the sinfulness of humanity, I am less certain that Kierkegaard's subsequent views may be regarded as "variants of liberalism and populism,"[7] insofar as they are so deeply informed by his understanding of the Bible.[8] Kierkegaard, however, kept apace of contemporary political developments to avoid an abstract or culturally irrelevant faith.

In *The Politics of Exodus: Kierkegaard's Ethics of Responsibility*, Mark Dooley risks severing Kierkegaard's "theological content" from his "ethical/ political" concerns. Dooley emphasizes "his more radically liberating idea of identifying the God-man as ethical prototype par excellence, the imitation of which engenders a sensitivity to the other qua neighbour" over "his tendency to advance the strictly Lutheran idea that the individual's private salvation is realized through an 'absolute relationship' to God."[9] Instead of analyzing the sphere of politics separately from his Christian beliefs or politicizing his faith,[10]

---

[5]   This explains Kierkegaard's deep pain at being ostracized following *The Corsair* scandal: "You common man! I have not segregated my life from yours, you know that; I have lived on the street, am known by all. Furthermore, I have not become somebody, do not belong to any class-egoism. So if I belong to anyone, I must belong to you, you common man …" (*TM*, p. 346). Evidently, Kierkegaard did not consider his independently wealthy status to be an obstacle to rubbing shoulders with the "common man" since, "[M]yself of humble descent, I have loved the common man or what is called the simple class …" (*PV*, p. 90). Kirmmse describes Kierkegaard as "half peasant, half urbane aristocrat" (*Kierkegaard in Golden Age Denmark*, p. 26).

[6]   Ibid., p. 4.

[7]   Ibid. Kirmmse states that Kierkegaard "in the end came not only to resign himself to the age of the common man, but positively to welcome it." I am more inclined to side with Robert Perkins that Kierkegaard grew increasingly sceptical that any sort of political reform could untangle the jumble of "reflection, constitutional discussion, chatter, an ill-proportion between authority and responsibility, and a mystification about where real political power lay" in the aftermath of 1848 ("Kierkegaard's Critique of the *Bourgeois* State," *Inquiry*, 27/2 [1984]: 211). See also Alastair Hannay, *Kierkegaard* (London, 1982), p. 286.

[8]   Kirmmse does identify strong Pietistic resonances in Kierkegaard. See *Kierkegaard in Golden Age Denmark*, p. 29.

[9]   Dooley, p. xv.

[10]   Michele Nicoletti addresses similar concerns in "Politics and Religion in Kierkegaard's Thought: Secularization and the Martyr," in George Connell and C. Stephen

I intend to foreground Kierkegaard's theological concerns to show how his theory of power is rooted in and stems from this theological core, hopefully avoiding the pitfall of his contemporary N.F.S. Grundtvig wherein "[p]olitics ('the human') remains related to religion ('the Christian') as its anteroom, its preparation."[11]

The Arrival of Christ

Throughout his life, Kierkegaard expressed a childlike wonder over the divine motivation which lies at the heart of the incomprehensible truth of Christianity.[12] As Climacus mused, "The absurd is that the eternal truth has come into existence in time, that God has come into existence, has been born, has grown up, etc., has come into existence exactly as an individual human being, indistinguishable from any other human being ... ."[13] It may appear counter-intuitive to include discussion of the Incarnation under the third tier and not confine it to either the cosmological tier or the anthropological tier, but there are two main reasons for this positioning. First, it illuminates the sovereign uniqueness and extreme heterogeneity of Christ, rendering it well-nigh impossible to slot him neatly within any categorical schema. Second, it accords with Kierkegaard's theocentric methodology, which strives to locate Christ at the center of Christian existence.[14] This chapter will demonstrate that, for Kierkegaard, the coming of Christ entails the "collision" of two types of authority. On the one hand, Christ embodies the perfect power of God, an omnipotence simultaneously manifested and masked by its inconspicuous nature. On the other hand, Christ embodies a perfected human power, one which does not seek its own interests, but seeks to guide and uphold

---

Evans (eds), *Foundations of Kierkegaard's Vision of Community: Religion, Ethics, and Politics in Kierkegaard* (New Jersey and London, 1992), p. 184.

[11] Kirmmse, *Kierkegaard in Golden Age Denmark*, p. 221. Kirmmse himself is well-aware of Kierkegaard's "prioritarian view"— "What is required is thus that one give eternity its due, that one respect its *priority*; then, far from being removed from one's worldly social responsibilities, one is better able to shoulder them" (ibid., p. 291). However, at times, in his justifiable eagerness to correct an "apolitical" interpretation of Kierkegaard, Kierkegaard's theological enterprise is seemingly subsumed by his political views. See, for example, p. 410: "[H]is entire authorship is informed and guided by his vision of politics and society and ... the concluding, polemical phase of his authorship must be understood as an expression of that vision in a post-1848 world."

[12] Michael Matthis observes that Kierkegaard's understanding of Christianity as paradox was formulated by the time he was 25 ("Kierkegaard and the Problem of the Social Other," *Philosophy Today*, 38/4 [1994]: 438, n. 11).

[13] *CUP*, vol. 1, p. 210. See also *BA*, p. 183; *SW*, p. 658 [1849]; *CI*, p. 221.

[14] As Mark C. Taylor states, "Kierkegaard's interpretation of Christ is the keystone of his entire philosophical and theological position" ("Christology," in Niels Thulstrup and M. Mikulová Thulstrup [eds], *Bibliotheca Kierkegaardiana: Theological Concepts in Kierkegaard* [16 vols, Copenhagen, 1980], vol. 5, p. 167).

the disempowered individuals around him. It is not surprising that both his inferred authority as God and his example of "proper" human authority posed a colossal threat to the temporal authorities of his day. The discussion will first probe Christ's revelation of authority, before investigating the differences between sensate and spiritual authority.

Christ as saviour: revelation of divine power as omni(m)potence
Of all the truths of Christianity, the Incarnation remains its incomprehensible central mystery, graspable only by faith.[15] As Anti-Climacus explained,

> The God-man is not the union of God and man—such terminology is a profound optical illusion. The God-man is the unity of God and an individual human being. That the human race is or is supposed to be in kinship with God is ancient paganism; but *that* an individual human being is God is Christianity, and this particular human being is the God-man.[16]

Kierkegaard subscribed to the orthodox doctrine of Christ's full divinity, insisting that it was not sufficient for God to put on a human "disguise" like Socrates' pretence to simplicity or a king in peasant's garb:

> For this is the boundlessness of love, that in earnestness and truth and not in jest it wills to be the equal of the beloved, and it is the omnipotence of resolving love to be capable of that which neither the king nor Socrates was capable, which is why their assumed characters were still a kind of deceit.[17]

Climacus contended that only "the god," whose life and teaching are one, can impart the condition for receiving the truth, enabling the learner to think the thought that thought cannot think.[18]

As the Son of God, Jesus came to influence a rebellious world that was in dire need of transformation. In order to combat the effects of sin, Kierkegaard argued that Jesus required the full power of God, the perfect mediation of divine holiness and compassion, which was "equally present in every moment, no greater when

---

[15]   *PC*, p. 77; *CUP*, vol. 1, p. 210.

[16]   *PC*, p. 82.

[17]   *PF*, p. 32.

[18]   See ibid., pp. 26–30. Murray Rae elaborates on the incommensurability of the Incarnation with human rationality: "The juxtaposition of time and eternity in the person of an individual human being strains the credulity of the Western mind in particular, which has long believed that time and eternity, the transcendent and the immanent, God and man, are terms which describe mutually exclusive realities … . It is to propose an absurdity which reason cannot accept" (*Kierkegaard's Vision of the Incarnation: By Faith Transformed* [Oxford, 1997], p. 68).

he breathed his last on the cross than when he suffered himself to be born."[19] In contrast to a kenotic emptying of power prior to the Incarnation, he contended that Christ's undiminished omnipotence was essential for at least three reasons. First, his loving omnipotence was always necessary to shield the temporal world from being overwhelmed by God directly entering into human history; subsequently, "[H]e uses the power of omnipotence to ensure his continually being nothing!"[20] Second, Christ's omnipotence protected him from succumbing to temptation or despair as his mission followed its arduous path to Calvary: "He uses equally great powers not to budge an inch from the position he has taken, where he will stand—before the eyes of all, in the middle of actuality where he wants to express: My kingdom is not of this world."[21] Third, Christ used his omnipotence to perform miracles which ensured that the attention of Israel would be riveted upon him as he effected his ultimate sacrifice.[22]

At the same time, Kierkegaard was careful to qualify this omnipotence as characterized by self-limitation and restraint, particularly with regards to respecting human freedom and eliciting a response which is genuine and unforced. In contrast to the sentiment that Christ's temptations were confined to his 40-day wilderness survival stint,[23] Kierkegaard maintained that "his whole life is a story of temptation," the temptation to "secularize his calling" by using his divine power to accomplish forcibly his goal while irrevocably transforming his kingdom into an "earthly" one.[24] Anti-Climacus marvelled,

> It is a strange kind of dialectic: that he, omnipotent, binds himself and does it so omnipotently that he actually feels bound, suffers under the consequence of his loving and free decision to become an individual human being—to that degree there was earnestness in his becoming an actual human being.[25]

Consequently, omni(m)potence did not entail a pleasurable, pain-free existence for Jesus. Rather, Christ's life was characterized by profound, unmitigated suffering, according to Kierkegaard. His "external" suffering consisted of the

---

[19]   *WL*, p. 107. See also *PC*, p. 301 [1849].

[20]   *FS*, p. 174. See also *PC*, p. 131; *SW*, p. 144; *PF*, pp. 32, 45; *EUD*, p. 310. Judge William stated that Supreme Power would have disrupted all normalcy had it not sent a representative on its behalf: "If his royal majesty had his lord chamberlain attend a christening party, it can perhaps heighten the mood of those present; but if the king himself were to attend, it perhaps would disturb …" (*SW*, p. 99).

[21]   *FS*, p. 174.

[22]   Ibid.; *PC*, p. 96. On Christ's substitutionary atonement, see *WA*, pp. 123, 181; *CD*, p. 299; *PF*, p. 16.

[23]   See Luke 4:1–13.

[24]   *FS*, pp. 58–9.

[25]   *PC*, p. 132. See also *PF*, pp. 31–2, 55.

scorn and derision he experienced from a sinful and rebellious world,[26] in addition to constantly battling every possible human temptation.[27] This was compounded *ad infinitum* by the ineffable, "internal" torment of being separated from God on Calvary; hence, Kierkegaard was shocked by "the sublimity under which (to put it as strongly as possible) even the Saviour of the world sinks—that God who is love yet can abandon him and do it out of love … ."[28] Furthermore, Kierkegaard argued that Jesus suffered from a profound awareness of the effects of his coming: the realization that he could not spare his followers from agony,[29] and the even more excruciating awareness that, by coming "in person," he would be intensifying the condemnation of those who obstinately rejected him. As Kierkegaard exclaimed, "What heavy suffering: to have to be the stumbling stone in order to be the Savior of the world!"[30] Consequently, omnipotence cannot forcibly secure its ultimate aim—that none should perish:

> [H]is whole life was sheer suffering of mind and spirit through belonging to the fallen human race, which he wanted to save and which did not want to be saved, that a living person cruelly chained to a corpse cannot suffer more torturously than he suffered in mind and spirit by being embodied as man in the human race![31]

Christ as servant: revelation of human power

Kierkegaard recognized the heterogeneous nature of Christ's sacrifice and perfect obedience to God which is humanly impossible to imitate.[32] However, in order to challenge the spiritual indolence reclining within a prevalent doctrine of "cheap grace," he underscored Christ's role as "Prototype" for human behavior.[33] For this

---

[26] *PC*, pp. 95, 271 [1848].

[27] *WA*, p. 122; *PV*, p. 161 [1848]. However, Kierkegaard carefully asserted, "[T]here is an eternal chasmic abyss between his suffering and the human being's" (*UD*, p. 281). See also *JP*, vol. 3, p. 571 [1849–51].

[28] Ibid., vol. 4, p. 583 [1854].

[29] *FS*, p. 174: "What torment, not to be able out of love to lower the price the least … ." See also *UD*, p. 224.

[30] Ibid., p. 254. See also *SD*, p. 159: "He can debase himself, take the form of a servant, suffer, die for men, invite all to come up to him, offer up every day of his life and every hour of the day, and offer up his life—but the possibility of offense he cannot take away."

[31] *CD*, p. 259.

[32] *TM*, p. 423 [1853]: "But he still is not altogether literally the prototype, because he is, of course, heterogeneous to an ordinary human being by a full quality … ."

[33] *WL* [revised], p. 471 [1847]. By raising the costs of following Christ, Kierkegaard hoped that individuals would existentially realize the impossibility of pleasing God by their actions and throw themselves daily upon the grace of God. Hence, he once wrote, "I want to apply the Christian requirement, imitation, in all its infinitude, in order to place the emphasis in the direction of grace" (*TM*, p. 425 [1853]). See also *FS*, p. 191.

reason, Kierkegaard once mused that if he could broadcast one sentence to the social-climbing, comfort-seeking Danish "Christians," it would be: "Our Lord Jesus Christ was a nobody."[34] Anti-Climacus attributed Christ's desire to adopt servant-form to self-mastery, "this superiority over oneself of wanting to be incognito in such a way that one seems much lowlier than one is."[35] However, Climacus had no patience for a "childish orthodoxy" which reduces the Christian paradox of power to Christ's social status as a humble carpenter; rather, the Incarnation itself—regardless of station—entailed inconceivable condescension: "It is not more adequate for God to be a king than to be a beggar; it is not more humiliating for God to become a beggar than to become an emperor."[36] For Kierkegaard, Christ's greatest pronouncements on power pertained not to his choice of career but to his absolute freedom from envy or thirst for sensate power. Hence, he once wrote,

> [O]ne could indeed say: He chose a differential, since he chose to be a poor and insignificant man rather than to be prominent. But this is not true, for he was not a poor and insignificant man in contrast to prominence and wealth; if that were the case he would have belonged to the solidarity of the poor and insignificant. He was purely and simply man, who felt no pressure to own anything (consequently he was not poor) and found blessedness in being nothing (consequently he was not insignificant, either).[37]

Christ's living example entails a divine revaluation of all that human beings—in their state of sinful autonomy—erroneously esteem.[38] Hence, Anti-Climacus posited, "Christ has never wanted to be victorious in this world. He came into the world in order to suffer; *that* he called being victorious."[39] Christ provided the ultimate demonstration that true power does not maintain a hierarchical distance but rather overcomes all obstacles to reconciliation and union. Kierkegaard contended, "Thus his life was retrogression instead of progression, the opposite of what the human mentality naturally thinks and covets. In a worldly way, a person

---

[34]   *JP*, vol. 3, p. 574 [1850]. See also *SD*, p. 124.

[35]   *PC*, p. 129.

[36]   *CUP*, vol. 1, p. 596.

[37]   *JP*, vol. 4, p. 172 [1850]. One of Kierkegaard's points is that the offence of Christ and the Gospel is not limited to "the establishment"—it is an affront to sinful human autonomy in all walks and stations of life. See, for example, ibid., p. 316 [1854]: "Christianity is the greatest, the most intense, the most powerful restlessness imaginable; it disturbs human existence at its deepest level … . It explodes everything, bursts everything."

[38]   He once posited that Christ's entire life consisted of "a terrible collision with the merely human concept of what love is" (*WL*, p. 115).

[39]   *PC*, p. 224.

ascends rung by rung in honor and prestige and power ... . But he, in reverse, descended rung by rung, and yet he ascended ... ."[40]

The loftiness and power of the heavenly kingdom manifests itself in sheer opposition to the loftiness and power celebrated by sinful humanity. The omnipotent delimitation of an otherwise overwhelming divine presence simultaneously lowers itself in order to raise others and patiently endures the most supreme injustice given the identity and authority of the recipient.[41] Kierkegaard emphasized, "He did not descend from heaven in order to become *poor*, but he descended in order to make others *rich*."[42] It is extremely significant that Jesus never sought to appropriate sensate authority for his own cause. Such qualitatively heterogeneous power can be neither a threat nor a boon to the Kingdom of God. Hence, Christ acknowledged political authority over non-religious matters—"rendering unto Caesar the things that are Caesar's"[43]—and rejected all attempts by the temporal powers that be to ratify, preserve, or "deify him."[44] The Danish theologian later concluded, "[I]t actually would be comical or ridiculous if Christ had come in earthly loftiness and splendor, because the loftiness he was supposed to express was the very opposite of that."[45]

Judging the "powers"

Since first-century Roman and Jewish authorities could do nothing to win divine favor, support Christ's cause, or obstruct God's purposes, Kierkegaard believed that Jesus' example conveys everything a Christian needs to know about power: "God has walked in lowliness on earth and in this way has judged all such worldly power and might to be nothing."[46] Hence, for Kierkegaard, Christ's coming in the form of a lowly servant expresses the vital truth that "no one should feel himself excluded or think that it is human status and respect among one's fellows that bring one closer to God."[47] Even the most historically disadvantaged Christian "believes

---

[40] *CD*, p. 277. Anti-Climacus emphasized that such radical identification with humankind is particularly indispensable in light of universal suffering: "If someone wants to invite the sufferer to come to him, he must either alter his condition and make it identical with the sufferer's or make the sufferer's condition identical with his own, for if not, the contrast makes the difference all the greater" (*PC*, p. 13).

[41] *JP*, vol. 4, p. 156 [1848]: "That supreme power is impotence is seen in the impotence of Christ, the only one who never got justice, for even his death became a benefaction, even to his murderers."

[42] *CD*, p. 123.

[43] Kierkegaard's exegesis of Mark 12:17 reads, "Christ clearly means this: 'If you want to be a Christian, then snap your fingers first and foremost and above all at politics'" (cited in Nicoletti, p. 186).

[44] *PC*, pp. 47–8.

[45] *JP*, vol. 3, p. 418 [1850].

[46] *CD*, p. 52.

[47] *SD*, p. 161.

that this prototype, if he continually struggles to resemble him, will bring him again, and in an even more intimate way, into kinship with God, that he does not have God only as a creator, as all creatures do, but has God as his brother."[48]

For those who value hierarchy and inequality over their "brethren," however, Christ's coming simultaneously represents a supreme rejection and judgment over sinful socio-political structures. For this reason, Kierkegaard declared that "Christianity is incendiarism,"[49] a fire that consumes the corruption of religious truth, since "Christendom is precisely the very thing Christ wanted to throw out entirely, the very thing he came into the world to annihilate."[50] Christ's example of non-truncated divine power in servant form further conveys a human model for true strength and leadership:

> Christ has no scepter in his hand, only a reed, the symbol of impotence—and yet at that very moment he is the greatest power. As far as power is concerned, to rule the whole world with a scepter is nothing compared to ruling it with a reed—that is, by impotence—that is, divinely.[51]

If Christ did not come to be served but to serve, Kierkegaard reasoned, how much more should Christians reject sensate means as an escape from service. However, such rejection does not entail violence.

> God does not use force to tear man out of the devil's power. No, Christ allowed himself to be born, to suffer, to die—to save man from the devil's power. Injustice also has its rights, and in considering injustice it is injustice to want to commit an injustice against it: it is simply unchristian. The essentially Christian is: in suffering to permit injustice to have all its rights down to the least detail—and thus to win, to conquer it.[52]

The heterogeneity of Christ's message and example is reflected in the hostility he evoked. Kierkegaard offered two suggstions for why Christ incurred the wrath of his contemporaries. First, the demonstration of the obvious power he possessed, as testified by his miracles, authoritative teaching, and massive following, intimidated the political and religious authorities, and incited them to envy. Understandably, the leaders recognized the direct and implicit challenge to their authority represented by his insuperable "collision of pietism with the established order": "Quite properly the established order poses the question: Who does he think he is?"[53] Second, Jesus' genuine independence and liberty from conventional means

---

[48]   *CD*, p. 43.

[49]   *TM*, p. 51. See Luke 12:49.

[50]   *JP*, vol. 3, p. 426 [1854].

[51]   Ibid., vol. 4, pp. 184–5 [1851].

[52]   Ibid., p. 401 [1851].

[53]   *PC*, p. 86.

of power sparked resentment in those who sought either to co-opt his influence for their own schemes of personal or nationalist aggrandizement,[54] or to indebt him to their service by assisting Christ's cause.[55] If Christ's "authority" hinges upon human recognition and endorsement, it ultimately reflects an anthropocentred power.

This raises an interesting question: who, in Kierkegaard's view, killed Jesus? Arguably, he attributed Christ's death to a collaboration of sensate authorities rising up against a common threat to sinful human autonomy. Anti-Climacus once alluded to such an alliance: "So the people turned away from him, and the powerful sprung their trap ... ."[56] A more complicated and *eo ipso* "Kierkegaardian" alternative would be that Christ's crucifixion resulted from the rebellion of these authorities working at times in collusion, at times in competition. Certain Jewish authorities felt threatened by Jesus and sought to employ Rome's political power by depicting Christ as a political threat. Rome [that is, Pilate] saw through this ruse and sought to keep Jesus alive because he threatened to destabilize the religious leaders' power base and would provide some political leverage or—at the very least—an amusing distraction.[57] As a goad against Jewish national identity and the local religious establishment, Jesus apparently galvanized the Roman political leadership of the day.[58] Vexed by Christ's refusal to seek political aid in securing his release, and stymied by the threat of imperial treason levied by the religious leaders and the incited crowds, Pilate's officiously washed hands relinquished Christ for crucifixion. Ironically, the Passover crowds, incited by the religious leaders, also cast their lot against Christ by rejecting Pilate's favored choice and voting for the release of the notorious insurrectionist Barabbas.[59]

Although this argument is an extrapolation from Kierkegaard's thought, it is consistent with his refusal to blame Christ's death entirely upon Israel or Christ's first-century contemporaries:

---

[54]   *JP*, vol. 4, p. 163 [1850]: "It is obvious that one of the factors in Christ's death was that he repudiated nationalism, wanted to have nothing to do with it."

[55]   He especially blamed the "crowd" for crucifying Christ "because he in no way wanted a crowd for support, ... would not form a party, did not allow balloting, but wanted to be what he was, the truth, which relates itself to the single individual" (*PV*, p. 109).

[56]   *PC*, p. 56. See also *WA*, pp. 59–60.

[57]   Kierkegaard soundly denounced Pilate's intended method of "saving" Christ: "Judas sold him for thirty pieces of silver, but Pilate wanted to sell him at an even lower price, wanted to make him a poor wretch of a man, an object of pity for the compassion of the raging mob" (*UD*, p. 255). Pilate then used the cross "to show the Jewish nation how wretched and weak it was" (*WA*, p. 62).

[58]   Luke 23:12: "That same day Herod and Pilate became friends with each other; before this they had been enemies."

[59]   Matthew 27:21–2. Even his closest friends were implicated by betraying or abandoning him in his moment of crisis.

> The death of Christ is the result of two factors—the Jews' guilt plus on the
> whole a demonstration of the world's evil … . Christ's fate is an eternal fate;
> it indicates the specific gravity of the human race, and the same thing would
> happen to Christ at any time. Christ can never express something accidental.[60]

In light of Christ's demonstration of true power and exposure of corrupted human
authority, it is necessary to explore the concept of sensate authority.

Struggling for Supremacy: Sensate Authority

Defining sensate authority
The attempt to assimilate divine authority is not confined to the time of Christ. From
the Tower of Babel to the systematic juggernaut of Hegelianism, human beings
have chronically engaged in "quantification" of the eternal, the arrogation of power
by the illusory negation of the qualitative abyss between God and temporality.[61]
Because of this nefarious blurring of the boundaries between the temporal and
the eternal, Kierkegaard strove to reinforce "the perhaps most important ethical-
religious concept: authority."[62] Anti-Climacus employed the term "sensate" to
denote the fallen human reality within the temporal order: "[T]he sensate, the
secular, the momentary, the multiple—in itself it is nothing, is empty. In the last
resort, it cannot be said to draw to itself; it can only deceive."[63] It is important to
clarify that, from Kierkegaard's perspective, all sensate authority is temporal—
that is, belongs to the created universe—and "fallen." However, not all temporal
authority is sensate, as Christ demonstrated by entering fully into temporality and
empowering his followers with spiritual authority, the means of contesting fallen
human authority. Furthermore, sensate authority does not encompass only brute
force;[64] instead, it represents a human-centered authority derived from human
recognition and directed towards human ends.

The pseudonym H.H. maintained, *"In the sphere of immanence, authority
is utterly unthinkable, or it can be thought only as transitory."*[65] In contrast to
an anthropocentric concept of authority, which relies upon fallacious because
transient "certainties," Kierkegaard once wrote,

---

[60]   *WA*, p. 208 [1847].

[61]   "Everywhere there is and must be existentially an either/or. And the demoralization
of our age is precisely the continuous substitution or quantification" (*JP*, vol. 4, p. 179
[1851]).

[62]   *WA*, p. 240 [1849].

[63]   *PC*, p. 158.

[64]   Hence, Kierkegaard acknowledged the temptation to become a "builder, a teacher,
or a disciplinarian" as a means "to rule over others" (*WL*, p. 206).

[65]   *WA*, p. 99.

"Authority" does not mean to be a king or to be an emperor or general, to have the power of arms, to be a bishop, or to be a policeman, but it means by a firm and conscious resolution to be willing to sacrifice everything, one's very life, for his cause; it means to articulate a cause in such a way that a person is at one with himself, needing nothing and fearing nothing. This infinite recklessness is authority. True authority is present when the truth is the cause.[66]

As opposed to spiritual authority, which cannot be proven externally, H.H. observed, "In the transitory relations of authority between persons *qua* human beings, authority will as a rule be physically recognizable by power."[67] Moreover, should a church leader attempt to impose her authority using sensate power, she would ineluctably compromise both the heterogeneity of the Gospel and the divine authority [*guddommelig Myndighed*] with which she was invested.[68]

Sensate authority proper: The state[69]
Although Kierkegaard was a rigorous opponent of totalizing systematization, he firmly believed in careful philosophical definitions and categorization. Many errors result when an individual unthinkingly transposes the assumptions and methodologies of one category onto another.[70] According to Kierkegaard, categories can be readily identified by their teleological trajectories. Hence, he once distinguished the political sphere from the religious as follows: "[T]he political begins on earth in order to remain on earth, while the religious, taking its beginning from above, wants to transfigure and then to lift the earthly to heaven."[71] In addition to their respective goals, the two spheres are ultimately distinguishable by their anthropocentric or theocentric power sources: "[P]olitically, everything turns on getting numbers of people on one's side, but religiously on having God on one's side."[72]

The Danish thinker seldom wrote exclusively on contemporary political and social affairs, since he regarded sensate glory, accomplishments, and power as

---

[66] *JP*, vol. 1, p. 73 [1847].

[67] *WA*, p. 105. Kierkegaard once advised that an individual "ought not be a ruler with direct recognizability as such," since "[t]his is a lower form of human existence ..." (*JP*, vol. 4, p.178 [1851]).

[68] *WA*, p. 105.

[69] This is not to suggest that the state represents the only proper sensate authority, as opposed to the Human Rights Commission, the World Health Organization, or the Royal and Ancient's authority on golf. Rather, it is the form with which Kierkegaard was most concerned.

[70] *PV*, p. 109. By contrast, when subjects are examined within their proper disciplines, the result is a "correct" concept as well as a "true" mood (*CA*, p. 14).

[71] *PV*, p. 103. For politics as "externality," see *TC*, pp. 54–5.

[72] *TM*, p. 537 [9 June 1855].

intoxicating "vapors."[73] However, Kierkegaard was no naive idealist who believed that states or cities can be run solely upon "spiritual" principles. Subsequently, he did not oppose all political authority, but rather sought to confine it within its proper bounds. Nicoletti rightly observes that Kierkegaard does not condemn politics but the "sacralization of politics," the absolutist utopianism to which it had been wed.[74] As Kirmmse explains, "Genuine politics has to do with associations of people who have been through the individuating process of religious inwardness, and such politics will not transgress upon the religious sphere ... ."[75] With regards to political systems, Kierkegaard was somewhat conservative, a firm supporter of the traditional monarchy,[76] which upheld—at least in principle—the dignity and importance of the individual chosen by "grace" rather than ability,[77] in contrast to recent democratic movements which, he felt, sacrificed the individual to a dehumanizing collectivism.[78] Originally, he agreed with Hegel that the state

---

[73]   *WL*, p. 160. Frater Taciturnus asserted, "It is a contradiction to be willing to sacrifice one's life for a finite goal, and in the eyes of poetry such behavior is comic, akin to dancing oneself to death ..." (*SW*, p. 410). Kierkegaard critiqued political platforms for equal human rights, asserting that such attempts to redefine true human egalitarianism—found only as individuals stand "before God"—merely produce a "counterfeit equality" (*BA*, p. 230 [October 1848]). On the impossibility of "external" equality, see *EUD*, p. 143. Kirmmse comments, "[I]t is of crucial importance that the reader note that—with the exception of SK's own personal judgment that, as a practical matter, worldly equality is unattainable— SK's stance is completely open and 'agnostic' on the question of politics *per se*, be they conservative, egalitarian, etc." (*Kierkegaard in Golden Age Denmark*, p. 324).

[74]   Nicoletti, p. 187.

[75]   Kirmmse, *Kierkegaard in Golden Age Denmark*, p. 272.

[76]   Climacus observed, "Of all forms of government, the monarchical is the best. More than any other form of government, it encourages and protects the secret fancies and the innocent follies of private persons" (*CUP*, vol. 1, p. 620). Kierkegaard once instructed King Christian VIII on how to rule properly (*JK*, pp. 155–7 [1849]). He was, however, less enamoured of politicians, comparing them to "the Church Fathers' descriptions of demons" (*JP*, vol. 4, p. 134 [21 May 1839]). Did Kierkegaard relinquish his monarchism for more democratic sympathies following the 1848 upheavals as Kirmmse contends? Although most of his explicitly monarchical statements were written prior to 1848, highly critical statements concerning populism and liberalism appear well after that year. Michael Plekon observes that Kierkegaard was not a "pure" conservative even before 1848 "precisely because his social theory focuses so nearly on the individual" ("Towards Apocalypse: Kierkegaard's *Two Ages* in Golden Age Denmark," in Robert Perkins (ed.), *International Kierkegaard Commentary: Two Ages* [Macon, 1984], p. 47). Moreover, he notes that Kierkegaard attacked both liberals and conservatives for endorsing "the synthesis of Christianity and culture" and "a capitalist political economy" (ibid., p. 48). In light of the increasing clamour for populist-driven reforms, it would arguably have been too risky for Kierkegaard's theological project to throw his hat into the "democratic" ring.

[77]   *JP*, vol. 4, p. 135 [8 August 1839].

[78]   He concluded that populism is an effective if deplorable means of securing power: "[T]o love the crowd or pretend to love it, to make it the authority for *the truth* is the way

represented the highest vehicle of virtue and amelioration,[79] but later chided himself for such "childish babble."[80]

Kierkegaard eventually concluded that the Danish state protects an indolent *status quo* and, though it often threatens the emergence of the individual,[81] it is a "necessary evil" which provides "a safeguard against egotism by manifesting a higher egotism which copes with all the individual egotisms."[82] The state can even exert a positive impact upon the development of the individual, for the innate pressures which the state directs upon individuals in order to maintain peace through conformity can serve as a vital stimulus to inculcate the necessary strength to stand alone. Thus, Kierkegaard opposed attempts either to subsume the individual within the state or to remove the individual from the state's jurisdiction.[83]

To the extent that sensate authority is confined to its proper sphere, Kierkegaard advised Christians to remain loyal to the state:

> Christianity teaches: "You shall fear God, honor the king"; a Christian is to be, if possible, His Majesty's best subject. But, *Christianly*, the king is not the authority; he is not and cannot and shall not and will not be the authority in relation to a kingdom that at no price wants to be of this world … .[84]

In a journal entry, he once wrote: "Christianity is political indifference; engrossed in higher things, it teaches submission to all public authorities."[85] For Kierkegaard, every Christian possesses, as George Pattison explains, "the double-citizenship of time and eternity,"[86] whereby he is a committed earthly citizen so long as this does

---

to acquire tangible power, the way to all kinds of temporal and worldly advantage—it is also untruth, since the crowd is untruth" (*PV*, p. 111). His worst nightmare was that the crowd is permitted "to vote on Christianity" (*PC* 365 [1851]). He blamed the lamentable rise of spurious populist movements and demands for reform on weak leaders in positions of authority (*BA*, p. 149).

[79]   *EO*, vol. 2, p. 485, n. 29.

[80]   *JP*, vol. 4, pp. 199–200 [1854]. For Kierkegaard's politics as a rebuttal to Hegel's deification of the state as the ultimate instrument of *Geist*, see Dooley, chapter 2, and Merold Westphal, "Abraham and Hegel," in Robert Perkins (ed.), *Kierkegaard's Fear and Trembling: Critical Appraisals* (Tuscalosa, 1981), p. 76.

[81]   *JP*, vol. 4, p. 147 [1848]. On history's oscillation between individuality and collectivism, see ibid., p. 130 [11 December 1836].

[82]   Ibid., p. 200 [1854].

[83]   Ibid., p. 184 [1851].

[84]   *TM*, p. 113.

[85]   *JP*, vol. 4, p. 176 [1851]. Perkins elaborates: the religious entails "political indifference" insofar as "[t]he religious has always the same struggle, whatever the politics: the creation of inwardness or perhaps even of a new being" ("Kierkegaard's Critique of the *Bourgeois* State," p. 216).

[86]   George Pattison, *Kierkegaard, Religion, and the Nineteenth Century Culture of Crisis* (Cambridge, 2002), p. x.

not compromise his identity as a "citizen of heaven."[87] Hence, Kierkegaard stated, "With responsibility before God and after having tested himself in his conscience, he [the ordinary Christian] attaches himself to the whole as a limb and takes it as his task to be faithful in the reproduction [of 'the established order in his life'], while the responsibility of eternity saves him from the purely animal category: to be the crowd ... ."[88] Accordingly, "The individual is primarily related to God and then to the community, but this primary relation is the highest, yet he does not neglect the second."[89] Kierkegaard did not forbid Christians from holding political positions, since such positions curry neither divine favor nor displeasure *per se*,[90] so long as "I don't allow what I become in the world to be the earnestness of life ... ."[91] From the perspective of the "merely human," however, he asserted, "[T]he state is the highest human authority."[92]

Limitations of sensate authority

Although Kierkegaard retained a life-long aversion to the "crowd," he acknowledged that political power in general and democracy in particular can play a vital role: "[W]ith regard to all temporal, earthly, worldly goals, the crowd can have its validity, even its validity as the decisive factor, that is, as the authority."[93] Rather, he vehemently opposed the erroneous conclusion that temporal successes within an appropriate sphere of activity justify its deployment in all aspects of human life. While reforms "in street lighting, in public transportation ... do perhaps best come from the public," he emphasized "but that a religious reformation should come from the public is untruth and, Christianly understood, a mutinous untruth."[94]

According to Kierkegaard, sensate authority is vastly limited for several reasons. First, because it is "accidental"—that is, possessed by "good fortune"— and not eternal, sensate authority "perishes" and can never be "truly" possessed.[95] Judge William declared, "[I]t is always despair to have one's life in something whose nature is that it can pass away."[96] Furthermore, Climacus argued that, basing one's individuality on "external" privileges, which are unavailable to all

---

[87]   *WA*, p. 100; *JP*, vol. 4, p. 154 [1848].

[88]   *BA*, pp. 149–50. However, the saint or "extraordinary individual" seeks to reform society itself "*by bringing a new point of departure* for it ... by submitting directly to God" (Ibid., p. 150).

[89]   *JP*, vol. 4, p. 139 [1846]. Due to the added temptations and risks of office, he emphasized the need to pray for political leaders: "[T]he higher a person stands, the more he needs God" (*EUD*, p. 305).

[90]   *CD*, p. 60; *WL*, p. 95.

[91]   *FS*, p. 167.

[92]   *TM*, p. 149.

[93]   *PV*, p. 106.

[94]   *FS*, p. 19.

[95]   *CD*, pp. 222, 225; *EUD*, pp. 169, 317.

[96]   *EO*, vol. 2, p. 236.

but the randomly privileged, constitutes existential "flabbiness" in contrast to the "ethical victory" of becoming an individual "in the same sense as everyone else is capable of being."[97]

Second, because sensate authority represents a finite means for finite ends, it can delude the possessor with its transient accomplishments, masking the despair of spiritual dissolution.[98] Whether the person whose motto is "Caesar or nothing" achieves that goal or not, Anti-Climacus insisted that the end result is despair over herself—either by becoming Caesar and thus "getting rid of herself," or by failing to attain this goal and thus being "stuck with herself."[99] Subsequently, sensate authority is powerless to liberate an individual from the thraldom of despair.

Third, sensate authority may be spectacularly thwarted by the most seemingly innocuous contingencies.[100] For instance, the use of sensate power may bolster an opposing cause as well as destroy it,[101] and even the best philanthropic ventures can unleash debilitating spiritual effects, compounding material poverty with spiritual impoverishment.[102] Hence, Vigilius observed that a person may be "an omnipotent *Ansich* [in-itself]" and yet be a slave to fate.[103]

Fourth, sensate authority is impotent in and of itself and must rely upon external opposing forces and resistances to strengthen and define itself against.[104] For this reason, Kierkegaard contended, "There is no earthly power for whom you are nothing ... ."[105] Even the most powerful tyrant rules precariously, since he must constantly convince his subjects that rebellion is against their better interests.[106] Kierkegaard believed,

> To rule secularly ... is an indulgence, and therefore is based upon and is possible only in proportion to this: that the far, far greatest number of people either are so completely unaware that they are not part of (political) life or God-fearing enough not to want to bother themselves with it.[107]

---

[97]   *CUP*, vol. 1, p. 356.

[98]   Climacus argued that willing only finite goals ultimately finitizes the will itself (*CUP*, vol. 1, p. 394).

[99]   *SD*, p. 49. See also *CD*, p. 74.

[100]   *EO*, vol. 1, p. 25.

[101]   *PV*, p. 43.

[102]   *WL*, p. 298; *EUD*, p. 146.

[103]   *CA*, p. 99.

[104]   *CUP*, vol. 1, p. 507.

[105]   *CD*, p. 128.

[106]   *JP*, vol. 4, p. 200 [1854].

[107]   *BA*, p. 235 [1848]. On account of increased public awareness via the media, Kierkegaard contended that "genuine" governing power was at an end. Kierkegaard's comment that "in our time each individual is already on the way to being too reflective to be able to be content with merely being *represented*" (cited in Nicoletti, p. 189) recalls Luther's warning: "[T]he common man is learning to think, and the prince's scourge, which

Furthermore, there are immense problems for the prospects of peaceful succession, since the successor must establish an independence from one's predecessor; thus, sensate authority, unlike divine authority, can seldom be bestowed without some degree of seizing or tendency towards a will to ingratitude.[108]

A closely related fifth limitation of sensate authority revolves upon its inherently "unjust" nature, in that it is based upon associations which unavoidably exclude or ostracize others and emphasize external imparities between individuals.[109] Because it belongs solely to the finite realm, Kierkegaard maintained that such authority is a "limited resource," which will always engender discord at some level: *"Every earthly or worldly good is in itself selfish, begrudging; its possession is begrudging or is envy and in one way or another must make others poorer—* what I have someone else cannot have; the more I have, the less someone else must have."[110] He continued,

> The unrighteous mammon (with this term we perhaps may indeed designate every earthly good, also worldly honor, power, etc.) is in itself unjust and makes for injustice (quite apart here from the question of acquiring it or possessing it in an unlawful manner) and in itself cannot be acquired or possessed equally.[111]

Climacus posited that once a person focuses exclusively on temporal accomplishments, the justification of immoral means follows "[a]s soon as the will begins to cast a covetous eye on the outcome."[112]

Sixth, sensate authority is unable to transcend itself; thus, the individual remains bound by her temporal limitations and abilities. According to Kierkegaard, sensate self-mastery is a mere illusion.[113] Denouncing Kant's ethical autonomy as an avenue for "lawlessness and experimentation," Kierkegaard exclaimed that a person cannot bind herself in earnest to a self-imposed law "any more than Sancho Panza's self-administered blows to his own bottom were vigorous."[114] Subsequently, he believed that the sensate can only truly be elevated by the eternal.[115]

Seventh, sensate authority is potentially all-enslaving, partially because any human life which does not consciously enter relationship with God is "as pitiable as children's play if it supposed to be earnestness."[116] In addition to distracting

---

God calls *contemptum*, is gathering force among the mob ..." (*Selections from His Writings*, ed. John Dillenberger [New York, 1962], p. 391).

[108] See *PF*, p. 155; *EUD*, p. 15.

[109] *UD*, p. 144.

[110] *CD*, p. 115.

[111] Ibid.

[112] *CUP*, vol. 1, p. 135.

[113] *EUD*, p. 18.

[114] *JP*, vol. 1, p. 76 [1850].

[115] For sensate authority's powerlessness to secure a soul, see *EUD*, pp. 171–2.

[116] Ibid., p. 265.

the ruling or ruled-over individual from the true basis of temporal authority—inwardness cultivated by consciously living in the presence of God—sensate authority constantly requires one to prove oneself. Contrary to God, who need not retaliate instantly against rebellion, Kierkegaard observed,

> Only a weak and soft person wants to have his rights at once, wants to be victorious in the external realm at once, simply because he is weak and therefore must have an external proof—that he is the stronger. The person who in truth has power and in truth is the stronger calmly grants the weak one a free hand … .[117]

Furthermore, such "proofs" unavoidably enslave individuals to the audience upon which proof of one's independence paradoxically depends![118] This criticism holds true regardless of whether the political system is a classic tyranny or a democracy, since the authority is still based on human recognition and submission. Hence, Kierkegaard argued, "Tyranny and democracy hate each other just as the one potter hates another—that is, it is the same form of government, only in tyranny one is the tyrant, in democracy, the masses."[119] Quidam observed that any government which relies upon physical force quickly finds itself enslaved to the "sword" rather than basing its rule upon creativity, love, and truth.[120]

Abuses of sensate authority

Kierkegaard considered sensate authority to be a necessity for civil and communal life in the world, provided it stayed within carefully categorical boundaries. The greatest abuse of sensate authority for Kierkegaard is its insistence upon either assisting or aborting the purview of spiritual authority. Such abuse stems from "a complete misconception of Christianity" as homogeneous with human power and history.[121] For Kierkegaard, this constitutes the most grievous infraction of Christendom: "[T]hey have shifted the sphere of the paradoxical religious back into the esthetic."[122] The consequence of this categorical error is chaos, according to Climacus:

> In our day everything is mixed together; one responds to the esthetic ethically, to faith intellectually, etc. One is finished with everything, and yet scant attention is given to which sphere it is in which each question finds its answer. This produces

---

[117]   *UD*, pp. 40–41.

[118]   *CUP*, vol. 1, p. 76. Climacus later noted that one may show powerlessness "simply in showing power" (ibid., p. 515].

[119]   *JP*, vol. 3, p. 486 [1854].

[120]   *SW*, p. 324.

[121]   *TC*, pp. 54–5. Hence, he lamented that "the Church and the state are treated exactly alike" (*JP*, vol. 1, p. 239 [1848]). See also *PC*, p. 223.

[122]   *BA*, p. 173. See also *TM*, p. 129; *PV*, p. 130.

even greater confusion in the world of spirit than if in civic life the response to an ecclesiastical matter would be given by the pavement commission.[123]

For this reason, Kierkegaard remained a passionate advocate for a carefully qualified separation of church and state: "[L]et us not secularize the religious but eternally separate the religious and the secular precisely by earnestly thinking about them together."[124]

According to Kierkegaard, sinful secularization seeks to secure human autonomy so that "we are governed, educated, and brought up according to mankind's conception of what it means to be a human being."[125] Kierkegaard identified two complex maneuvers which occur in this process of secularization: the "nonchurch" appropriates what it desires from the church, while the church appropriates what it desires from the nonchurch. In both movements, however, the church is rendered "unchurchlike," disempowered of its eternal heterogeneity, and ignominiously reduced to "a kingdom of this world."[126] In nineteenth-century Denmark, this resulted in the "finitization" of Christian faith primarily through three avenues: its intellectual conflation with philosophy, the political amalgamation of church and state, and the existential blurring of personal security and sacrifice.

Intellectual finitizing: philosophy and faith
In his unpublished treatise on Reverend Adolph P. Adler, Kierkegaard attributed the universal upheavals of the nineteenth century to widespread rebellion:

> The calamity of our age in politics, as in religion and as in everything, is disobedience, not being willing to obey. One only deceives oneself and others by wanting to make us think that it is doubt that is to blame for the calamity and the cause of the calamity—no, it is insubordination—it is not doubt about the truth of the religious but insubordination to the authority of the religious. But dialectically self-willfulness has two forms: either to want to overthrow the ruler or to want to be oneself the ruler … .[127]

In light of this revolt, Anti-Climacus accused speculative philosophy of arrogantly eradicating the heterogeneity between God and humankind, exhibiting—in Virginia Rumble's felicitous phrase—the "speculative forgetfulness of finitude":[128]

---

[123]   *CUP*, vol. 1, p. 324.

[124]   *UD*, p. 125.

[125]   *FS*, p. 86. See *SD*, p. 114.

[126]   *FS*, p. 171.

[127]   *BA*, p. 5.

[128]   Vanessa Rumble, "Eternity Lies Beneath: Autonomy and Finitude in Kierkegaard's Early Writings," *Journal of the History of Philosophy*, 35/1 (1997): 89.

What has gone basically wrong with Christendom is really Christianity, that by
being preached day in and day out, the doctrine of the God-man (safeguarded
in the Christian understanding, be it noted, by the paradox and the possibility
of offence) is taken in vain, that the difference in kind between God and man is
pantheistically revoked (first with an air of superiority in speculative philosophy,
then vulgarly in the streets and alley-ways).[129]

When humans attempt to speculate on the realm of the eternal, the result is invariably
a metaphysics or religiousness of immanence ("Religiousness A"), a mythological
projection of human traits and desires upon a cosmic canvas, a subtle self-celebration
of human act and creativity in which "to be God becomes a direct superlative of what
it is to be a human being."[130] Kierkegaard was particularly sensitive to the duplicitous
nature of this "existential ventriloquism" in his era. As Vigilius observed, "[N]o age
has been more skilful than our own in producing myths of the understanding, an age
that produces myths and at the same time wants to eradicate all myths."[131]

Kierkegaard identified Hegelianism in particular as the predominant intellectual
incursion upon the religious sphere, whose proponents "understand carelessly what
Hegel has carelessly taught, that his philosophy was the highest development of
Christianity."[132] He criticized the epistemological "imperialism" at the heart of the
Hegelian systematizer, which sought to disregard and negate particularity while
grasping after totalizing universalities: "[W]hen the phenomena are paraded, he
[Hegel] is in too much of a hurry and is too aware of the great importance of his role
as commander-in-chief of world history to take time for more than the royal glimpse
he allows to glide over them."[133] Ironically, in attempting to "preserve" Christian
faith within a philosophical system, Hegel had severed the "wildflower" from its
roots and pressed it into the pages of his tomes, "preserving" while destroying its
vitality in one fell swoop.[134]

Kierkegaard was well aware of the tremendous power of intellectual authority
in present-day Europe. Contrary to the Romantic era of passionate revolution, he
asserted, "An age that is revolutionary but also reflecting and devoid of passion
changes the expression of power into a *dialectical tour de force: it lets everything
remain but subtly drains the meaning out of it* ... ."[135] Although many of the Christian
forms were retained, devoid of passion, they remained as lifeless as children's toys
without batteries: "[W]e are willing to keep Christian terminology but privately

---

[129]   *SD*, p. 150.

[130]   *PC*, p. 104.

[131]   *CA*, p. 46.

[132]   *BA*, p. 94. He particularly abhorred Hegel's condescending attitude towards faith
as a more "primitive" stage of existence which humankind must "move beyond" (*JP*, vol. 4,
p. 458 [1851]); *SW*, p. 486; *FT*, p. 37; *CA*, p. 10).

[133]   *CI*, p. 222.

[134]   In keeping with Hegel's controversial term, *aufheben*. See *CA*, p. 225, n. 16.

[135]   *TA*, p. 77.

know that nothing decisive is supposed to be meant by it."[136] In an upbuilding discourse, Kierkegaard insisted, "To place a crown of thorns on his head and spit on him is blasphemy, but to make God so lofty that his existence becomes a delusion, becomes meaningless—that, too, is blasphemy."[137] He deplored that God had become a figurehead on the "good ship" Humanity—ceremonially leading the throng, with absolutely no bearing upon the rudder.

According to Kierkegaard, the roots of this sensate assault on the eternal extended back to the Greek philosophers, whose systems presupposed the homogeneity between faith and intellect as solely human-based, human-centered activities, and who remained optimistic that "if we only understand the right it follows automatically that we do it."[138] However, once faith is relegated to the realm of the human mind, decision and action are forever aborted in endless deliberation over what constitutes true proof that faith is indeed warranted.[139] Subsequently, demonstrations are open to unceasing debate and subject to the unquestioned authority of human reason; "oughts" are cannily transformed into "thoughts."[140]

By definition, Kierkegaard maintained that faith can never be proved or disproved, otherwise faith is commensurable with human reason, and human beings become the higher authority who judge eternal truth.[141] He was especially critical of "Christian" and biblical scholarship which reduced the life of Christ to historical data for "scientific" scrutiny. To evaluate Christ solely for his socio-political impact is blasphemous, since it reduces him to a mere human participant.[142] It is also blasphemous to ask whether Christ was "profound," "as if he were up for examination and should be catechized instead of being the one to whom all power is given in heaven and on earth."[143] As H.H. explained, "To ask if a king is a genius, and in that case to be willing to obey him, is basically high treason, because the question contains a doubt about submission to authority."[144]

By contrast, Anti-Climacus insisted that faith does not pertain primarily to the intellect but to the will: "Faith is: that the self in being itself and in wanting to be itself is grounded transparently in God."[145] Hence, he argued that sin is not "weakness, sensuality, finitude, ignorance," but a being-wide rebellion against

---

[136]   Ibid., p. 81.

[137]   *EUD*, p. 208.

[138]   *FS*, p. 116.

[139]   "[T]he very first beginning of deliberation over it [Christianity] is defection, rebellion" (*JP*, vol. 4, p. 408 [1852]).

[140]   *CD*, p. 205.

[141]   *FS*, pp. 18, 125; *WL*, p. 273; *CUP*, vol. 1, pp. 11, 30; *CA*, p. 139.

[142]   *PC*, p. 23; *CUP*, vol. 1, p. 599.

[143]   *BA*, p. 183.

[144]   *WA*, p. 101.

[145]   *SD*, p. 114.

God which can only be acknowledged pending "a revelation from God."[146] If faith and "subjective" commitment are supplanted by deliberation and "objective" content, Christianity quickly collapses into a functional gnosticism, a "professorial-scholarly Christianity" whose chief power-broker is the "assistant professor."[147]

By presumptuously applying itself to categories which only a religiousness of transcendence can address, philosophy misconstrues both doubt—rendering it a thought category instead of an existential act of rebellion—and freedom. Thus, Vigilius contended:

> When freedom is apprehended in this way [i.e., as the capacity to do as one pleases], it has necessity as its opposite, which shows that it has been conceived as a category of reflection. No, the opposite of freedom is guilt, and it is the greatness of freedom that it always has to do only with itself, that in its possibility it projects guilt and accordingly posits it by itself. And if guilt is posited actually, freedom posits it by itself. If this is not kept in mind, freedom is confused in a clever way with something entirely different, with *force*.[148]

By offering its "protective" services to Christian faith, human rationality in general and Hegelian philosophy in particular assumed a higher authority over God and theology.[149] In return, theology achieved a dubious respectability and short-lived legitimacy from this intrinsically "Faustian" arrangement.

Political finitizing: church and state
The second avenue of the "finitization" of the Christian faith involves the incredible degree of fusion between the Danish government and the state church. As Kirmmse observes, "Except for such few exceptions as the Crown might make, official Danish 'citizenship' during the absolutist period (1660–1849) was extended only to baptized and confirmed members of the Lutheran State Church."[150] The

---

[146] Ibid., pp. 129–30.

[147] *FS*, p. 195.

[148] *CA*, p. 108.

[149] Klaus-M. Kodalle argues that this, in no way, represents a fideistic jettisoning of rationality, since "the task with the paradox is to grasp its unthinkableness and that requires full use of the categorical power of reason" ("The Utilitarian Self and the "Useless" Passion of Faith," in Alastair Hannay and Gordon Marino [eds], *The Cambridge Companion to Kierkegaard* [Cambridge, 1998], p. 407).

[150] Kirmmse, *Kierkegaard in Golden Age Denmark*, p. 27. It is telling that Bishop Mynster once ordered the mandatory baptism of Baptist children on the grounds that sacramental independence from the state church entailed "political disloyalty to the crown" (Robert Perkins, "Climacan Politics: Person and Polis in Kierkegaard's *Postscript*," in Robert Perkins (ed.), *International Kierkegaard Commentary: Concluding Unscientific Postscript to "Philosophical Fragments"* [Macon, 1997], p. 48).

church had merely become "another arm of royal administration."[151] Kierkegaard highlighted the church's usefulness to the state as a means of political unification: "The state thought it prudent to accommodate this teaching of eternity and instructions about another world in order to tranquilize people and thus be better able to control them."[152] Contrary to the message of the suffering Messiah, Christianity was marketed as a strategy for material blessing: "To be a Christian, so it was said, is sheer happiness ... . Indeed, to be a Christian is the only thing that really gives meaning to life, savor to joys, and relief to sufferings."[153] This unfortunate union fostered the revaluation of the eternal based on an "aesthetic fallacy" whereby "every striving for the infinite is measurable by finite rewards and advantages ... ."[154]

Within the context of "Golden Age" Denmark, Robert Perkins observes that "Christendom" entailed "a combination of the 'conservative' forces that included the 'liberal' state and the cultural institutions, ... which had as its aim the maximum possible preservation of the social and cultural arrangements of pre-1848 Denmark in a post-revolutionary parliamentary democracy."[155] Kierkegaard contended that, regardless of political system, people truly seek a means of christening their desires and actions with the "champagne" of divine approval, "a divine confirmation of the pursuit of the finite."[156] This results in what Anti-Climacus called the "deification of the established order": "the smug invention of the lazy, secular human mentality that wants to settle down and fancy that now there is total peace and security, now we have achieved the highest."[157] However, Kierkegaard derided the self-proclamation of any "Christian nation" as illusory,[158] and predicted that the

---

[151]   Kirmmse, *Kierkegaard in Golden Age Denmark*, p. 28. Walter Lowrie recounts how Kierkegaard once had to seek the king's permission to withdraw his request for a parish (*A Short Life of Kierkegaard* [2nd edn, Princeton, 1965], p. 59).

[152]   *JP*, vol. 4, p. 203 [1855].

[153]   *TM*, p. 190. Kierkegaard declared that objectifying God by transforming him into a means of attaining temporal success "is not venturing in reliance upon God; this is taking God in vain" (*FS*, p. 100).

[154]   *TM*, p. 330. This is why Kierkegaard denounced medieval asceticism as a societally sanctioned means of attaining honor and prestige (*FS*, p. 205; *SW*, p. 253; *CUP*, vol. 1, p. 407).

[155]   Robert Perkins, "Habermas and Kierkegaard: Religious Subjectivity, Multiculturalism, and Historical Revisionism," *International Philosophical Quarterly*, 44/4 (2004): 492.

[156]   *TM*, p. 453 [1854]. See also *PV*, p. 130. This included the "hierarchical 'People's Church,'" the newly christened Danish state church under the 1849 constitution (Robert Perkins, "Habermas and Kierkegaard: Religious Subjectivity, Multiculturalism, and Historical Revisionism," p. 492).

[157]   *PC*, p. 88. He considered the deification of worldly cunning to be "precisely the idolatry of the age."

[158]   *TM*, p. 36; *SD*, p. 134. This was particularly vexing for Kierkegaard, since the illusion that everyone was Christian was safeguarded by the "guardian illusion" that the church and the state are one (*TM*, p. 107).

commandeering of the eternal for the purpose of statecraft will inevitably end in revolt.[159] The consequences for the church are equally foreboding. The merging of church and state imbues the state with divinely sanctioned "infallibility," thus "abolishing the authority of Christianity and substituting the authority of the state."[160] The final result, he contended, is "a sophisticated esthetic and intellectual paganism with an admixture of Christianity."[161] Subsequently, he raged,

> The ordinary kind of Christianity is: a secularized life, avoiding major crimes more out of sagacity than for the sake of conscience, ingeniously seeking the pleasures of life—and then once in a while a so-called pious mood. This is Christianity—in the same sense as a touch of nausea and a little stomachache are cholera.[162]

The state's use of the church is not one-sided, however, for this symbiotic relationship allows for a cozy settlement which secures government salaries and pensions for its ministers.[163] Furthermore, Kierkegaard charged that government "protection" "teaches Christianity the most loathsome bad habits: in the name of Christianity to use police force."[164] The intolerable alliance likewise has a detrimental impact upon sensate authority, rendering it as "ludicrous" as if a mayor were to offer protection to a citizen who turns out to be the king in civilian clothes.[165]

Kierkegaard believed that the most invidious assault of sensate authority upon spiritual authority entails the former's attempts to "protect" the latter. The deleterious effects of this compromise are two-fold. First, "deplorable confusion" arises, since it implies that God, like Napoleon, needs assistance to achieve his aims. Instead, Kierkegaard exclaimed, "God does not need anything at all in order to be victorious; he is from eternity to eternity the strongest."[166] Moreover, such a

---

[159]   *JP*, vol. 4, p. 203 [1855].

[160]   *TM*, p. 556 [1855]. Kierkegaard graphically compared "official Christianity" to the hollow husk of a caterpillar that has been consumed by a wasp larva from the inside out (*JP*, vol. 4, p. 189 [1853]).

[161]   *PV*, p. 78.

[162]   *FS*, pp. 202–3.

[163]   *TM*, p. 556 [1855]. Hence, Jesus becomes "the greatest monetary object that ever appeared in the world" (ibid., p. 44). Kierkegaard stridently compared those "sheer worldlings" who sought to make a "career" of ministry to "cannibals" feasting upon the bloody sacrifices of the martyrs (ibid., p. 321).

[164]   Ibid., p. 159.

[165]   Ibid., pp. 112–13.

[166]   *BA*, p. 255 [1846–47]. He criticized Luther, who "became impatient" and "accepted the help of the princes, *i.e.* he really became a politician, to whom victory is more important than 'how' one is victorious; for religiously the one important thing is the 'how,' just because the religious person is infinitely certain that he or his matter will be victorious, indeed that it is already won ..." (*JK*, p. 204 [1850]).

human-brokered relation to the eternal inevitably "usurps" the eternal it is intended to "establish."[167] Subsequently, Kierkegaard scathingly posited,

> The formula is very simple: a cause which is served by the refusal of human assistance—yes, it may be arrogance, but it may also be God's cause; but a cause which is served in such a way that one accepts the assistance of men is politics. To set God's name to it does not turn the scales any more than to say: Now in God's name I am going out to steal, or—in the name of our Lord Jesus Christ I shall go out and hang myself.[168]

Anti-Climacus bluntly observed that such veneration of human aid constitutes a worship of one's own ingenuity and, subsequently, "makes a fool of God."[169] Kierkegaard thus concluded, "Just as many a cause may have been lost because the world's assistance failed to come, so also is many a cause ruined because the world was allowed to help."[170]

A second deplorable effect of sensate authority's "assistance" in the Christian "cause" is an over-realized eschatology, which prematurely heralds the historical actualization of Christ's reign on earth, supplanting the "church militant" with the "church triumphant."[171] As a result, the church can enjoy maximum comfort in this life as well as the next—a temptation to which Luther allegedly succumbed.[172] Climacus soundly castigated this "singing and ringing" triumphalism,[173] while Anti-Climacus scoffed, "[I]n short, we hear nothing but sermons that could more appropriately end with 'Hurrah' than with 'Amen.'"[174] Subsequently, Kierkegaard contended, "[T]he 'Church triumphant' has triumphed over the world in an external sense, that is, it has in a worldly way triumphed over the world."[175] On account of this spiritual smugness, Kierkegaard maintained that contemporary Christians behave "even more sensately" than pagans "because they have this confounded security that basically they are Christians."[176]

---

[167]   *CUP*, vol. 2, p. 161 [1850].

[168]   *JP*, vol. 4, p. 189 [1853].

[169]   *PC*, p. 92.

[170]   *UD*, p. 340. See also *FS*, p. 127; *UD*, pp. 61, 338.

[171]   *PC*, p. 207.

[172]   *JP*, vol. 4, p. 189 [1853]. Bishops J.P. Mynster and H.L. Martensen receive similar censures (*TM*, p. 6).

[173]   *PF*, p. 107.

[174]   *PC*, p. 107. He later hypothesized on the diabolical origins of this contagion of complacency: "Then Satan said to himself: I shall not conquer in this way [by overt persecution]; and he changed his method. Little by little he deluded the Christian Church into thinking that now it had been victorious, now it should have a good rest after the battle and enjoy the victory" (ibid., pp. 229–30).

[175]   *CD*, p. 229.

[176]   *PV*, p. 48.

In light of the predominance of sensate authority, Kierkegaard underscored the complete incommensurability between the means and the ends of church and nonchurch: "[T]he Christianity of the New Testament, which teaches asceticism, voluntary renunciation, requires the most unconditional heterogeneity to this world, abhors all use of worldly power ... ."[177] Because he believed that authentic Christianity had all but expired in his world, Kierkegaard compared his polemic battles to those of Don Quixote, "an individual struggling to uphold some venerable, idealistic cause ... that can no longer be said to 'exist.'"[178]

Existential finitizing: security and sacrifice

While the previous avenue of finitization of the Christian faith focused primarily on political and religious leaders, the third avenue pertains to the personal lives of priests and laity alike: the Gospel is duplicitously shorn of its self-abnegating, risk-taking elements and transformed into a bourgeois, "eternal life" insurance policy. Kierkegaard was scandalized that "[t]here is always a secular mentality that no doubt wants to have the name of being Christian but wants to become Christian as cheaply as possible."[179] On account of such complacency, he asserted, "To have lived this human life in such a way that we have let others be sacrificed for us and to have lived this human life in such a way that we have been sacrificed for others—between these two lies an eternal qualitative difference."[180] He did not completely disregard the spiritual solace provided by Christian faith, but emphasized that such periodic respites constitute temporary "rest stops," not permanent "rest homes."[181] Hence, he wrote, "Christianity is taken in vain, however, when the *infinite* requirement is either made finite ... or it is even left out completely and *grace* is introduced as *a matter of course* ... ."[182]

Intriguingly, Kierkegaard broke with Christian tradition by blaming the apostles for reducing the cost of Christian discipleship: whereas Jesus amassed 11 followers in three-and-a-half years, the disciples gained three thousand "in one hour." He exclaimed, "Either the follower is here greater than the Master, or the truth is that the apostle is a bit too hasty in striking a bargain, a bit too hasty about propagation; thus the dubious already begins here."[183] In an attack against

---

[177]   *TM*, p. 504 [January 1855].

[178]   Eric Ziolkowski, "Don Quixote and Kierkegaard's Understanding of the Single Individual in Society," in George Connell and C. Stephen Evans (eds), *Foundations of Kierkegaard's Vision of Community: Religion, Ethics, and Politics in Kierkegaard* (New Jersey and London, 1992), p. 139.

[179]   *FS*, p. 16. See also *TM*, p. 151.

[180]   *JP*, vol. 3, p. 335 [1854].

[181]   *TM*, p. 408 [1850].

[182]   *PV*, p. 16. Ludwig Feuerbach similarly railed against "spiritual freedom ... which demands no sacrifice, no energy" (*The Essence of Christianity*, trans. George Eliot [New York, 1957] p. 163).

[183]   *TM*, p. 181.

church leaders, Kierkegaard maintained that this apostolic compromise has been "faithfully" followed by their successors throughout the centuries. As a result, "Instead of whales, we have caught sardines—but countless millions of them."[184] He once accused Bishop Mynster of allowing the Christian ideal to vanish via a "Hezekian" compromise in order to secure a "worldly" peace which would "last the few years I have to live."[185] Kierkegaard denounced Mynster and his successor, H.L. Martensen, for "playing at Christianity"; that is, "to remove all dangers (Christianly, *witness* and *danger* are equivalent), to replace them with power (to be a danger to others), goods, advantages, abundant enjoyment of even the most select refinements."[186]

In view of this fatal compromise of the Danish church, Kierkegaard indignantly concluded, "No, whatever true Christianity there is to be found in the course of the centuries may be found in the sects and the like, except that being a sect outside the Church is no proof of being true Christianity."[187] Having examined the detrimental impact of the church's "merger" of mediocrity, we will turn to the traditional dichotomy of sensate roles, before exploring how these roles blur in Kierkegaard's analysis of sensate authority.

Positions of sensate authority
According to Stephen Esquith and Nicholas Smith, ancient populations were typically divided into two main categories: those in control, the "masters," who largely determine the goals of a society and allocate resources to achieve those objectives; and those in submission, the "slaves," who largely supply the means whereby these goals are attained.[188] On one level, Kierkegaard acknowledged this division of human society. Commenting on first-century Israel, he wrote, "[T]hat little nation ... is divided, as tends to be the case, into two groups: the mighty and what is called the masses."[189] For Kierkegaard, however, the predominant struggle of history is not the clash between masters and slaves, but rather the existential rebellion of sinfully autonomous humans against the incontestable power of God. As a result, the distinction between master and slave becomes significantly blurred in Kierkegaard's writings. The inherent futility of basing human independence and well-being on an anthropocentric foundation for power constitutes what may be termed "the myth of mastery."

---

[184]   *JP*, vol. 3, p. 338 [1854]. See also ibid., vol. 6, p. 538 [1854]; *FS*, p. 259 [1851].

[185]   Ibid., p. 258 [1851]. See II Kings 20:19.

[186]   *TM*, p. 6. He especially denounced the revaluation of genuine acts of "earnestness" as spiritual "showboating" (*FS*, p. 34) and the eradication of Christian risk-taking on the grounds that "[t]o venture beyond the bounds of probability is to tempt God" (ibid., p. 102).

[187]   *JP*, vol. 3, p. 183 [23 September 1855].

[188]   Stephen Esquith and Nicholas Smith, "Slavery," in Edward Craig (ed.), *Routledge Encyclopaedia of Philosophy* (10 vols, London, 1998), vol. 8, pp. 803–7.

[189]   *FS*, p. 171.

The "slave"

Kierkegaard claimed to be nonprejudicial when it came to associating with individuals regardless of whether they were kings or cobblers. However, he remained antagonistic towards anything to do with "the masses" as a category, which became synonymous with mediocrity, whether spiritual or otherwise.[190] Attempts at populist politics were soundly criticized, since they were still based upon human recognition and servitude; instead of one tyrant, however, the nation was ruled by the tyrannical will of a faceless abstraction—public opinion.[191] Hence, Kierkegaard critiqued communism[192] and democracy with equal fervour: "[I]t [democracy] flatters their arbitrariness that the government they obey is of their own making. It is like a pagan worshiping the god he himself has made—it is about the same as worshiping oneself."[193]

Kierkegaard also criticized political egalitarianism which seeks to level all individual distinctions and reduce humankind to a collective of clones "as exchangeable as a coin of the realm."[194] He acerbically observed that, by banishing "first place," the "second class students" are *de facto* promoted to "number 1" without any merit on their part.[195] This, in Perkins' pithy phrase, is "equality with a vengeance,"[196] where exceptionality and extremities are supplanted by a dehumanizing conformity and moderation—the abhorrent "everything to a certain degree."[197] Subsequently, Kierkegaard complained that any attempts to distinguish oneself from the crowd are condemned as "elitist" due to a hyper-politicization of reality: "Everything is understood politically (but 'they' do not necessarily have a great understanding of politics), with the result that the religious person comes to be hated as being proud, aristocratic, and the like."[198] Even an over-ambitious "sinner" is more preferable to "mediocrity's sensate enjoyment of life."[199] Hence, Anti-Climacus stated, "The person who gets lost in possibility soars with the boldness of despair; but the person for whom all has become necessary strains his back on life, bent down with the weight of despair; but the petty bourgeois mentality spiritlessly triumphs."[200]

---

[190]   *JP*, vol. 3, p. 179 [1855].

[191]   Ibid., vol. 4, p. 147 [1848]: "But another form of tyranny is a corollary of equality—fear of men." See also *PC*, p. 16.

[192]   *SD*, p. 61; *JP*, vol. 4, p. 148 [1848].

[193]   Ibid.

[194]   *SD*, p. 64. See also *TA*, p. 87.

[195]   *TM*, p. xvii.; *FS*, p. 199.

[196]   Robert Perkins, "Envy as Personal Phenomenon and as Politics," in Robert Perkins (ed.), *International Kierkegaard Commentary: Two Ages* (Macon, 1984), p. 125.

[197]   *TM*, p. 93.

[198]   *JP*, vol. 4, p. 164 [1850].

[199]   *TM*, p. 460 [1854].

[200]   *SD*, p. 72. See also *EUD*, p. 143.

The "master"

Compared to the lower classes, Kierkegaard's attitude towards the master class appears somewhat ambivalent. On the one hand, he advocated that everyone must be treated altruistically: "One ought to exist for all men and not caste-consciously and egotistically to seek his own advantage."[201] He once hypothesized that *The Corsair* scandal transpired because the poor derided him for refusing to act elitist, while the privileged ironically withheld their support for the exact same reason.[202] On the other hand, the populist upheavals of 1848 initially incited him to support the monarchy in light of the moral and religious vacuum which ensues following populist uprisings. Hence, his indignation rose against "a people who each day provide new evidence that there is no public morality in the land—a people who must either be saved by a tyrant or by a few martyrs."[203]

Like Nietzsche, Kierkegaard could indulge in a measure of romanticism by idealizing the self-assured aristocrat of a vanished, glorious past.[204] The importance of individual identity in Kierkegaard's theology afforded a natural affinity with the nobility's proclivity for manicuring strong personalities.[205] He once acknowledged the veracity of Plato's principles for how rulers should exercise power:

> [G]iven the presupposition that there is competence, the disinclination to rule is an excellent guarantee that the ruling will be true and competent, whereas the power-seeker too easily becomes one who misuses his power in order to tyrannize, or one whom the desire to rule brings into a concealed relation of dependency on those whom he is supposed to rule, so that his ruling actually becomes an optical illusion.[206]

Rather than incite a revolution, Kierkegaard sought to "support" "governing by those who are officially appointed and called, that fearing God they might stand firm, willing only one thing—the good."[207] He attributed the political tumult of 1848 to two deplorable factors: "the mistake from above," a government founded

---

[201] *JP*, vol. 4, p. 140 [1846]. He especially criticized the upper class for "playing at Christianity" and thus succumbing to "the most aristocratic of diseases, to admire socially what one personally regards as trivial, because the whole thing has become a theatrical joke …" (*TA*, p. 73). Judge William criticized elitists who used brazen evils to distinguish themselves from "the common herd" (*EO*, vol. 2, pp. 226–7).

[202] *PV*, p. 62. Kierkegaard's inherited wealth located him in the privileged class of society. He once identified himself as a "master," who lacked "the authority to order his servant to go to a place of disrepute" (*TC*, p. 184).

[203] *JP*, vol. 4, p. 146 [1848].

[204] For example, see his criticism of the "new Napoleon" who conducted himself more like a "tense gambler" than a "self-contained hero" (ibid., p. 186 [1851]).

[205] *JK*, p. 244 [August 1854].

[206] *TM*, p. 91.

[207] *PV*, p. 18.

upon secular "sagacity" rather than fear of God, and "the mistake from below," a disastrous desire by the masses to reject all forms of true government.[208]

Fearing that unchecked rebellion against the masters would foster further insurrection against higher authorities including God, Kierkegaard sided with the ruling elite: "As the crowd intimidates the king, as the public intimidates counsellors of state and authors, so the generation will ultimately want to intimidate God, constrain him to give in, become self-important before him, brazenly defiant in their numbers, etc."[209] This anxiety led to a rare breech of principle whereby sensate authority, albeit indirectly, "bolsters" eternal authority. Perhaps Kierkegaard feared the onset of early Israelite chaos: "In those days there was no king in Israel; all the people did what was right in their own eyes."[210]

On account of his desire for genuine internal reform over external revolt, Kierkegaard originally argued that, rather than undermining the Danish church, his highly critical book *Practice in Christianity* "is certainly the potential defence for an established order if it understands itself."[211] With regards to ecclesiastical hierarchy, he did not seek to topple bishops or minimize their spiritual authority— if anything, church leaders were guilty of being too lenient and granting too many concessions to the increasingly powerful masses.[212] On the contrary, he believed that power must rightfully be wielded by an educated elite over the chaotic masses, and always "in the service of an idea" so as to qualify as "the best power."[213] Subsequently, Kierkegaard sought to convert the ecclesiastical leaders to his own understanding of faith so that, through their considerable influence, they might sway the rank and file.[214]

---

[208]   Ibid., p. 19.

[209]   *CD*, p. 385 [20 November 1847]. See also Plekon, "Towards Apocalypse: Kierkegaard's *Two Ages* in Golden Age Denmark," p. 46: "He supported an orderly hierarchical structure reflecting God's rule over creation, one in which the monarch rules with authority in matters of state and the church governs in the religious realm."

[210]   Judges 21:25. Joe Jones claims that Kierkegaard falls prey to a "vicious" circularity: "[W]e need a usable criterion for identifying what does have God's authority, and we seem confronted with either deriving the criterion from relative authorities or with justifying the criterion by appeal to God's authority" ("Some Remarks on Authority and Revelation in Kierkegaard," *Journal of Religion*, 57/3 [1977]: 245).

[211]   *PV*, p. 19.

[212]   Hence, he advised them to repent of their weakness and "grasp the reins again" (*PC*, p. 360 [1850]).

[213]   *CD*, p. 321.

[214]   *TM*, p. 440 [March 1854]. This explains why he waited in silent anticipation for Mynster's recantation and did not publish any further criticisms of the church until the elderly prelate's death.

The myth of sensate authority

Within the sphere of sensate authority, Kierkegaard favored a strong centralized leadership which kept the dangerous forces of depersonalizing collectivism in check. However, within the sphere of spiritual authority, Kierkegaard theologically undermined all political distinctions. While he upheld the temporal differences between rulers and subjects, he vigorously championed the spiritual equality of all individuals before God. In an attack on elitist society, he once charged, "[H]ow are you really any different from what you most detest—lack of culture, the coarseness of the masses? You differ in that you do the same as they do, but you observe good form, do not do it with unwashed hands—O human culture!"²¹⁵ Kierkegaard did not naively regard sensate power as a prelude to greatness. Rather, as Tacitus observed of Agrippa, the possession of power often highlights the mediocrity of the bearer.²¹⁶ Contrary to sensate proclivities towards hierarchy, the Gospel has irreversibly levelled all socio-political power distinctions. On account of Christ's teaching and example, the nobility can no longer live in exclusivity, but must accept responsibility for the welfare of all others.²¹⁷

In addition to the spiritual equality of every individual before God, any delineation between "master power" and "slave power" is problematic from Kierkegaard's perspective for four primary reasons. First, they are both founded upon human premises which are instilled by and instill fear in others, the envy and angst of comparison.²¹⁸ Subsequently, he did not differentiate between the soul-damaging capacity of sensate authority possessed by the masters and the slaves' craving for the same:

> Far be it from us to strengthen anyone in the presumptuous delusion that only the mighty and the famous are the guilty ones, for if the poor and weak merely aspire defiantly for the superiority denied them in earthly existence instead of humbly aspiring for Christianity's blessed equality, this also damages the soul.²¹⁹

---

²¹⁵ *FS*, p. 64.

²¹⁶ *TC*, p. 164 [7 January 1846]: "[J]ust as Tacitus detected the contemptible slave mind in the Jewish King Agrippa, because he exercised tyrannical power, so contemptibleness is always seen most readily when it possesses power." As "lord of the flies," Domitian also exemplified small-minded obsession despite immense power (*WL* 253). See Pascal, *Pensées*, trans. A.J. Krailsheimer (London, 1966), p. 43, where he chuckled at how "[t]he mind of this supreme judge of the world" may be disrupted by a buzzing fly.

²¹⁷ *WL* [revised], p. 411 [1847]: "The aristocrats take for granted that there is always a whole mass of people who go to waste. But they remain silent about it, live secluded, and act as if these many, many human beings did not exist at all. This is the wickedness of the aristocrats' exclusiveness—that in order to have an easy life themselves they do not even make people aware."

²¹⁸ Kierkegaard regarded envy as "the *negatively unifying principle* in a passionless and very reflective age" (*TA*, p. 81).

²¹⁹ *WL*, p. 81.

Although conceding that the populist demands for "external" equality may eradicate all of the ancient "tyrannies"—"emperor, king, nobility, clergy, even money tyranny"[220]—he argued that they merely establish a new tyranny, "the omnipotence of public opinion," whereby one is still enslaved by "the other."[221] Populist power is especially insidious "in part because it is not directly obvious and attention must be called to it."[222] Furthermore, he regarded "tyranny of the equal" to be "the most dangerous slavery" because it seeks to eradicate individual differences and thus "do away with every individual's relation to God."[223] Whether a person seeks to accentuate "aesthetic" differences—like certain "masters"—or to eliminate those differences—like certain "slaves"—external differences still remain the basis for human existence. In fact, contrary to Hegelian distinctions, so-called "master" power represents the artful deployment of so-called "slave" power, according to Kierkegaard:

> The people is the force which has demolished kings and emperors; kings and emperors again have sometimes used the people to demolish the nobility or the clergy. The people has demolished the clergy, and the clergy has used the people to demolish the nobility, and the nobility has used the people to demolish the clergy. But always "the people."[224]

The second reason why distinguishing between master power and slave power is problematic for Kierkegaard is that both easily become expressions of sinful human autonomy. Although he is speaking specifically about material wealth, Kierkegaard's words arguably apply to sensate power:

> It is corruption when the poor man shrivels up in his poverty so that he lacks the courage of will to be built up by Christianity. It is also corruption when a prominent man wraps himself in his prominence in such a way that he shrinks from being built up by Christianity. And it is also corruption if he whose distinction is to be like the majority of people never comes out of this distinction through Christian elevation.[225]

Any temporal element—whether wealth, power, prestige, or the lack thereof—which becomes an "obstacle" between God and the individual has entered the realm of the sensate. While sinful separation from God allows individuals to take more liberties over other humans with apparent impunity, Kierkegaard believed

---

220　*CD*, p. 383 [1848]
221　Ibid., p. 403 [27 March 1848]; *TA*, p. 108.
222　*CD*, p. 383 [1848].
223　*UD*, pp. 326–7.
224　*JP*, vol. 4, p. 146 [1848].
225　*WL*, p. 85.

that such people ultimately squander their opportunities to become more fully human and to embrace true freedom through obedient submission to God.[226]

Based on the inexorable limitations of sensate power, a person cannot exercise autonomy without elevating herself above other individuals, without infringing upon the personhood of those around her and relegating them to abstraction—"the public." Kierkegaard once wrote, "The tyrant was egotistically the individual who inhumanly made the others into 'the masses,' and ruled over the masses ... ."[227] He believed that the social elite are particularly susceptible to this pernicious posturing: "[T]his distinguished corruption teaches the man of distinction that he exists only for distinguished men, that he shall live only in their social circle, that he must not exist for other men, just as they must not exist for him."[228] Although a tyrant may do this overtly, even the lowliest slave may participate in the negation of the other: "The inhumanness and unChristianness of this does not consist in the manner in which it is done but in wanting to deny one's relationship in the human race with all men, with absolutely every man."[229]

In response, Kierkegaard dismissed all attempts to become a self on one's own terms—or avoid doing so on God's terms—as profoundly rebellious and futile, whether by masters elevating themselves above the masses or by slaves "losing themselves" in the crowd.[230] In the throes of human cunning, even disempowerment can serve as a powerful distinction for excusing oneself from basic existential responsibilities owed to God and neighbor.[231]

The third reason why the distinction between master power and slave power is obscured in Kierkegaard's writing is that both remain "enslaved to the outcome."[232] The most self-assured master is precariously enslaved to the uncontrollable vicissitudes of fortune, external successes, and the submission—whether voluntary or coerced—of the masses over which he rules.[233] Even the mightiest monarch remains a slave to circumstance,[234] a pawn of power, a concierge to soul-eroding comparison with "the others."[235] For this reason, Kierkegaard recalled Solon's wisdom that a person can only be said to have enjoyed a happy life after he has

---

[226] Ibid., p. 253.

[227] *JK*, p. 151 [1848].

[228] *WL*, p. 85.

[229] Ibid., p. 84.

[230] Ibid., p. 93.

[231] Ibid., pp. 128–9.

[232] *CUP*, vol. 1, p. 398.

[233] *WA*, p. 215 [1848]; *BA*, p. 157.

[234] *CUP*, vol. 1, p. 137.

[235] See *SD*, p. 111: "[A] master who is a self directly before slaves, indeed really ... is not a self—for in both cases there is no standard for measurement." This standard can only be supplied by God, "that directly in the face of which it is a self."

died and is safe from temporal mutability.[236] Moreover, in *Christian Discourses*, Kierkegaard compared the reliance upon sensate power, honor, and prestige to Caesar's "Praetorian guard": once employed, ostensibly to serve some higher cause, it quickly becomes the controlling cause—the preservation of its own domain against all threats—and shackles him whom it professes to serve.[237] Any vestige of legacy or public recognition is subsequently illusory:

> [L]ike the world's contempt, the world's honour is a vortex, a play of confused forces, a deceptive element in the divisiveness, an illusion, as when a swarm of insects in the distance seems to the eye like one body, an illusion, as when the noise of a crowd in the distance seems to the ear like one voice.[238]

In addition to the masters' tenuous hold on power over the masses, Kierkegaard also recognized that individuals can undermine the authority of even the most ruthless dictator with the bitter blade of passive resistance: "But a disguise of hidden exasperation and a remote intimation of painful dejection will transform the power and glory and eminence into a plague for the mighty, the honoured, the eminent, who nevertheless cannot find anything specific to complain about."[239] The Danish theologian knew that victimhood can paradoxically become a position of power, particularly since a heavy-handed response by persons in authority inadvertently legitimizes the "weak" as a threat, heaping further ridicule and antipathy upon those in power.[240] Hence, Kierkegaard contended that there is strength behind sensate "weakness" and weakness behind every exertion of sensate "strength."[241]

The fourth reason for the obfuscation of "master" versus "slave" power distinctions in Kierkegaard's thought is that all humans, regardless of position and power, possess the most terrible power of all—the ability to reject God. For this reason, no one is truly powerless.[242] As Anti-Climacus explained, "The powerful can cruelly have a person be tortured—but the weak can cruelly make it impossible for love to help them, alas the only thing for which love asked and so ardently."[243] This represents "true" if tragic power for Kierkegaard, the power to withhold one's self from the Ground of All Being and thereby lose one's immortal soul. Hence, he dismissed sensate authority and privilege as mere pretence. The actor

---

[236]   *WL*, p. 46; *CD*, p. 255. Hence, only the dead possess true strength, "the strength of unchangeableness" (*WL*, p. 327).

[237]   *CD*, p. 48.

[238]   *UD*, p. 28.

[239]   *WL*, p. 90.

[240]   *TA*, p. 108; *SW*, p. 213.

[241]   *JK*, p. 155 [1849]. See also *SW*, p. 51.

[242]   *CD*, p. 128.

[243]   *PC*, p. 77. This resonates with Christ's impassioned plea over Jerusalem in Luke 13:34. Masters and slaves also wield the ominous power of being able to compound transgressive damage by willingly withholding forgiveness (*WL*, p. 275).

who plays a king or the child pretending to be emperor becomes ludicrous and pathetic when he expects obeisance in real life "[b]ecause the play and the child's game are a nonreality. But neither is it reality, in the Christian sense, to be eminent in actuality; the real is the eternal, the essentially Christian."[244] Subsequently, Kierkegaard criticized sensate power whether wielded by master or slave:

> What else is worldly power but dependence; what slave in chains was as unfree as a tyrant! No, the worldly is not one thing; multifarious as it is, in life it is changed into its opposite, in death into nothing, in eternity, into a curse upon the person who has willed this one thing.[245]

In short, master power *per se* is, therefore, a myth since the masters are never truly powerful. Slave power is, likewise, a myth since the slaves are never truly powerless.

Striving for Service: Spiritual Authority

Defining spiritual authority

Whereas sensate authority is bound to the temporal sphere both in its foundation and its goals, Kierkegaard posited that spiritual authority is conjoined with the eternal as both its basis and its *telos* in the cause of serving truth.[246] Although Kierkegaard insisted that both types of authority are necessary, provided that they respect their mutual boundaries, spiritual authority is "superior," for it does not issue from the realm of temporality but from God,[247] and is not dependent upon the talent, lineage, or intellect of the recipient. Climacus distinguished between two categories of truth: temporal truths, which require talent to expose and express; and spiritual truths, which can only be disclosed by authority from God.[248] As H.H. contended,

---

[244]   *CD*, p. 53. Compare with Pascal, p. 217: "If they [Plato and Aristotle] wrote about politics it was as if to lay down rules for a madhouse. And if they pretended to treat it as something really important it was because they knew that the madmen they were talking to believed themselves to be kings and emperors."

[245]   *UD*, pp. 29–30.

[246]   *JP*, vol. 1, p. 73 [1847]. On the impotence of power without purpose, see *EUD*, p. 91. Stephen Dunning identifies five features of "divine authority": transcendence, paradoxicality, heterogeneity, the tendency towards offence, and the tendency towards reduplication in the apostle's life ("Who Sets the Task? Kierkegaard on Authority," in George B. Connell and C. Stephen Evans [eds], *Foundations of Kierkegaard's Vision of Community: Religion, Ethics, and Politics in Kierkegaard* [New Jersey and London, 1998], p. 23).

[247]   *JP*, vol. 1, p. 74 [1847]. See also ibid., vol. 4, p. 128 [23 December 1834]: "A great man is great simply because he is a chosen instrument in the hands of God."

[248]   *PF*, p. 152.

Authority, however, is something that remains unchanged, something that one cannot acquire by having perfectly understood the doctrine. *Authority is a specific quality that enters from somewhere else and qualitatively asserts itself precisely when the content of the statement or the act is made a matter of indifference esthetically.*[249]

For this reason, spiritual authority has no need for eloquence, brute force, or human genius. As soon as an individual seeks to embellish or rationalize an authoritative statement, that authority is ineluctably contested.[250] The only proper response, for Kierkegaard, is immediate compliance: "I should show him [a prophet] religious submission, ... I should imprison my judgment in obedience under his divine authority."[251] Although spiritual authority is not qualitatively inferior to sensate authority, the latter may ironically obstruct an individual's receptivity to the former.[252] As the individual's identity is "transplanted" from the soils of sinful autonomy to the ground of divine love, "we become lesser while God becomes greater in our lives."[253] Until that transformation has taken place via individual encounter with God, sensate authority will invariably misinterpret divine authority and sinful individuals will confuse life for death.[254] Hence, Johannes de silentio stated, "Abraham was the greatest of all, great by that power whose strength is powerlessness, great by that wisdom whose secret is foolishness, great by that hope whose form is madness, great by that love that is hatred to oneself."[255]

Kierkegaard drew upon the biblical motifs of stewardship and service to define this authority which does not rightfully belong to or proceed from human sources.[256] Although humankind is intended to be "the ruler of creation,"[257] he

---

[249]   *WA*, p. 98.

[250]   Ibid., p. 101.

[251]   *BA*, p. 26. See *JP*, vol. 2, p. 587 [1847]: "[T]he very first beginning of deliberation about it is deflection, rebellion." See also *WA*, p. 24; *BA*, p. 22; *JP*, vol. 4, p. 459 [1851].

[252]   *FS*, p. 77. Subsequently, Kierkegaard believed that the Holy Spirit actively strips individuals of anthropocentric power "in order to become the power in us" (ibid., p. 87).

[253]   See *CUP*, vol. 1, p. 55: "[A]n eternal happiness is specifically rooted in the subjective individual's diminishing self-esteem acquired through the utmost exertion." See also *JP*, vol. 3, p. 550 [14 May 1839]: "God in heaven, let me rightly feel my nothingness, not to despair over it, but all the more intensely to feel the greatness of your goodness." For Kierkegaard's sheer amazement that the Holy Spirit can reside in "infinitely inferior," "self-deceptive" individuals, see ibid., p. 572 [1850].

[254]   In an 1854 journal entry, he identified "this fundamental idea in Christianity, that which makes it what it is: transformation of the will" (ibid., vol. 4, p. 551 [1854]).

[255]   *FT*, pp. 16–17. See also *WL*, p. 144.

[256]   *EUD*, p. 148.

[257]   Ibid., p. 84.

asserted, "[H]e is not the lord in such a way that he is not also a servant ... ."[258] Spiritual authority is also linked with the theme of descending in order to ascend, which reaches its paradoxical apex in the doctrine of the Incarnation, and Christ's death and resurrection.[259] Contrary to corrupted sensate authority, which seeks to rule by usurping God's position, spiritual authority seeks to rule by "serving" God, in the sense of "obedience to" rather than "facilitating the cause of."[260]

Because the person invested with spiritual authority represents the interests of God, not humankind, she does not seek the approval of her audience.[261] In stark contrast to sensate authority, which is measurable by temporal accomplishments and tangible displays of power, Kierkegaard espoused a liberation from dependence upon external effects: "What, then, is true human greatness? Sure it is greatness of heart. We do not by rights say that someone is great who has much power and dominion ... . [T]he more profound person does not allow himself to be disturbed by externality."[262] This does not preclude a "great man" from exerting a great influence in the world. However, "[T]his would not occupy him at all, because he would know that the external is not in his power and therefore means nothing either *pro* or *contra*."[263] For this reason, Kierkegaard stated that the religious life view

> does not overlook suffering, does not rashly hope in the world, but religiously wants success and failure to signify equally much, that is, equally little, and does not want the religious to have significance by way of or along with something else, but wants it to have absolute meaning in itself.[264]

For those who demand concrete proof of spiritual authority, "no sign will be given."[265] By rejecting the "crutches" of temporal appearances and results, spiritual authority demonstrates both its independence from temporal limitation and its heterogeneous origins, according to Kierkegaard:

---

[258] Ibid., p. 85.

[259] For example, Johannes explained how, by subordinating himself to the universal domain of ethics, the single individual may be raised above it (*FT*, p. 56).

[260] *JK*, p. 249 [1854]. For an interesting parallel, see Michel Foucault's notion of "pastoral power" in *Religion and Culture by Michel Foucault*, ed. Jeremy Carrette (Manchester, 1999), pp. 122–3.

[261] He wrote that "if you fast out of fear of men, it is precisely not Christianity, and if men seek to browbeat you to give up fasting, then Christianity can mean fasting" (*JP*, vol. 2, p. 336 [1854]).

[262] *CD*, p. 291.

[263] *CUP*, vol. 1, pp. 135–6.

[264] *TA*, p. 13.

[265] Climacus alluded to Matthew 16:4 in *CUP*, vol. 1, p. 414.

> Do you know, my reader, any stronger expression for superiority than this, that
> the superior one also has the appearance of being the weaker? *The stronger* who
> looks like the stronger sets a standard for his superiority; but he who, although
> superior, appears as the weaker negates standards and comparisons—that is, he
> is infinitely superior.[266]

Such freedom from results does not issue from a humanly generated stoicism or
will-to-passivity. Rather, it is rooted in the utter incontestability of divine power:
"For one all-powerful cannot be a co-worker with you, a human being, without its
signifying that you are able to do nothing at all; and on the other side, if he is your
support, you are able to do everything."[267] Subsequently, Kierkegaard posited,
"What a man achieves or does not achieve is not within his power. He is not the
One who shall steer the world; he has one and only one thing to do—to obey."[268]
By her liberation from slavery to the outcome through faith in God's ultimate
victory, the Christian has thus "conquered the changeable."[269]

Kierkegaard insisted that freedom from basing one's worth and authority upon
external effects can only come from a transcendent source. Nor can an individual
break free from the sinful human autonomy in which she is paradoxically
enslaved:

> [A]nd is it not doubt's stratagem to make a person believe that he by himself can
> overcome himself, as if he were able to perform the marvel unheard of in heaven
> or on earth or under the earth—that something that is in conflict with itself can
> in this conflict be stronger than itself![270]

Because sin is a matter of rebellion rather than ignorance, Kierkegaard contended,
"Those with authority, therefore, always address themselves to the conscience,
not to understanding, intelligence, profundity—to the human being, not to the
professor."[271] People possessing spiritual authority thus transfix the listener like

---

[266]   *WL*, p. 228.

[267]   Ibid., p. 333. See also *EUD*, p. 307: "[T]he highest is this: that a person is fully
convinced that he himself is capable of nothing, nothing at all. What rare dominion … ."

[268]   *WL*, p. 93. For this reason, he considered prayer to be "[t]he weapon of the
powerless" (*EUD*, p. 311). For biblical parallels on freedom from temporal results, see
Judges 7:7, II Chronicles 20:17, Ephesians 6:13. Kierkegaard made specific reference to
Romans 8:37 (*BA*, p. 232 [October 1848]) and Psalm 103:15–16 (*CUP*, vol. 1, p. 135) in
this regard.

[269]   *EUD*, p. 19. See also *JP*, vol. 3, p. 553 [1840–41] and *CI*, p. 319.

[270]   *EUD*, p. 128.

[271]   *JP*, vol. 1, p. 73 [1847]. David Aiken contends, "This Authority is concrete
and personal insofar as it is grounded in the God-Man and his appointed witnesses, the
apostles; but it is also objective insofar as these Sources proclaim and enact a teaching
whose content stands over against both the private judgment of the theoretical thinker and

Coleridge's "ancient mariner": "[D]ivine authority … is like the single eye; it constrains the person addressed to see who is talking with him and then fastens its piercing look on him and says with this glance, 'It is you to whom this is said.'"[272] However, Anti-Climacus dourly lamented the loss of such authority in Christendom:

> There was a time when it [Christianity], with divine authority, exercised dominion over people, when it addressed each individual briefly, tersely, commanding authoritatively with "*You shall*"; when it shocked every individual with a rigorousness that hitherto was never known: eternal punishment. This rigorousness helped; in fear and trembling before the inescapable hereafter, the Christian was able to disdain all the dangers and sufferings of this life as child's play and a half-hour prank … .[273]

According to Kierkegaard, all Christians are to be characterized by "righteousness," which he defined as the unwavering commitment to "seek first God's kingdom": "Neither is righteousness power and dominion, because no human being stands so high that he is higher than righteousness, so high that he would need to lay down his crown in order to have the opportunity to practice righteousness."[274] Instead, he argued, "It is said that by learning to obey one learns to rule … ."[275] Christians must always oppose the universal rebellion of fallen humankind, but

> not, of course, with shouts and conceited importance, not by domineering and wanting to force others to obey God, but by unconditionally obeying as an individual, by unconditionally holding fast to the God-relationship and the God-demand and thereby expressing for his part that God exists and is the only master … .[276]

The church's reliance upon any method of sensate authority, whether his majesty's prisons or reason's "proofs," instantly transforms Christianity into precisely its opposite—an earthly kingdom.[277]

---

the evanescent spirit of the age to which that judgment is beholden" ("The Decline from Authority: Kierkegaard on Intellectual Sin," *International Philosophical Quarterly*, 33/1 [1993]: 28).

[272]   *WL*, p. 104.

[273]   *PC*, p. 229.

[274]   *UD*, pp. 210–11.

[275]   *WA*, p. 24.

[276]   *WL*, pp. 121–2.

[277]   *JP*, vol. 1, p. 77 [1850]: "This is the way Christianity came into the world; it was substantiated by authority, its divine authority; consequently the authority is higher. Now for

In contrast to conventional apologetics, Anti-Climacus contended that the model for the church is not that of a "defence attorney" but a "lover":

> A believer, after all, is someone in love; indeed, when it comes to ardor, the most infatuated of lovers is as a stripling compared with a believer … . [D]on't you think he would find it disgusting to speak in such a way as to offer three reasons for concluding that there was after all something to being in love—more or less as when the pastor gives three reasons for concluding that it pays to pray, as though the price of prayer has fallen so low that three reasons were needed to help give it some crumb of esteem?[278]

Accordingly, a proper apologetics must always emphasize Christianity's heterogeneity with human development and history: "Every defence of Christianity that understands what it wants must do the very opposite and with all its might and with a qualitative dialectic assert the *improbability* of Christianity."[279] Moreover, the would-be apologist should wisely heed the words of Johann G. Hamann: "There is doubt that must be dismissed with no reasons or replies but simply with a Bah!"[280] Given the apparently superior nature of spiritual authority, it is necessary to probe further Kierkegaard's understanding of its paradoxical loss through an unholy reliance upon sensate defences.

Benevolent blasphemy: the "apologetic" compromise
One of the ultimate indignations for the Christian faith, according to Kierkegaard, is the arrogance of individuals who either seek to employ spiritual authority for temporal means, thus rendering the infinite "finite,"[281] or endeavor to defend spiritual authority by use of sensate authority, whether by imperial edict or human reasoning. In both cases, the faith is "secularized," its heterogeneity compromised by a quantifiable commensurability with the temporal order, its transcendence inexorably supplanted by a religiousness of immanence or worse. Kierkegaard once sardonically remarked that Christianity is the only religion in world history which has been destroyed precisely by "flourishing."[282] Because the subject of employing spiritual authority as a means to temporal gain has already been explored,[283] the use of temporal authority to "protect" spiritual authority will now be examined.

---

a long time the relationship has been reversed: men seek on rational grounds to demonstrate, to substantiate the authority. And yet this is supposed to be the same religion."

[278]   *SD*, p. 135.

[279]   *BA*, p. 40. See also *SW*, p. 662 [1850].

[280]   *SW*, p. 695, n. 9.

[281]   *TM*, p. 408 [1850]. On the cheapening of grace, see ibid., p. 151; *JP*, vol. 3, p. 335 [1854]; *PV*, p. 16; *FS*, p. 16.

[282]   *TM*, p. 160.

[283]   See this chapter, "Positions of Sensate Authority."

Kierkegaard's primary accusation against the Danish state church was that, by endeavoring to bolster faith with reason and material rewards, misguided ecclesiastical leaders had conflated God's rule with that of a human ruler who consolidates power by conferring favors upon his subjects.[284] In addition, the church had rendered faith commensurate with human reason in order to justify Christian belief to non-Christians.[285] Hence, he sarcastically charged, "They are embarrassed by obeying God because he is God; and so they obey him— because he is a very great genius, perhaps almost the greatest, greater even than Hegel."[286] Kierkegaard regarded such rationalization as existential treason against God, a form of benevolent blasphemy in which one appears to be "doing God a favour," thus reducing God to a ludicrous dependence upon the human defender. Kierkegaard eviscerated such megalomaniac presumption whereby "God in heaven has to sit and wait for the decision on his fate, whether he exists, and finally he comes into existence with the help of a few demonstrations ... ."[287] Ironically, the most fervent defender unwittingly joins forces with the abject atheist's aim "to make *Christianity probable*"; that is, to "demythologize" any supernatural claims and render it subject to human definitions of temporal plausibility.[288] For this reason Anti-Climacus once denounced apologetics as the "second betrayal of Christ":

[H]ow extraordinarily stupid it is to defend Christianity, how little knowledge of humanity it betrays, how it connives if only unconsciously with offence by making Christianity out to be some miserable object that in the end must be rescued by a defence. It is therefore certain and true that the person who first thought of defending Christianity in Christendom is *de facto* a Judas No. 2; he too betrays with a kiss, except his treason is that of stupidity. To defend something is always to discredit it.[289]

Moreover, this apologetic maneuver tacitly implies that certain Christians or offices are more "valuable" to God than others,[290] and the spiritual authority of

---

[284]   *TM*, pp. 44, 321, 556 [1855].

[285]   *JP*, vol. 4, pp. 463–4 [1850]: "Men simply refuse to be satisfied with acknowledging the absurd; so they substitute the most profound profundity and the most sublime sublimity ... ."

[286]   Ibid., vol. 1, p. 74 [1847].

[287]   *EUD*, p. 242.

[288]   *BA*, p. 39.

[289]   *SD*, p. 119. Anti-Climacus' sentiment is a reflection of Pascal: "The extreme sin is to defend it [truth]" (p. 339). Climacus posited that the only way to account properly for paradox was to highlight its paradoxicality—not attempt to resolve it (*CUP*, vol. 1, p. 219).

[290]   *TM*, p. 43; *CD*, p. 86; *CUP*, vol. 1, p. 78.

the apostle is surreptitiously replaced by the sensate genius of the commentator.[291] Hence, Kierkegaard lashed out vehemently against the Danish clergy: "You rag of velvet, did Christianity come into the world in order to have help from human beings, or in order to help them … ."[292]

Kierkegaard once compared the sheer preposterousness of offering God assistance to "a child's giving his parents a present, purchased, however, with what the child has received from his parents."[293] However, the truly monumental achievement of human cunning is to transfer the nexus of faith from the realm of the personal/existential to the abstract/intellectual, whereby obedience becomes contingent upon sensate proofs and credentials. Instead, Kierkegaard contended,

> It is claimed that arguments against Christianity arise out of doubt. This is a total misunderstanding. The arguments against Christianity arise out of insubordination, reluctance to obey, mutiny against all authority. Therefore, until now the battle against objections has been shadowboxing, because it has been intellectual combat with doubt instead of being ethical combat against mutiny.[294]

Kierkegaard strongly believed that no reliance upon sensate authority will benefit the Christian cause.

Effects of Spiritual Authority

Suffering and persecution

In stark contrast to those wielding sensate authority, bearers of spiritual authority do not receive wealth, power, and honor, but rather pain, disdain, and rejection: "In this mediocre, wretched, sinful, evil, ungodly world the truth must suffer—this is Christianity's doctrine … ."[295] Climacus once asserted that "religious existence is suffering, and not as a transient element but as a continual accompaniment."[296] For the Christian, persecution is an unavoidable fact of life in a world of sinful autonomy and "grandiloquent illusions"[297] which are fundamentally threatened

---

[291]   *BA*, p. 5.

[292]   *TM*, p. 44. See also *UD*, p. 87.

[293]   *TM*, p. 392 [1847].

[294]   *PF*, p. 332, n. 30. For obedience as a precursor to Christian understanding and not vice versa, see *WA*, p. 24.

[295]   *TM*, p. 321. See also *JP*, vol. 4, p. 155 [1848]; *UD*, p. 99; *CUP*, vol. 1, p. 402.

[296]   Ibid., p. 288.

[297]   *CD*, p. 385 [20 November 1847]. Anti-Climacus carefully delineated between "authentic Christian suffering" and "ordinary human suffering": "What is decisive in Christian suffering is voluntariness and *the possibility of offense for the one who suffers*" (*PC*, p. 109). He earlier asserted that non-Christians are ignorant of what "genuine" suffering entails [that is, separation from God] (*SD*, p. 38). Kierkegaard concurred in *CD*, p. 102: "All temporality's suffering is a mirage … ."

by Christian truths. Regarding the non-Christian response to Christian witness, Kierkegaard contended, "Even if you say nothing, he notices, you may be sure, that your life contains, if it is truly related to God's demand, an admonition, a demand on him—it is this which he wants to do away with."[298] Subsequently, the obvious and inexorable value differences between Christians and non-Christians seldom elicit mutual tolerance: "[H]ow could the living, who cling with all their souls to this life and all that belongs to it, calmly put up with the presence of someone who has died."[299]

Kierkegaard once declared that persecution is not a precursor to victory but rather its result: "*Christianly* one has in advance already been more than victorious. Therefore one does not suffer in order to be victorious, but instead because one has been victorious … ."[300] Plainly, for Kierkegaard there is no divine "witness protection program": "[P]eople look on the world's opposition as an accidental relationship to Christianity rather than as an essential relationship."[301] Suffering unjust treatment in a world hostile to God is such an intrinsic aspect of the Christian life that it represents a rare exception to Kierkegaard's cardinal principle of incommensurability between spiritual inwardness and externalities: "[T]he degree of one's faith is demonstrated only by the degree of one's willingness to suffer for one's faith."[302] He even stated that, whereas suffering on behalf of righteousness constitutes a believer's "privilege," "it is his [God's] disfavor which allows these rich and powerful ones etc. to become more rich and powerful."[303]

Instead of undermining spiritual authority, external opposition inadvertently underscores it, according to Kierkegaard:

> To transform hardships into a witness for the truth of a teaching, to transform disgrace into glory for oneself and for the believing congregation, to transform the lost cause into a matter of honor that has all the inspiring force of a witness—is this not like making the cripples walk and the mute speak![304]

---

[298]   *WL*, p. 130.

[299]   *FS*, p. 116. For accusations of the world's "jealousy" over the believer's love for God, see *WL*, p. 125.

[300]   *BA*, p. 233 [October 1848].

[301]   *WL*, p. 187. See also *PC*, p. 87; *BA*, p. 148.

[302]   *TM*, p. 324. See also *PC*, p. 173; *JP*, vol. 4, p. 548 [1850]. For suffering as "road signs" that the Christian is on the "straight and narrow," see *UD*, pp. 227, 297; *BA*, p. 154; *CUP*, vol. 1, p. 507.

[303]   *JP*, vol. 4, p. 408 [1852].

[304]   *EUD*, p. 83. See also *WA*, p. 215 [1848]; *SW*, p. 454. Ironically, both Pascal and Feuerbach agreed that "[s]uffering is a Christian's natural condition" (ibid., p. 460).

Furthermore, persecution unites the believer contemporaneously with Christ and the prophets of old, and "translates" Calvary into the present.[305]

Suffering injustice, thus, serves both apologetic and evangelistic purposes. Kierkegaard hoped that the illusions of some non-Christians might be jarred by witnessing such abject injustice.[306] He once paradoxically mused: "Truly Christianity does not want to force anyone. No, but Christianity wants its followers, suffering, to force the world to become Christian."[307] The greatest endorsement of spiritual authority is martyrdom for the Gospel, which not only conveys the conviction of the witness,[308] but also highlights both the impotence of sensate authority in eradicating belief[309] as well as the wickedness of society.[310] Due to its original refusal to compromise in the face of death, "Christianity became power, power, became the power that was able to transform the world."[311] Hence, Kierkegaard triumphantly proclaimed, "In suffering, bold confidence is able to take power from the world and has the power to change scorn into honor, victory into downfall!"[312] As Nicoletti poignantly summarizes, "[R]eligion must relate itself inversely to politics, not through a direct superiority but through a 'suffering superiority.'"[313]

True equality: the power of love

In addition to engendering persecution, which both strengthens the believer and ultimately weakens the opposing powers, spiritual authority reflects the universal equality of everyone in the sight of God. Because external threats merely emphasize the heterogeneity of spiritual authority, and spiritual authority is freely available to all who follow Christ, the only person who can deny anyone from receiving spiritual authority is the person herself.[314] Kierkegaard emphasized that God judges individuals on the basis of who they become, not on biology or beginnings,[315] and nobody is denied the possibility of living in love, "the strongest

---

[305]   Kierkegaard described true contemporaneity as "to make present the life of the departed glorious one in such a way that you thereby would come to suffer as you would have suffered in contemporaneity if you had acknowledged a prophet to be a prophet" (*TM*, p. 289). See also *PC*, p. 171.

[306]   *TM*, p. 208; *BA*, p. 234 [1848].

[307]   *JP*, vol. I, p. 243 [1851].

[308]   *PV*, p. 51.

[309]   *WA*, p. 74. Kierkegaard even [playfully?] mused over the possibility of his own martyrdom for disturbing the "false peace" of Christendom (*CD*, p. 187).

[310]   *TC*, p. 203.

[311]   *FS*, p. 129.

[312]   *UD*, p. 331. This is another example of Christian revaluation via redemption whereby, "the language a whole race speaks in unanimous agreement is still turned upside down ..." (ibid., p. 333).

[313]   Nicoletti, p. 191.

[314]   *UD*, p. 123. See also *SW*, p. 443; *TA*, pp. 62–3; *EUD*, p. 335.

[315]   *CD*, p. 26.

power in a man."[316] Moreover, the Danish thinker maintained that true personal distinction entails excelling at something which everyone can theoretically do, rather than distinguishing oneself in a proficiency in which few can participate. Thus, he exclaimed, "Is it really so glorious to become *the* superior person no one else can become; is it not disconsolate instead!"[317]

In proclaiming spiritual egalitarianism, Kierkegaard was remaining true to his Protestant heritage. Luther himself criticized the potential abuses and misunderstanding of an artificial dichotomy:

> It has been devised that the Pope, bishops, priests and monks are called the spiritual estate; princes, lords, artificers and peasants are the temporal estate. This is an artful lie and hypocritical device, but let no one be made afraid by it, and for this reason: that all Christians are truly of the spiritual estate, and there is no difference among them, save of office alone.[318]

Unlike sensate power, talents, and knowledge, which elevate a person above the others, Kierkegaard claimed, "Love is not an exclusive characteristic, but it is a characteristic by which or in virtue of which you exist for others."[319] In light of Christ's commandment to "love your neighbour," Kierkegaard regarded love as the great equalizer in the temporal world.[320] To transform one's enemy into one's friend and "vanquish" them with love, Kierkegaard argued, is precisely what St. Paul meant by "more than conquering."[321] This radical love does not have its source in immanence; rather,"[K]inship of all men is secured by every individual's equal kinship with and relationship to God in Christ."[322]

Because everyone has an equal opportunity for actualizing "the possibility of the good ... at every moment,"[323] Kierkegaard condemned the withdrawal of hope for another person's eternal well-being as tantamount to "spiritual murder."[324] However, he insisted that the neighbor cannot even be acknowledged prior to the

---

[316]   *WL*, p. 160.

[317]   *UD*, p. 226. See Pascal, p. 75: "[T]he true good must be such that it may be possessed by all men at once without diminution or envy, and that no one should be able to lose it against his will."

[318]   Martin Luther, *Documents of Modern History*, ed. E.G. Rupp and Benjamin Drewery (London, 1979), p. 43.

[319]   *WL*, p. 211.

[320]   *PV*, p. 111.

[321]   *UD*, p. 303.

[322]   *WL*, pp. 80, 158; *UD*, p. 85.

[323]   *WL*, p. 239.

[324]   This explains his fascinating exegesis of Matthew 5:21–2, where Jesus criticizes hatred of one's brother: "Even if one does not take murder upon his conscience, he nevertheless gives up the hated one as hopeless and consequently takes possibility away from him. But does this not mean to kill him spiritually?" (ibid., p. 240).

life-transforming deflation of an individual's sinful autonomy: "It is only in dying to the joys and happiness of the world in self-denial that the 'neighbour' comes into existence."[325] As a "spiritual" possession, love is an eternally renewable, eternally renewing resource.[326] Because of the inexhaustible reservoir of divine love, he maintained,

> Already sin feels its powerlessness; it cannot withstand love any longer; it wants to tear itself away; then it insults love as painfully as possible, because it thinks that even love cannot forgive more than seven times. But see! Love could forgive seventy times seven times, and sin grew weary of occasioning forgiveness more quickly than love grew weary of forgiving.[327]

For Kierkegaard, then, Christian love can never be defeated—it can only be fled.

Positions of Spiritual Authority

The apostle
Within the parameters of spiritual authority, Kierkegaard recognized two primary positions of spiritual authority: the apostle and the truth-witness. Because of his insistence upon Christianity's heterogeneity with the sensate world and its intrinsic power hierarchies, he believed that it is categorically erroneous to distinguish oneself as an "extraordinary Christian,"[328] for one cannot possess faith "in an *extraordinary* degree, since the ordinary degree is the highest."[329] Because everyone is spiritually equal before God, nobody can introduce qualitative distinctions between followers of Christ. However, throughout history God has freely chosen to communicate Godself directly to specific individuals whereby "God empowers a particular human being, makes him his instrument."[330] Kierkegaard adopted the New Testament designation, "apostle," to describe such individuals.

---

[325]   Ibid., pp. 359–60, n. 17.

[326]   *CD*, p. 116. See also *EUD*, p. 143 on "the divine equality that opens the soul to the perfect and blinds the sensate eye to the difference, the divine equality that like a fire burns ever more intensely in the difference without, however, humanly speaking, consuming it."

[327]   Ibid., p. 64. See also *SW*, p. 384; *EUD*, p. 380.

[328]   *TM*, p. 421 [1852]. Kierkegaard could be inconsistent on this point. See *BA*, p. 150, where he distinguished the "ordinary" individual from the "extraordinary" through whom God "brings a new point of departure for the established order," and *PV*, p. 120, where he argued against his own status as "a truth-witness in the stricter sense."

[329]   *WL*, p. 48.

[330]   *TM*, p. 424 [1853].

The pseudonym H.H. defined an apostle as "a man who is called and appointed by God and sent by him on a mission."[331] Kierkegaard did not relegate the apostolic office to the canonical past:

> In our age, just as in every previous one, there can indeed be true extraordinaries appointed by God. But the world's changes will still have a great influence on the outer appearance, even though the essence remains the same. Accordingly, for example, it would be suspicious if in our time a prophet appeared who resembled one of the ancient ones right down to the beard.[332]

In contrast to the genius or religious poet, who relies on personal ability to present her message, the only "prerequisite" for the apostle is "a noble and pure simplicity ... which is the condition for being the instrument of the Holy Spirit."[333] Hence, anyone can potentially be an apostle, if chosen by God.[334] H.H. insisted that it is not possible to attribute the apostle's message to the natural development of human thought or history:

> The apostle has something paradoxically new to bring, the newness of which, just because it is essentially paradoxical and not an anticipation pertaining to the development of the human race, continually remains, just as an apostle remains for all eternity an apostle, and no immanence of eternity places him essentially on the same line with all human beings, since essentially he is paradoxically different.[335]

Unsurprisingly, the apostle seeks no support from either sensate authority or temporal "proofs." Instead, H.H. contended that the apostle possesses "no other evidence than his own statement, and at most his willingness to suffer everything joyfully for the sake of that statement."[336] For this reason, the apostle never seeks to emulate sensate leadership, but concerns himself primarily with his personal

---

[331]   *WA*, p. 95. Apostles were by no means faultless. See *TM*, pp. 605–6 [23 August 1855]; 457 [1854].

[332]   *BA*, p. 25. It is highly significant that Kierkegaard never upbraided Rev. A.P. Adler for claiming to have received a personal revelation. Instead, he criticized him for obfuscating the heterogeneous boundaries between transcendence and immanence by announcing that his "revelation" needed further revision—a mark of human agency.

[333]   *TM*, p. 464 [1854]. This accounts for his derision of pulpit "theatrics" (*WA*, p. 104), criticism directed specifically at Danish pastor and reformer Nicolai F.S. Grundtvig (*BA*, p. 185). For his deprecation of "hell-fire" evangelism as "aesthetic," see *CD*, p. 192.

[334]   See *WL*, p. 126: "[T]he less promising the apostle was as a man the greater was the impression of divine authority granted to him ... ."

[335]   *WA*, p. 94.

[336]   Ibid., p. 105. See also *BA*, p. 154.

relationship with God.[337] Accordingly, the apostle must faithfully convey his message without taking responsibility for any results, proclaiming

> [I]t is God himself or the Lord Jesus Christ who is speaking, and you must not become involved presumptuously in criticizing the form. I cannot, I dare not compel you to obey, but through the relationship of your conscience to God, I make you eternally responsible for your relationship to this doctrine by my having proclaimed it as revealed to me and therefore by having proclaimed it with divine authority.[338]

Although he believed that he was supplying a vital corrective for the Danish church, Kierkegaard assiduously denied any personal claims of apostleship: "I am no apostle or the like; I am a poetical-dialectical genius, personally and religiously a penitent."[339] He further elaborated,

> I do not have an immediate God-relationship to appeal to, nor do I dare to say that it is God who directly contributes the thoughts to me, but that my relationship to God is a relationship of reflection, inwardness in reflection, since reflection is the predominant quality of my individuality … .[340]

Whereas the apostle's authority stems directly from God regardless of any natural talents he possesses,[341] Kierkegaard's role as church "auditor" was based on "ordinary" intellectual prowess.[342] Subsequently, Kierkegaard could hone his

---

[337] *UD*, p. 334; *BA*, p. 187; *EUD*, p. 330. Climacus asserted that the apostle is "a solitary man" who does not even consult other apostles on what he should do (*CUP*, vol. 1, p. 57). Because of his under-articulated ecclesiology, Kierkegaard underemphasized the fact that the office of apostle is a gift from God for *building up the church*, and that church unity is a fundamental concern for the apostles in the New Testament, further exposing himself to Bishop Martensen's criticism of "Dr. S. Kierkegaard, whose Christianity is without Church and without history, and who seeks Christ only in the 'desert' and in 'private rooms'" (*TM*, p. 362).

[338] *BA*, p. 177. Because faith is contingent upon authority rather than "having all the facts" of Jesus' life, Climacus famously proclaimed, "Even if the contemporary generation had not left anything behind except these words, 'We have believed that in such and such a year the god appeared in the humble form of a servant, lived and taught among us, and then died'—that is more than enough" (*PF*, p. 104).

[339] *PV*, p. xv. Kierkegaard also claimed to possess "too much imagination and much too much of the poet to dare to be called a truth-witness in the stricter sense" (ibid., p. 120). He was partly motivated to publish explicitly non-religious works to prevent people from making this erroneous assumption, "something I am a very long way from being" (*CD*, p. 418 [1848]).

[340] *PV*, p. 74.

[341] *WA*, p. 95; *BA*, pp. 86–7.

[342] *TM*, pp. 463–4 [1854].

message using human artistry and reason, since even his devotional writings were mere "Christian addresses without divine authority."[343] Only ordained ministers could deliver sermons, which operate "absolutely and entirely through authority, that of Holy Writ and of Christ's apostles."[344]

The Truth-witness

Introduction: the importance of witness

Although they are specifically chosen by God for authoritative communication, those with apostolic authority receive no special spiritual privileges. All human beings—including apostles—are called to lives of "proper" pietism, "in the sense of witnessing for the truth and suffering for it."[345] If Christ received so brutal a reception in life, how could his followers expect better?[346] Kierkegaard's understanding of witness diverged from the traditional Christian emphasis insofar as he questioned the "self-security" of evangelists who allegedly believe, "My soul is safe, so now I can preoccupy myself solely with saving others."[347] Because grace can only be directly communicated by God himself, Johannes de silentio insisted that "[t]he true knight of faith is a witness, never the teacher."[348] The truth-witness is, in no way, to exert power over his neighbors, since his reward is "to be satisfied with ruling over himself instead of over the world, to be satisfied as a pastor to be his own audience, as an author to be his own reader, etc."[349] For Kierkegaard, the greatest Christian testimony is the necessary correlation between word and deed, doctrine and praxis, an unwavering commitment to living the truth regardless of material advantage or disadvantage.[350] Hence, he contended, "[T]he highest a person is capable of is to make an eternal truth true, to make it true that it is true—by doing it, by being oneself the demonstration, by a life that perhaps will also be able to convince others."[351]

According to Kierkegaard, every Christian must share the apostle's personal courage and immunity to prestige: "The qualification *truth-witness* is a very imperious and extremely unsocial qualification and scrupulously allows itself to be joined only with: being nothing otherwise. *Truth-witness* relates to Christianity's

---

[343]   *WL*, p. 11.

[344]   Ibid.

[345]   *JP*, vol. 3, p. 524 [1850].

[346]   *FS*, p. 169; *CD*, p. 172; *UD*, p. 338.

[347]   *TM*, p. 607 [23 August 1855]; *CUP*, vol. 1, p. 454.

[348]   *FT*, p. 80. As Quidam retorted, "[F]ortunate is the person who is so sure of himself that he dares to accept money for teaching" (*SW*, p. 258).

[349]   *TA*, p. 89.

[350]   *PV*, p. 119; *FS*, p. 10.

[351]   *CD*, p. 98. Kierkegaard sought to avoid both cheap grace and works righteousness. Hence, he emphasized, "No, infinite humiliation and grace, and then a striving born of gratitude—this is Christianity" (*FS*, p. xi).

heterogeneity with this world ... ."[352] He acknowledged that there is an element of paradoxical pride in dissociating oneself from others: "Christian humility, as with everything Christian, involves a dialectic, so that its humility presupposes a pride which carries its head higher than proud human humility but which then humbles itself."[353] Although the Christian boasts a superior "power source," her authority is dedicated to uplifting, not overthrowing, those around her. Therefore, Kierkegaard declared, "But all true helping begins with a humbling. The helper must first humble himself under the person he wants to help and thereby understand that to help is not to dominate but to serve ... ."[354] In doing so, the truth-witness demonstrates "abilities" which God has granted to everyone, should they choose to follow his ways.[355]

Methods of bearing witness to the truth are as myriad as the individuals God calls, for Christ "does not unconditionally require of everyone that he must be *the disciple*."[356] In a personal reflection, he once mused, "No, there is not one single person alive who shares my task, and, in my opinion, not one person among these millions shares a task with another ... ."[357] Because every individual must pursue the truth in an individually truthful manner, intellectual Christians are not to denigrate the simplicity of other believers, nor are the "simple" to indulge in anti-intellectual elitism.[358]

Responding to context: task of the truth-witness
In order for the truth-witness to bear humble yet relevant testimony, she must respond carefully to her particular historical and cultural context:

> Above all, generality is not for upbuilding, because one is never built up in general, any more than a house is erected in general. Only when the words are said by the right person in the right situation in the right way, only then has the saying done everything it can to guide the single individual to do honestly what one otherwise is quick enough to do—to refer everything to oneself.[359]

For Kierkegaard, human history is characterized by movements which veer between extremes: "[A]s Luther says, the world continues to be like the drunken peasant who, helped up on one side of the horse, falls off the other side."[360] He contended

---

[352]   *TM*, p. 10. On the heterogeneity between truth-witnessing and "politics," see *PV*, p. 109.

[353]   *JP*, vol. 3, p. 176 [1854].

[354]   *PV*, p. 45.

[355]   *JP*, vol. 6, p. 535 [1854]; *TC*, p. 195.

[356]   *FS*, p. 99. However, all must become disciples (ibid., p. 207). See also *CD*, p. 186.

[357]   *JP*, vol. 6, p. 535 [1854]. In his own life, writing became not only a vocation but also a means of living the truth Christianly, Kierkegaard's "divine worship" (*PV*, p. 73).

[358]   *CUP*, vol. 1, p. 228.

[359]   *EUD*, p. 276.

[360]   *JP*, vol. 3, p. 727 [1846–47].

that during the Romantic period, society sought representative individuals who fully embodied its ideals and conventions, whereas the Enlightenment responded to the excesses of powerful individuals by advocating a "cosmopolitan system" which attempted to unify diverse elements.[361] In turn, Kierkegaard viewed his theological task as supplying a counter-balance or "corrective" to contemporary extremes.[362] In his own time, spiritual security and material gain had partially contributed to redefining "faith" as unthinking intellectual assent to a set of abstractified tenets safely removed from practical daily living, a religion by rote. Because such a "pendulum swing" is particularly pronounced when a culture is preoccupied with "finite objectives," the proper Christian response in nineteenth-century Christendom is that "eternity should be continually introduced counteractingly."[363]

Kierkegaard maintained that Christianity itself is not exempt from the pendulous exaggerations of the prevailing culture and must, therefore, continuously adjust its message accordingly, since "the ensuing corruption always corresponds proportionately to what is introduced."[364] Further imbalances result when previous correctives are transformed into universal, authoritative truths regardless of changing contexts.[365] Hence, he once warned, "Lutheranism is a corrective—but a corrective made into the normative, into the sum total, is *eo ipso* confusing in the following generation (where that for which it was a corrective does not exist … ."[366] For this reason, Kierkegaard emphasized the provisional nature of Christian doctrine to counter this contextual exaggeration.

Kierkegaard's willingness to set aside significant doctrines would have alarmed more conservative dogmatists. For instance, he was perfectly willing to divert attention from the salvific role of Christ's death to focus on Christ as exemplar in order to inflate the bargain prices of "cheap grace" which permeated the indolent church:

> The misfortune of Christianity is clearly that the dialectical factor has been taken from Luther's doctrine of faith so that it has become a hiding-place for sheer paganism and Epicureanism; people forget entirely that Luther was urging the claims of faith against a fantastically exaggerated asceticism.[367]

---

[361]   Ibid., vol. 4, p. 19 [March 1836].

[362]   *JK*, p. 200 [1850].

[363]   *JP*, vol. 6, p. 202 [1855].

[364]   Ibid., p. 531 [1854].

[365]   See, for example, his criticism of Luther's endorsement of marriage: "In this context it is distressing to me that an eminent person like Luther came to such an erroneous position. He should have understood that his marriage was an exceptional act, a corrective …" (ibid., vol. 4, p. 578 [1854]).

[366]   *TM*, p. 452 [1854].

[367]   *JK*, p. 166 [1849]. See also *JP*, vol. 1, p. 325 [1849]; *FT*, p. 121. Kierkegaard believed that Luther had rightly responded to medieval monasticism, which had reduced faith to a series of "petty observances" (*FS*, p. 16). However, the institutionalization of

He once qualified his own exaggerated emphasis on the individual to counteract the corrupted communitarianism of his day: "[E]stablishing a party and forming a school may be something inferior to what I am doing ... and it can be something superior, as with Socrates and Christ. It depends on the situation in which or the stage at which a person does it."[368] Due to the withering religiosity which arose from contemporary biblical studies, he once quipped, "In the main a reformation which sets the Bible aside would have just as much validity now as Luther's breaking with the pope."[369] Near the end of his life, he even criticized Protestantism itself as a necessary correction for a certain time which was then wrongfully institutionalized.[370]

Ultimately, contextual exaggeration is paradoxically the proper response to contextual exaggeration. In contemplating the backlash to his "anti-communitarianism," Kierkegaard responded,

> The person who is to provide the "corrective" must study the weak sides of the established order scrupulously and penetratingly and then one-sidedly present the opposite—with expert one-sidedness .... Nothing is easier for the one providing the corrective than to add the other side; but then it ceases to be precisely the corrective and itself becomes the established order.[371]

He also forewarned future readers not to misjudge his polemical stridency: "You have scarcely any idea of the degree to which the whole established ecclesiastical order is, Christianly, an untruth, and, what makes it worse, the degree to which the persons involved are themselves aware of it. Therefore judge slowly if you see me press so hard ... ."[372]

Luther's emphasis on "grace alone" culminated in a spiritual laxity which took grace for granted (*FS*, pp. 194–5). Hence, Kierkegaard asserted, "When the 'monastery' is the deviation, faith must be affirmed; when 'professor' is the deviation, imitation must be affirmed" (ibid., p. 196).

[368]   *JP*, vol. 4, p. 191 (1854). In supplying a corrective to Kierkegaard's corrective, one might posit: "When 'society' is the deviation, the individual must be affirmed, but when 'self' is the deviation, community must be affirmed." Another contextual exaggeration, the Hegelian appropriation of *Geist,* may have partially contributed to Kierkegaard's understated pneumatology.

[369]   Ibid., vol. 1, p. 84 [1848].

[370]   *TM*, p. 41. Kierkegaard's "dialectical dogmatics" could be construed as an argument for relativism, were it not for his assiduously maintained core of theological non-negotiables: notably, the character of God, human sinfulness, creation *ex nihilo*, the heterogeneity of Christianity, the full deity and humanity of Christ, and the need for self-risk and sacrifice among believers. Climacus carefully differentiated the religious dialectic from the Hegelian dialectic which rendered everything "sophistically relative (this is mediation)" (*CUP*, vol. 1, p. 525).

[371]   *TM*, p. 403 [1849].

[372]   Ibid., p. 525 [1855]. See also *UD*, p. 340.

In response to the oversimplified, complacent Christianity of his contemporaries, the Danish theologian deliberately strove to make things "more difficult." His intentions were partially to fend off potential "followers," partially to avoid igniting a misguided because merely "external" reform.[373] This strategy also ensured that "that single individual" did not place her trust in yet another human doctrine or teacher, but solely upon God. As Frater Taciturnus contended, "[B]elieving is just like swimming, and instead of helping one ashore the speaker should help one out into the deep."[374] Perhaps Kierkegaard even consciously or unconsciously reprised the role of Abraham in *Fear and Trembling* by playing the theological "bogeyman" for the benefit of the next generation's "Isaac," reckoning that "it is better that he believes me a monster than that he should lose faith in you [God]."[375] Nevertheless, like Nietzsche, craven imitation of Kierkegaard's thoughts and behavior was expressly forbidden.

Indirect communication: the means of the truth-witness
Although the Christian's life centers on bearing witness to the truth with keen contextual sensitivity, Kierkegaard carefully qualified this witness within the rubric of indirect communication. If the predominant philosophical problem facing Socrates was, "How does a man learn something he does not know and therefore cannot recognize?,"[376] the ultimate Kierkegaardian quandary was, "How does a person teach another individual something that is intrinsically 'unthinkable' and can only be learned from God?"[377] How can the eternal be conveyed in temporal formulations without compromising its heterogeneity with the contingent world and merging with paganism?[378] Furthermore, in an age where external authority has been thoroughly corrupted and misused, how does someone oppose sensate authority without themselves becoming a sensate authority?[379] Kierkegaard rigorously wrestled with the pedagogical paradox of how to teach people to think

---

[373]   See *CUP*, vol. 1, p. 186 and *CD*, pp. 385–6 [20 November 1847]: "As long as I am living, I cannot be acknowledged, for only a few are able to understand me, and if people began trying to acknowledge me, I would have to exert all my powers in new mystifications to prevent it."

[374]   *SW*, p. 443. See also *PC*, p. 289 [1849].

[375]   *FT*, p. 11.

[376]   *PF*, p. 9.

[377]   In Vigilius' words, to "allow thought to collide with the unthinkable" (*CA*, p. 27).

[378]   *CUP*, vol. 1, p. 243.

[379]   "The unrecognizables recognize the servants of levelling but dare not use power or authority against them, for then there would be a regression, because it would be instantly obvious to a third party that the unrecognizable one was an authority, and then the third party would be hindered from attaining the highest" (*TA*, p. 109).

for themselves without enslaving them to dependence on his instruction or himself. How could he, in good conscience, "command" them to be individuals?[380]

Although direct communication is appropriate for conveying temporal information, as well as previously unknown truths in the case of the apostle,[381] Kierkegaard believed that it is impossible for one individual to communicate spiritual truth directly to another individual for five reasons. First, given the heterogeneity between God and sinful humankind, an individual can only recognize the truth after she first receives the condition for receiving truth—a condition which God alone can bestow.[382] Second, no Christian may be so self-assured that she can neglect her personal pursuit of the truth and focus upon others since "there can be no schoolmaster, strictly understood, in the art of existing."[383] Third, intimations of "direct" communication of truth translate into sensate power, which ineluctably indebt the learner to the human "teacher" instead of God. Consequently, Climacus exclaimed,

> [T]he secret of communication specifically hinges on setting the other free, and for that very reason he must not communicate himself directly; indeed, it is even irreligious to do so … if the communicator is not God himself or does not presume to appeal to the miraculous authority of an apostle … .[384]

Otherwise, instead of proclaiming "good news to the poor, healing to the broken-hearted, and freedom for the captives,"[385] the speaker generates further fear, obligation, and dismay.[386] Kierkegaard meticulously heeded Socrates' crucial lesson: "[T]here is no direct relation between the [human] teacher and the learner … ."[387] Fourth, the direct communication of Christian truth without

---

[380]　This plight is marvellously depicted in *Monty Python's Life of Brian*, when Brian, the reluctant "messiah," shouts at his unwa(rra)nted followers, "You are all individuals!" to which they bray, "We … are … all … individuals …" After a brief pause, a paradoxical voice squeaks, "I'm not!" A likely candidate for Kierkegaard's favourite cinematic moment.

[381]　*CUP*, vol. 1, pp. 76, 243. The apostle must still be careful lest "the believer would enter into a direct relation to him, not into a paradoxical relation" (*BA*, p. 186).

[382]　*PF*, pp. 14–15; *EUD*, p. 136. Hence, Climacus vehemently opposed the "halo effect," any notion that Jesus' divinity was eminently recognizable, otherwise "he is *eo ipso* a mythological figure" (*CUP*, vol. 1, p. 600).

[383]　Ibid., vol. 2, p. ix. See also ibid., vol. 1, p. 74. However, Kierkegaard felt confident that he was applying the proper corrective: "That I have understood the truth I am presenting—of that I am absolutely convinced" (*PV*, p. 25).

[384]　*CUP*, vol. 1, p. 74.

[385]　Isaiah 61:1.

[386]　See *EUD*, pp. 15, 382; *PF*, p. 12.

[387]　*CUP*, vol. 1, p. 247. See also *PF*, p. 10. The epistemological humility of Socrates' maieutic method profoundly influenced Kierkegaard's model of indirection. See *TM*, p. 341 [1 September 1855]: "The only analogy I have before me is Socrates; my task is a Socratic

apostolic warrant negates existential immediacy and tends towards abstraction, robbing truth of its "inward" urgency towards decisive action.[388] As David Aiken observes, "[A]ny attempt to impart Christianity by direct means of communication, such as professional lecturing, is a 'monstrous error,' insofar as evangelical truth is not a possession of the mind but a form of being."[389] Fifth, direct communication may fatally disrupt the listener's appropriation of the message by riveting her attention upon the messenger.[390] For Kierkegaard, this is as detrimental as shouting, "Watch what you are doing!" to a person using a chainsaw, who immediately looks at the shouter, maiming herself in the process.[391]

The solution to Kierkegaard's great dilemma was, "[I]n suffering to serve, to help indirectly."[392] In order to love the beloved without imprisoning him in dependence upon the lover, Kierkegaard posited, "[T]he greatest benefaction cannot be accomplished in any way whereby the recipient gets to know that he is indebted."[393] Without a direct relationship, Anti-Climacus claimed that there is no assertion of power on the part of the author: "There is no direct communication and no direct reception: there is a choice. It does not take place, as in direct communication with coaxing and threatening and admonishing ... . [T]o deny direct communication is to require faith ... ."[394]

Kierkegaard's personal strategy for implementing indirect communication had three facets. First, he assiduously strove to eliminate any direct dogmatic statements in his writings: "I do not have a stitch of doctrine—and doctrine is what people want. Because doctrine is the indolence of aping and mimicking for the learner, and doctrine is the way to sensate power for the teacher, for doctrine collects men."[395] Furthermore, emphasis on doctrine is both detrimental

---

task, to audit the definition of what it is to be a Christian—I do not call myself a Christian (keeping the ideal free), but I can make it manifest that others are that even less." Following Socrates' precedent was also contextually appropriate, given the proliferation of "sophistry" which plagued both ancient Greece and nineteenth-century Christendom (ibid.).

[388]   *CUP*, vol. 1, p. 236. This was a favourite tactic of Christendom, according to Kierkegaard (*PV*, p. 52).

[389]   Aiken, p. 24.

[390]   *UD*, pp. 160–61; *CUP*, vol. 1, p. 100.

[391]   See ibid., p. 277. This explains Kierkegaard's problem with venerating ethical "geniuses": "People should not admire an ethicist; they should be precipitated by him into an ethical life" (*WL* [revised], p. 422 [1847]).

[392]   *TA*, p. 109.

[393]   *WL*, p. 256.

[394]   *PC*, pp. 140–41. See also *PF*, p. 103.

[395]   *JP*, vol. 6, p. 535 [1854]. Hence, reducing Christianity to "an objective doctrine" helps render it "a kingdom of this world" (*FS*, p. 171). This also explains Climacus' injunction not to cite his book authoritatively by direct quotation, since this misses the crucial point of indirection (*CUP*, vol. 1, p. 618).

to Kierkegaard's project of emphasizing praxis over intellectually acknowledged "beliefs," as well as unnecessary: "My position has never been an emphasis on 'doctrine': my view is that the doctrine is very sound."[396] Second, Kierkegaard strove to remain personally enigmatic and politically aloof, eschewing direct relations with foes and followers alike.[397] He also vigorously renounced all authoritative titles and "heroic" personal feats: "[W]hen he [an author] says: I am a poet, only a poet—he is saying: Look at me and see that I am not great, I am not the ideal—but look at the ideal."[398] Third, Kierkegaard concocted a pantheon of pseudonymous speakers. As Louis Mackey explains, "A Kierkegaardian pseudonym is a *persona*, an imaginary person created by the author for artistic purposes, not a *nom de plume*, a fictitious name used to protect his personal identity from the threats and embarrassments of publicity ... . [H]is purpose was not mystification but distance."[399] However, the pseudonyms do assist in preserving mystery to great religious effect, as Kodalle observes: "[T]he existential center of the individual remains a mystery, kept intentionally from the inquisitive looks of others. Making it communicable would jeopardize the possibility of the absolute individuality of the other, who has the task of finding his own unique path."[400]

These existential personas presented spiritual truths beneath "aesthetic" camouflage,[401] creatively enabling Kierkegaard to embody world views which were not representative of his own Christian understanding,[402] and further preventing direct relationships with his readers.[403] This rhetorical strategy incorporated topics as well as perspectives intended to "lure" aesthetically-

---

[396]   *JP*, vol. 6, pp. 402–3 [1851].

[397]   For example, *BA*, p. 336 [March 1855]: "I am not very directly understandable and will never be understood by those who want to have anything direct." Kierkegaard jubilantly claimed to have removed all perilously personal references from his papers (*JP*, vol. 5, p. 226 [1843]).

[398]   Ibid., vol. 4, p. 178 [1851].

[399]   Cited in *FT*, pp. x–xi, n. 3. Kirmmse states that Kierkegaard's identity would hardly have been a secret among the estimated three to four thousand people who comprised his "cultivated audience" (*Kierkegaard in Golden Age Denmark*, p. 79). It is somewhat comical to envision Kierkegaard's towering Saul-like figure vainly attempting to conceal itself behind the "baggage" of contemporary Danish literature. See I Samuel 10:22–3.

[400]   Kodalle, p. 402.

[401]   Kierkegaard attributed the idea for the pseudonyms to Schleiermacher's written experimentation (*CI*, p. 425 [October 1835]), and may have styled his epistemological approach after Christ's parables, which stymied opponents while offering illumination "to the person who is honestly seeking" (*PV*, p. 34).

[402]   *FT*, p. x. For Kierkegaard's "representational perspectivism" via the pseudonyms, see Pattison, pp. 238–41.

[403]   *SW*, p. 648 [1845]. In the case of Anti-Climacus' heightened Christian ideal, Kierkegaard could "regard myself as a *reader* of the books, not as the author" (*PV*, p. 12).

minded readers to his more explicitly religious writings.[404] Since Christendom maintained the illusion that all were Christians,[405] Kierkegaard dismissed any direct assault, since it "only strengthens a person in the illusion and also infuriates him," instead advising that "one who is under illusion must be approached from behind."[406] Because Danish "Christians" were existentially "choking" on undigested "truth,"[407] Kierkegaard sought to perform a hermeneutical "Heimlich maneuver" to dislodge the obstruction.

There was also a subtle polemics behind his methods of indirection: by "wholeheartedly" inhabiting an opposing ideal within a poetic personage, Kierkegaard was able to expose its intrinsic short-comings. He once explained his "motif operandi" behind Johannes Climacus as follows:

> By means of the melancholy irony, which did not consist in any single utterance on the part of Johannes Climacus but in his whole life, by means of the profound earnestness involved in a young man's being sufficiently honest and earnest enough to do quietly and unostentatiously what the philosophers say (and he thereby becomes unhappy)—I would strike a blow at [modern speculative] philosophy.[408]

The pseudonyms, thus, supplied a series of "masks," each of which allows the truth-seeking reader to adopt imaginatively an existential life view, comprehend its limitations from an "insider's" perspective,[409] and safely discard it without incurring any detrimental consequences in actuality.

Reforming temporality

In a journal entry, Kierkegaard once warned that there are two perils in attempting to influence people: "(1) men are lukewarm and indolent, difficult to set in motion; (2) once they are set in motion, there is nothing they are more inclined to do than to mimic."[410] He remained suspicious of external reform, contending that it typically distracted individuals from true reform—the reform of each individual through

---

[404]   *TM*, p. 130; *PV*, p. 44. Thus, he was wary of giving too many clues into his methods: "A fisherman would not tell the fish about his bait, saying 'This is bait'" (ibid., p. 182 [1849]).

[405]   Ibid., p. xi.

[406]   Ibid., p. 43. See also *CUP*, vol. 2, p. 157 [1849–50], and *BA*, p. 142, where he cautioned against revivalist "thundering" "which can so easily embitter people instead of bettering them."

[407]   *CUP*, vol. 1, p. 275.

[408]   *PF*, p. xiii.

[409]   Westphal calls this "the determinate negation of positions which cannot survive the critical scrutiny of being compared to their own, self-imposed standards" ("Kierkegaard's Politics," p. 323).

[410]   *JP*, vol. 3, p. 727 [1847].

a personal and "inward" relationship with God.[411] In light of the "disastrous confusion of politics and Christianity,"[412] he carefully qualified his position:

> Permit me to add the following, lest what I say be misunderstood, as if it were my view that Christianity consists purely and simply of putting up with everything in regard to external forms, without doing anything at all, as if Christianity did not know very well what is to be done ... . There are situations, therefore, in which an established order can be of such a nature that the Christian ought not put up with it, ought not to say that Christianity means precisely this indifference to the external.[413]

Kierkegaard's challenging of *The Corsair*'s unbridled media power[414] and unrelenting demands for the separation of church and state comprise two such personal appeals for "justified" external reform.

Nevertheless, Kierkegaard's aversion to employing sensate authority for spiritual ends strongly influenced his approach to temporal reforms. He once confessed, "I am indeed suspicious of these politically achieved free institutions, especially of their saving, renewing power."[415] He scathingly criticized religious reformer N.F.S. Grundtvig for employing government power to enact ecclesiastical reform, maintaining: "[H]e actually has fought only for something earthly, civil freedom for himself and his adherents ... ."[416] Although Kierkegaard believed that God can anoint a particular individual to challenge the external order,[417] he

---

[411]   Furthermore, attempts to alleviate temporal differences [such as equitable distribution of goods, equal rights for women] are "futile" since they are impossible to achieve and ironically inflate the importance of those differences (*TM*, pp. 444–5 [1854]; *FS*, p. 131; *PV*, pp. 103–4; *CD*, p. 60; *WL*, pp. 87, 139–40, 145; *BA*, pp. 158, 230; *CUP*, vol. 1, p. 504; *TC*, p. 57; *EUD*, p. 330). However, his admonitions to the poor to "reconcile themselves to their position" (*JP*, vol. 4, p. 181 [1851]) ring hollow, coming from a highly educated, independently wealthy European male who never had to work a day in this life. As Aleksandr Solzhenitsyn rightly observed, "How do you expect a man who's warm to understand one who's cold?" (*One Day in the Life of Ivan Denisovich*, trans. Ralph Parker [London, 2000], p. 23). Lowrie, p. 52, cites an entry dated 13 October 1853, which expounds his long-standing belief that, "I should never be tried by having to work for my living—partly because I thought that in consideration of my peculiar cross God would spare me this suffering and problem."

[412]   *TC*, p. 53.

[413]   Ibid., p. 56.

[414]   Kierkegaard anticipates Derrida's indictment on media and public opinion. See Dooley, pp. 14–17.

[415]   *TC*, p. 54. Johannes de silentio criticized much social activism as egotism masquerading as sympathy (*FT*, p. 80).

[416]   *TM*, p. 208. See also *WL*, p. 342.

[417]   *BA*, p. 150.

deemed it inappropriate to pine for such a leader,[418] and chose to err on the side of conservatism: "[I]f there is no such man among us, then let us hold to the established order … ."[419] True reform transpires through personal sacrifices and voluntary suffering, which only the individual can choose for herself.[420] Moreover, faith must be worked out in meticulous response to one's particular historical context. He once observed, "Christ did not come *in order to* abolish slavery, even though that will follow and does result from it … ."[421]

Amidst the traumatic political events of 1848, Kierkegaard speculated on the possibility of a Christian society, which would only occur if God were related singly to every individual:

> God now comes to be related to individuals neither through abstractions nor through representative individuals but becomes the one who, so to speak, takes it upon himself to bring up the generation's countless individuals, becomes himself the schoolmaster who watches over everyone, each one individually. Here thinking halts. The shape of the world would resemble—well, I do not know to what I should compare it—it would resemble an enormous Christianfeldt … .[422]

With no small irony, he observed that "the two most powerful opponents"— communism and pietism—would offer starkly similar visions for society:

> [T]here must be no distinction between persons; we should be brothers and sisters, have everything in common; wealth, position, art, science, etc. are of evil; all people should be alike …, dressed alike, … going to bed by the clock, eating the same food out of one dish in a definite rhythm, etc. etc.[423]

Kierkegaard did not expand upon this societal vision, presumably to counterbalance the exaggerated clamor for political reform which was currently disrupting Danish society. He once declared,

---

[418] *TA*, p. 89.

[419] *FS*, p. 212. See also *TM*, pp. 444–5 [1854]: "I am—in this respect—so conservative that if I might have my way, not so much as one button will be changed on the assistant gravedigger's frock, even if the opposition ever so zealously insisted upon it."

[420] *BA*, p. 101.

[421] *UD*, p. 242.

[422] *WA*, p. 215 [1848]. This was a small town founded by the Moravian Brethren, with whom Kierkegaard's father and his friend Emil Boesen had connections (ibid., p. 296, n. 18). Kierkegaard's description strongly echoes Old Testament prophecies of eschatological reform. See Jeremiah 31:33–4; Isaiah 11:9, 54:13.

[423] *WA*, p. 216 [1848].

> [W]hen existence itself undertakes to preach for awakening as it is doing now, I do not dare to jack it up even more in that direction; something extraordinary like that has not been entrusted to me and scarcely can be entrusted to any human being. In a soft, refined, overcultured time, I was and ought to be for awakening. At present I ought to draw nearer to the established order.[424]

Subsequently, he continued to supply a politically "conservative" corrective to the contextual exaggeration of his day and never postulated further what a Christian society might look like.

In *Kierkegaard in Golden Age Denmark*, Kirmmse describes Kierkegaard as "a 'populist' in his view of culture and *Dannelse*, ['the education which forms character'[425]] a pragmatic 'agnostic' in his view of political arrangements, and a 'liberal' with respect to his sink-or-swim individualistic notion of salvation."[426] However, from the view point of sensate authority, it is surely an "armed agnosticism," given the prioritization of the individual's relationship with God which supersedes all externalized political formations, his suspicion of populist power, and his endorsement of the early church's model of "praying for the emperor" without subscribing to nationalist self-deifications or "household gods."

If one is to criticize Kierkegaard for failing to prescribe a thorough blueprint for social change or government infrastructure, his reticence may be attributed to the "over-politicization" of life in nineteenth-century Europe, the prevalence of false "authority," the fear of initiating yet another misguided—because solely exterior— reform movement, and the New Testament's own precedent in obviating socio-political, ethnological distinctions, conventions, and structures in order to attend to the pressing spiritual needs common to every person.[427] Westphal identifies a passage from *Practice in Christianity* as "Kierkegaard's politics in a nutshell":

> Every human being is to live in fear and trembling, and likewise no established order is to be exempted from fear and trembling. Fear and trembling signify that we are in the process of becoming; and every single individual, likewise the

---

[424]   Ibid., 216–17 [1849].

[425]   Kirmmse, *Kierkegaard in Golden Age Denmark*, p. 273.

[426]   Ibid., p. 276. See also p. 327, where he discusses Kierkegaard's response to women's equal rights: "Here, as elsewhere, *SK* seems quite the classical liberal, non-dogmatic and agnostic with respect to political solutions, so long as they respect individual rights … ." Similarly, Hannay deems him a "social nominalist" (p. 300): as long as the political structures allow individuals to be "accountable personally for their bureaucratic actions and political decisions, the framework can be allowed to stand" (p. 295).

[427]   As Perkins observes, "Kierkegaard's vision of community is of a kingdom not yet come and so is open to multiple political interpretations" ("Kierkegaard's Critique of the *Bourgeois* State," p. 217). This also places existential responsibility upon the reader to think up and implement strategies consistent with the Gospel. See Perkins, "Climacan Politics: Person and Polis in Kierkegaard's *Postscript*," p. 36, and Hannay, p. 278.

generation, is and should be aware of being in the process of becoming. And fear and trembling signify that there is a God—something every human being and every established order ought not to forget for a moment.[428]

Kierkegaard came closest to expounding a governing principle for forming such a society when he once wrote, "If Christianity is supposed to be culture, it must be the culture of character, or education and culture aimed at becoming persons of character."[429] According to Kirmmse, "The most general, basic rule SK lays down for ordering the religious-private and the political-social spheres in their proper relation is that one must relate infinitely only to the eternal."[430]

One final observation is necessary before concluding this chapter. A pronounced tension is implicit in the temporal/sensate division. At times, spiritual authority appears as a purely "transcendent" incursion into the world of temporality and the apostle apparently bears an utterly incommensurable authority from "beyond." However, in other instances, Kierkegaard wrote of spiritual authority as if it was a "redeemed" version of "sensate authority," which tends to downplay the "Christian" "chasm of incommensurability" between the divine and the created universe, and verges upon the Socratic "maieutic" pattern. Are human beings passive recipients of spiritual authority or do they participate in the redemption or emancipation of sensate authority? Part of the incongruity is due to the artificiality of my terminological bifurcations, imposed in order to elucidate the dynamic components of a highly sophisticated life view. However, part of the ambiguity is also based upon the fact that issues of freedom and authority involve a complex dialectic for Kierkegaard, who himself emphasized one side or the other depending on the context. When confronting the rebelliousness of sinful autonomy and the incursions of human rationality or nationalist politics into the sphere of Religiousness B, he adamantly upheld God's incommensurability with humankind and its self-serving interpretative schemas. However, concerning Christian responsibility towards the neighbor, he accentuated the vital role of passionate commitment and altruistic involvement. Hence, in *Works of Love*, he wrote,

> Therefore, giving thanks to God, he [the helper] declares: Now this individual is standing by himself—through my help. But there is no self-satisfaction in the last phrase, because the loving one has understood that essentially every human being indeed stands by himself—through God's help—and that the loving one's self-annihilation is really only in order not to hinder the other person's God-relationship, so that all the loving one's help infinitely vanishes in the God-relationship.[431]

---

[428] Cited in Westphal, "Kierkegaard's Politics," p. 324.

[429] *FS*, p. 256 [1850].

[430] Kirmmse, *Kierkegaard in Golden Age Denmark*, p. 323.

[431] *WL* [revised], p. 278.

Casting a sidelong glance at Hegel, Kierkegaard left no doubt as to the origins of Christian practice: "It certainly must never be forgotten that Christ also helped in temporal and earthly needs. It is also possible falsely to make Christ so spiritual that He becomes sheer cruelty. After all, 'spirit,' absolute spirit, is the greatest of cruelties for us poor men."[432]

What is essential to understanding Kierkegaard is, first, to be cognizant of these two fundamental loci of divine initiation/empowering and human participation which he endeavors to hold together in his comprehension of freedom within the contingent realm of creation. Second, we must recognize that Kierkegaard never conflated the Gospel with its socio-political applications or Christian ethical practices.[433] Within its prescriptive homilies and treatises, organized religion typically employs a "slippery" intransitive; for example, "To be before God *is* to minister to the poor." In such formulations, caring for the poor or advocating universal rights can easily be equated with standing before God, so that human activity tacitly supplants the role of divine grace upon which such activity is based. However, in his refusal to dictate specific actions for the church, Kierkegaard strove to remind his contemporaries of the Gospel imperative to enter a right personal relationship with God—possible only through the efficacy of Christ's life, death, and resurrection—as the only proper grounds for passionate, "existential" Christian praxis. Subsequently, he did not seek to question the value of social action but rather to situate it theologically as *following from* faith or as an *expression of* faith rather than being *confused for* or *equated with* faith.[434] Hence, the pith of his "political" message is aptly summarized by Nicoletti: "[T]he political sphere cannot satisfy the needs of a being capable of infinity."[435]

---

[432] From a 1849 journal entry cited in Søe, pp. 67–8.

[433] I am deeply indebted to Prof. Alan Torrance for this insight.

[434] Christopher Hamilton regards Kierkegaard as advocating a "religious spiritual stance of resignation" ("Kierkegaard on Truth as Subjectivity: Christianity, Ethics, and Asceticism," *Religious Studies*, 34 [1998]: 77). Against Hamilton, see Nicoletti, pp. 186–9. She concludes, "Mysticism wants to remove both finitude and politics; mundanity wants to remove infinity. To realize a real government it is necessary to retain the specificities of the two poles and their dialectical relation" (p. 191).

[435] Ibid., p. 189.

Chapter 6
Worlds Apart: Comparing Perspectives

The following two chapters will attempt to reconstruct a dialogue between Nietzsche and Kierkegaard with regards to their cosmology, anthropology, and concepts of authority. The first half of each section will briefly outline Nietzsche's contentions with regards to Christianity and the second half will contain Kierkegaard's possible rejoinders and counter-criticism. The final chapter will articulate some of the strengths and weaknesses of both positions and conclude with their relevance for contemporary discussions on power.

Cosmological Objections: The Accusation of Cowardice

Throughout Nietzsche's corpus, there are two primary objections which he leveled at Christianity: the lack of objective truth in its tenets, and its devaluation of the temporal universe in light of otherworldly delusions.

Nietzsche

Christian doctrine as myth
If he had read Kierkegaard's writings, Nietzsche may have delighted in encountering a Christian with a robust passion, imagination, and intellect, although he would vehemently oppose the majority of Kierkegaard's postulations about the cosmos. Providence,[1] sin,[2] revelation,[3] God,[4] the Incarnation,[5] salvation,[6] and free will[7] are all presuppositions which he resolutely rejected. According to Nietzsche, the human self consists of fractured inconsistencies, competing drives, and "a multiplicity of persons,"[8] and constitutes the ultimate construction of the

---

[1] *TI*, p. 137; *BG*, p. 111; *HA*, p. 77.
[2] Ibid., p. 76.
[3] Ibid., p. 88.
[4] Ibid., p. 89.
[5] Ibid., pp. 84, 102.
[6] *WP*, p. 212 [1888]; *Z*, p. 59; *HA*, p. 85; *BT*, p. 8.
[7] *WP*, p. 86 [1888], 357 [1883–88]; *GS*, p. 169; *HA*, pp. 26, 43.
[8] *WP*, p. 408 [1888].

imagination.[9] Christianity plays upon this fabrication, "raising to a principle the counterfeiting of psychological interpretation."[10] He derided Christianity as,

> [a] traffic between imaginary *beings* ("God," "spirits," "souls"); an imaginary *natural* science (anthropocentric; complete lack of the concept of natural causes); an imaginary *psychology* (nothing but self-misunderstandings, interpretations of pleasant or unpleasant general feelings, for example the condition of the *nervus sympathicus*, with the aid of the sign-language of religio-moral idiosyncrasy—repentance," "sting of conscience," "temptation by the Devil," "the proximity of God"); an imaginary *teleology* ("the kingdom of God," "the Last Judgment," "eternal life").[11]

For Nietzsche, such postulations are merely human falsehoods, existential "night lights" to comfort frail-hearted individuals in a darkened cosmos devoid of divine love and purpose.[12]

According to Nietzsche, human beings remain hopelessly entrenched within their biological and historical context,[13] not so much acting as "acted upon" by the inescapable forces and counter-forces which comprise the temporal realm.[14] Within this environment, even self-knowledge becomes illusory.[15] Nietzsche had little tolerance for the use of paradoxes to explain apparent inconsistencies: "[F]or what are paradoxes but assertions which carry no conviction because their author himself is not really convinced of them and makes them only so as to glitter and seduce and in general cut a figure."[16]

In contrast to this existential cowardice which fails to face fully the harsh realities of existence, Nietzsche found reason to celebrate, to triumph over the "telos-lessness" of nature. The truly powerful individual is able to accept unflinchingly this state of affairs, to recognize the arbitrariness of human formulations of truth, "to grasp that injustice is inseparable from life,"[17] to forsake his "astrological pride"[18] and transcend the challenges of existence. As Michael Tanner explains, Nietzsche juxtaposed "unblinking recognition of the frightfulness of life with a stubborn determination not to be subdued by it ... ."[19] By defiantly acting in the face of life's eternal "ends-lessness," humankind faces fate with stentorian

---

[9]   Ibid., pp. 263–4 [1887–88].

[10] Ibid., p. 94 [1887].

[11] *TI*, p. 137.

[12] *BT*, p. 22.

[13] *GS*, p. 121.

[14] Ibid., 168; *BT*, p. 18.

[15] *UM*, p. 129.

[16] Ibid., p. 134.

[17] *HA*, p. 9.

[18] That is, the belief that "the heavens revolve around the fate of man" (ibid., p. 16).

[19] *BG*, p. 16.

gravitas and nobility, simultaneously shaking a fist at the void while embracing its vicissitudes and vagaries with relish.

Christian devaluation of life

Nietzsche remained hyperbolically suspicious of any doctrine which erodes significance from the natural world in favor of an illusory hereafter. For Nietzsche, this "sin against life" is indubitably the "unforgivable sin."[20] Such transcendental escapism engendered his unmitigated scorn for Christian "afterworldsmen."[21] Neither would he admit any theological impediments to the free expression of humankind's natural instincts. "For what is freedom?" he once asked: "That one has the will to self-responsibility."[22] Subsequently, he rejected Christianity for attempting to imprison what is free, domesticate what is fierce, and foster "*hostility to life*, a furious, vindictive distaste for life itself."[23] The Christian attempt to impose an ethical structure on the intrinsically amoral universe and its creation of a false psychology of guilt and fear poisons the bloodlines of human vitality.[24]

In light of these contentions, Nietzsche would probably accuse Kierkegaard of cocooning his existential fears within the "swaddling clothes" of superstition and hermeneutical hocus-pocus: "When a misfortune strikes us, we can overcome it either by removing its cause or else by changing the effect it has on our feelings, that is, by reinterpreting the misfortune as a good, whose benefit may only later become clear."[25] Moreover, he would have adduced Kierkegaard's sundry references to guilt, fear and trembling, and self-torment[26] as symptomatic of Christianity's diseased, counterfeit psychology. As a proponent of nature, health, and happiness in material reality, the German philosopher subsequently sought to jolt the inert human world with the defibrillators of "dangerous knowledge."[27] He would likely cite several instances where the Danish thinker "denigrated earthly life" by espousing "hatred for the world" for the sake of chimerical eternal values, and upbraid their anti-naturalism.[28] Kierkegaard would, thus, be a coward on two accounts: for rejecting the "real" world of life and vitality, and for embracing an illusory world spawned by fear and spineless escapism.

---

[20]   *TI*, p. 167. See also *HA*, pp. 85, 230.

[21]   *Z*, p. 59.

[22]   *TI*, p. 103.

[23]   *BT*, p. 8.

[24]   Ibid., p. 9.

[25]   *HA*, p. 77. See also *GS*, p. 196.

[26]   See, for example, *TM*, p. 427 [1853]; *JP*, vol. 3, p. 574 [1850]; the centrality of despair in *The Concept of Anxiety* and *Sickness Unto Death*, and Quidam's assertion that he could not dispel his depression since it "becomes a religious point of departure" (*SW*, p. 375).

[27]   *BG*, p. 53.

[28]   For example, *TM*, pp. 312, 335; *WL*, p. 124; *FT*, p. 292 [1843–44].

Kierkegaard

Affinity

Nietzsche's response would likely constitute a refreshing change for Kierkegaard. Unlike scores of self-styled "Christians," Nietzsche's outrage at the preposterousness of Christianity indicated that the German philosopher better comprehended the Christian faith and its radical implications than many of its so-called adherents.[29] In a journal entry, Kierkegaard once lamented, "[T]he state of Christianity has long been such that one cannot find out what Christianity is in the so-called Christian church … but has to seek it among the freethinkers."[30] From Kierkegaard's viewpoint, Nietzsche's indignation at Christianity's hostility towards the amoral naturalism he espoused is both justified and understandable as the perspective of fallen humankind pursuing a reckless independence from God.[31] Because Christian revelation is completely incommensurable with human history, thought, and culture, it ineluctably aggravates the human spirit in its "normative" quest to celebrate its own powers, standards, and creativity.[32] For Kierkegaard, this constitutes offence at the Gospel, the "natural" response of anyone who lives in defiant autonomy: "All of 'humankind's' sagacity aims at one thing: to be able to live without responsibility [to God]."[33] In other words, Nietzsche's response to Christianity was far from radical, but rather conventional and predictably "human, all too human."

Furthermore, Kierkegaard would have concurred with much of Nietzsche's diagnosis of "diseased" Christendom, including the false psychological distortions which supplant theological content with false sentiment,[34] and the horrendous hypocrisy of self-love masquerading as love for spouse, society, and God.[35] Kierkegaard also condemned otherworldly escapism as indicative of a supreme "distrust in God" for provision in this life.[36] In fact, Nietzsche would

---

[29]   On the heterogeneity of Christianity, see *WA*, p. 100; *SD*, p. 159; *CD*, p. 63; *WL*, p. 41; *TM*, pp. 10, 393 [1847]; *BA*, pp. 20, 175; *CUP*, vol. 1, pp. 100, 213–14; *SW*, p. 440; *CA*, p. 19; *PF*, p. 36; *FT*, p. 53.

[30]   *JP*, vol. 6, p. 532 [1854].

[31]   *TM*, p. 177. See also ibid., p. 335; *JK*, p. 254 [1854]; *CD*, p. 97; *WL*, p. 340; *JP*, vol. 3, p. 733 [1851]; *CUP*, vol. 1, p. 461.

[32]   Kierkegaard separated the transcendent truth of the Gospel from the historical foibles of the church by affixing "an unshakable qualitative difference" between "*the historical in Christianity* (the paradox that the eternal once came into existence in time, this paradoxical fact)" and the "*history of Christianity*" (*BA*, p. 38).

[33]   *TM*, p. 350. See also *FS*, pp. 35, 140; *PC*, pp. 81, 94; *SD*, p. 155; *WL*, p. 70.

[34]   For example, individuals who attribute the gradual dissipation of strong emotions to "divine forgiveness" (*HA*, p. 93).

[35]   Ibid., p. 100; *WL* [revised], p. 473 [1847].

[36]   *JP*, vol. 4, p. 52 [1840–41]. See also *FS*, p. 169; *CD*, p. 261; *JP*, vol. 4, p. 145 [1848]; *CUP*, vol. 1, p. 432; *EUD*, pp. 259–60; *CI*, pp. 328–9; *BA*, p. 212 [4 July 1840].

have served Kierkegaard as an ally both directly and indirectly. He would be a direct ally by critiquing the fallibility of human notions of love and ethics, as well as Christendom's fallacious representation of Christ's teachings. The Danish theologian observed,

> [H]ow seldom Christianity is presented in its true form, how those who defend it most often betray it, and how rarely attackers actually hit it, although they often … superbly hit Christendom, which certainly might rather be called the caricature of true Christianity or an enormous quantity of misunderstanding, illusion, etc. sprinkled with a sparse little dash of true Christianity.[37]

Nietzsche would be an indirect ally by providing what Pascal called an "indirect demonstration" of Christian truths on account of his "natural" resistance to its "otherworldly" demands for personal sacrifice and servanthood.[38]

Rebuttal
Seldom one to pass up a polemical challenge, Kierkegaard would have subjected Nietzsche's cosmology to rigorous criticism and highlighted several crucial problems and inconsistencies.

Christendom versus Christianity
Kierkegaard would first take issue with Nietzsche's underlying presupposition that Christendom is Christianity.[39] Instead, Kierkegaard maintained that Christendom is the sensate world's cunning means of overthrowing true Christianity.[40] Furthermore, he would strongly contest Nietzsche's "facile" identification of Christendom with the desires and interests of the lowest classes of society. Rather, the church's transcendent mission had been compromised by plying it with temporal power and wealth—a decisive tactic of those in affluent positions who were able to disseminate such privileges. According to Kierkegaard, the "slaves" are not to blame for the church's plight: "But in 'Christendom' it is actually the favored ones who have taken possession of Christianity, the rich and powerful who in addition to all their enjoyment of life also want all their power and might and wealth interpreted as proof of God's grace and a sign of their piety … ."[41] Nor would Kierkegaard allow the admitted shortcomings of the visible church to excuse Nietzsche's unbelief, since "I regard it as an illusion for someone to imagine that it is external conditions and forms that hinder him in becoming a Christian … ."[42] To the degree that Nietzsche was repelled by "the good," a life of

---

[37] *PV*, p. 80.

[38] Blaise Pascal, *Pensées*, trans. A.J. Krailsheimer (London, 1966), pp. 163–4.

[39] *TM*, p. 107.

[40] Ibid., pp. 39, 188; *CUP*, vol. 1, pp. 555–6.

[41] *JP*, vol. 4, p. 408 [1852].

[42] *TC*, p. 54.

obedience to God, he was trapped in a "demonic" relation of fear and opposition towards the good.[43]

Mythical creatures

A second objection pertains to Nietzsche's anticipated future. Nietzsche once criticized Christianity's belief in a "non-existent" God by declaring, "There is not enough love and kindness in the world to permit us to give any of it away to imaginary beings."[44] However, Kierkegaard would quickly point out that Nietzsche's alternative violated his own principle—the adoration of an *über*-being who has yet to appear in world history.[45] In *Works of Love*, Kierkegaard declared, "The shrewd foolishly think that one wastes his time in loving imperfect, weak men ... . But to be unable to find an object, to waste love in vainly seeking, to waste it in empty space by loving the invisible [the perfect man]—this is truly to waste it."[46] In light of Nietzsche's accusation that God is merely an anthropomorphic "projection," Kierkegaard might also point out the suspicious resemblance between these exceptional specimens and a certain German philosopher.[47] Ironically, Nietzsche might not have evaded his own criticism directed against Romantic pessimism:

> It [the will to immortalize] can also be the tyrannic will of one who suffers deeply, who struggles, is tormented, and would like to turn what is most personal, singular, and narrow, the real idiosyncrasy of his suffering, into a binding law and compulsion—one who, as it were, revenges himself on all things by forcing his own image, the image of his torture on them, branding them with it.[48]

---

[43]   *CA*, p. 119.

[44]   *HA*, p. 89.

[45]   *Z*, p. 117. Ironically, Hollingdale speculates that Nietzsche modeled his concept of the *Übermensch* after God himself: "What the Christian says of God, Nietzsche says in very nearly the same words of the Superman, namely: 'Thine is the kingdom, and the power, and the glory, for ever and ever'" (ibid., p. 29). In "The Babylonian Captivity of the Church," Luther derided the bishops as "these high and mighty supermen" (*Selections from His Writings*, ed. John Dillenberger [New York, 1962], p. 325). The parallels in sentiment are striking: "The clergy can almost be said also to regard the laity as lower animals, who have been included in the church along with themselves. Thus it arises that they make bold to command and demand, to threaten and urge and oppress, as they please" (ibid., p. 345).

[46]   *WL*, p. 161.

[47]   See, for example, *WP*, p. 520 [1888]: "He enjoys the taste of what is wholesome for him ... . [H]e has illnesses as stimulants of his life; he knows how to exploit ill chances ... . [H]e does not submit; he is always in his *own* company, whether he deals with books, men, or landscapes; he honors by choosing, by admitting, by trusting."

[48]   *GS*, p. 330.

Self-referential incoherence

If Nietzsche is correct that human beings are unable to comprehend themselves, much less the world around them,[49] if thinking is truly "a quite arbitrary fiction, arrived at by selecting one element from the process and eliminating all the rest, an artificial arrangement for the purpose of intelligibility,"[50] if there is no semblance of truth but merely constructed realities and competing hermeneutics with varying degrees of usefulness which clash for ideological supremacy,[51] Kierkegaard would likely repeat God's Edenic exclamation to Nietzsche: "Who told you?"[52] If this is actually the case, how can Nietzsche himself confidently prognosticate the development of "a new habit" which will produce "wise, innocent (conscious of their innocence) men" over the course of millennia?[53] Despite Nietzsche's assertions, he is unwilling to relinquish the optimism that progress is possible, an optimism that underscores his own "priestly" role of offering true—if "human"—sacrifices on the altar of species transcendence.[54]

If, as Zarathustra maintained, the human will constructs its own volitional fictions out of the ashes of everyday haphazardness,[55] what prevents his interpretation from being yet another delusional attempt to conjure order from the churning caldron of chaos in which we stew? Why should Nietzsche's assessment of the human situation be privileged above that of Saint Augustine or Don Quixote? The Nietzschean world seems riddled with the pyrrhic victories of inter-subjectivist politics, where truth and what matters most is reduced to metaphysical "muscle-flexing."[56]

Moreover, if Christianity is derided for its endorsement of indemonstrable hopes, Kierkegaard would likely ask what confidence Nietzsche possessed in forcefully declaring teleology to be illusion[57] and life to be an endless cycle of recurrences with neither redemption nor resolution.[58] To argue that one "necessary fiction"—the tenet of *bellum omnium contra omnes*,[59] for example—is better than another—the Christian doctrine of divine love—is to presuppose that there is an element of truth in the world by which such statements can

---

[49]   *WP*, pp. 263 [1886–87], 269 [1885–86].

[50]   Ibid., p. 264 [1887–88]. See also ibid., p. 315 [1888].

[51]   For example, *GS*, p. 300; *WP*, p. 330 [1885–86].

[52]   Genesis 3:11.

[53]   *HA*, pp. 76, 224.

[54]   Nietzsche is thus able to reconcile himself with the contemporary glut of "unwise, unfair men" by regarding them as *"the necessary first stage, but not the opposite of those to come"* (ibid., p. 76).

[55]   *Z*, p. 163.

[56]   *WP*, pp. 224–5 [1883–88]. See also *HA*, p. 253.

[57]   Ibid., p. 266.

[58]   *WP*, p. 549 [1888].

[59]   Tanner claims that this concept was "never abandoned, though he often modified his formulations of it" (*BG*, p. 17).

be measured. By "making the metaphysical statement that there are no true metaphysical statements,"[60] Nietzsche assumed that he inherently possessed the criteria of truth by which to justify such a grand pronouncement. On this account, Nietzsche was firmly entrenched in a humanistically informed strand of Western philosophy, which presumes that human beings inherently possess the aptitudes, attitudes, and "requisite conditions" for recognizing truth[61]—a presupposition Kierkegaard seriously contested in conjunction with the Christian doctrine of human sinfulness.

In one way, Kierkegaard was far more "perspectivistic" than Nietzsche in his scepticism of human reason and interpretation.[62] With no small irony, Kierkegaard criticized the preposterous self-myopia of the Cartesian thinking subject who, basing epistemology and self-awareness on doubt, treats everything doubtingly except doubt itself.[63] In light of the reality of self-deception and distortion, Kierkegaard insisted that continuous relationship with God, the ultimate Subjectivity, is the sole means of escaping the errors and prejudices of rebellious human subjectivity, the only true way to become oneself.[64] In response to Nietzsche's famous declaration, "God is dead. God remains dead. And we have killed him … ,"[65] Kierkegaard would likely reply: "To slay God is the most dreadful suicide; utterly to forget God is a human being's deepest fall … ."[66]

From Kierkegaard's perspective, a politically and socially self-centered world is unavoidable when humankind attempts to quantify God, obviating the divine Other within the constructs of immanence. This merely highlights the inestimable need for grace to liberate human beings from the shackles of their own crippling self-reliance, to situate the existential "escape artist" within the all-encompassing embrace of God, to free her from her own broken attempts at "freedom." However, Kierkegaard did not foresee a sympathetic receptivity towards these veracities: "'Do become reasonable, come to your senses, try to become sober'—thus does the secular mentality taunt the Christian. And the Christian says to the secular

---

[60]   Susan Parsons, "Conceiving of God: Theological Arguments and Motives in Feminist Ethics," *Ethical Theory and Moral Practice*, 4 (2001): 376.

[61]   *CA*, p. 16. Climacus traced this confidence in self-immanent truth to Socrates (*PF*, pp. 11–12).

[62]   Hence, he consistently applied the hermeneutic of suspicion to everyone, including himself (*FS*, p. 44).

[63]   Ibid., p. 68. See Pascal, p. 64.

[64]   *FS*, p. 106; *SD*, p. 59; *CD*, p. 40; *WL*, p. 253; *CUP*, vol. 1, p. 244.

[65]   *GS*, p. 181.

[66]   *CD*, p. 67. Nietzsche himself acknowledged an internal coherence in Christian faith, though he doubted the veracity of its tenets: "If Christianity were right in its tenets of a vengeful god, general sinfulness, predestination, and the danger of an eternal damnation, it would be a sign of stupidity and lack of character *not* to become a priest, apostle, or hermit, and, with fear and trembling, work exclusively on one's own salvation" (*HA*, p. 86). Obviously, many Christians would not endorse those "core beliefs" as Nietzsche articulated them.

mentality, 'Do become reasonable, come to your senses, become sober.'"[67] Subsequently, Kierkegaard concluded that the proper corrective to widespread doubt is not apologetics but authority:[68] "Christianity by no means presupposes a direct need and desire for Christianity in the natural man (be he profound or simple) and therefore believes that it must itself command every man to become Christian, for otherwise he never becomes one."[69]

Losing the world

A fourth criticism pertains to the ultimate devaluation of temporal life. Kierkegaard would have approved of Nietzsche's emphasis on "becoming" over "being" so long as it is restricted to fallible, transient human forms and does not undermine faith in the existence of immutable eternal truths.[70] With regards to Nietzsche's accusation that Christianity ultimately devalues the natural world, Kierkegaard would claim that God's radical love and freedom, as epitomized in the humanly inconceivable entrance of the eternal into history in the person of Jesus Christ, constitutes the ultimate valuation and preservation of the temporal world, and furnishes the template for loving engagement with the world as neighbor. By contrast, Nietzsche's focus on the self as the sole grounds for love and truth risks reducing the world to a mere "vanishing point" in the spiraling egocentric preoccupation for self-actualization and empowerment.[71] Although Nietzsche intended to endorse the virtues of courageous action and existential heroism in defiance of a world-without-ends,[72] his efforts were irreversibly undermined by positing an artificially reconstructed world, where notions of truth and justice are mere secretions upon which humanity slips across the jagged cobblestones of amoral temporality. If Josephus is correct in asserting that the belittling of an adversary withers the laurels of the victor,[73] Kierkegaard may ask how true heroics can possibly emerge in a world whose existence "is *justified* only as an aesthetic

---

[67]   *FS*, p. 96. On the "disruption" of the ego-centered, autonomous self as the condition for receiving truth, see *JK*, p. 202 [1850]; *CD*, p. 386 [1847]; *WL*, p. 173; ibid. [revised], p. 407 [1846]; *PF*, pp. 14–15; *EUD*, p. 59.

[68]   *WL*, p. 11; *BA*, p. 5. Concurring with one of his main theological influences, he wrote: "Pascal says: The reason it is so difficult to believe is that it is so difficult to obey" (*JP*, vol. 3, p. 418 [1846]).

[69]   Ibid., vol. 3, p. 587 [1847].

[70]   See Climacus' critique of Hegel in *CUP*, vol. 1, p. 307.

[71]   Climacus traced this anthropocentric focus, which must ineluctably devalue the created order as a means or occasion for human self-awareness and expression, to Socrates: "In the Socratic view, every human being is himself the midpoint, and the whole world focuses only on him because his self-knowledge is God-knowledge" (*PF*, p. 11).

[72]   *GS*, p. 219.

[73]   Flavius Josephus, *The Jewish War*, trans. G.A. Williamson (London, 1959), pp. 21–2.

phenomenon."[74] Rather than Christianity abandoning the world, Kierkegaard would castigate Nietzsche's "aestheticizing" as "an emigration from reality."[75]

By contrast, Vigilius contested that it takes genuine courage for an individual to face the reality of his inescapable sinfulness in the presence of a holy, all-knowing God.[76] Kierkegaard would probably accuse Nietzsche of futilely attempting to evade the mercy and justice of God, since he believed that genuine ignorance of God simply does not exist within corrupted Christendom.[77] He also based this assertion on the providential goodness of God: "Truly, no more than God allows a species of fish to come into existence in a particular lake unless the plant that is its nourishment is also growing there, no more will God allow the truly concerned person to be ignorant of what he is to believe."[78] Furthermore, Kierkegaard may question the effectiveness of Nietzsche's aesthetic gambols with the satyr chorus in light of the brokenness, dejection, and hopelessness in the world. The great Dionysian revel might itself seem a superlative act of denial, a heavily romanticized dodge, a wild assertion "that whatever superficial changes may occur, life is at bottom indestructibly powerful and joyful."[79] Mr. A's commentary on Don Giovanni seems uncannily apt:

> When one throws a pebble in such a way that it skims the surface of the water, it can for a time skip over the water in light hops, but it sinks down to the bottom as soon as it stops skipping; in the same way he dances over the abyss, jubilating during his brief span.[80]

Delusion under despair

A final concern pertains to the latent despair in Nietzsche's view. In a critique of "a lust for life based on despair," Kierkegaard once commented, "This very remark ['Eat, drink, and be merry...'] echoes with the anxiety about the next day, the day of annihilation, the anxiety that insanely is supposed to signify joy although it is a shriek from the abyss."[81] Accordingly, he might inquire as to whether the Nietzschean esprit can redeem life from inherent meaningless. Nietzsche himself wrote that the "free spirits," precursors to his doctrine of the *Übermensch*, were "imaginary" friends intended to comfort him in a time of evident hopelessness in human potential.[82] He ecstatically envisioned their advent: "I already see them

---

[74]   *BT*, p. 8.

[75]   *CI*, p. 297.

[76]   *CA*, p. 102.

[77]   *JP*, vol. 3, p. 662 [1844].

[78]   *CD*, p. 244.

[79]   *BT*, p. 39.

[80]   *EO*, vol. 1, pp. 129–30.

[81]   *CD*, p. 77. See also *SD*, pp. 126–7.

[82]   *HA*, p. 5. See also ibid., p. 4: "[W]hen I could not find what I *needed*, I had to gain it by force artificially, to counterfeit it, or create it poetically." For the *Übermensch* as a

coming, slowly, slowly; and perhaps I am doing something to hasten their coming when I describe before the fact the fateful conditions that I see giving rise to them, the paths on which I *see* them coming."[83] For Kierkegaard, however, the attempt either to grasp the finite infinitely or to measure the eternal against the temporal can only begin and end in despair.

Anthropological Objections: The Accusation of Enslavement

Nietzsche

Christianity as slavery to mediocrity
With regards to their understandings of humankind, the main accusation which Nietzsche would level against Christianity in general and Kierkegaard in particular is that of forcibly confining the human race to the "backwaters" of slave morality and, consequently, intellectual and spiritual mediocrity. Although Nietzsche once conceded that Christianity has been distorted by being coerced "to propel the mills of state power,"[84] he generally equated the Christian religion with hypocrisy, narrowness, and untruth.[85] Christianity achieves its nefarious aim, according to Nietzsche, by undermining the noble values of the ruling classes through revaluation, "the most intelligent revenge,"[86] as well as by subverting human vitality and instinct through "a certain false psychology, a certain kind of fantasy in interpreting motives and experiences … ."[87]

> All psychological inventions of Christianity work toward this sick excess of feeling, toward the deep corruption of head and heart necessary for it. Christianity wants to destroy, shatter, stun, intoxicate: there is only one thing it does not want: *moderation*, and for this reason, it is in its deepest meaning barbaric, Asiatic, ignoble, un-Greek.[88]

Such slavish *réssentiment* is reflected in the gospels' repeated attack upon the "privileged class" of Pharisees and scribes.[89] According to Nietzsche, the ultimate hermeneutical revaluation for Christians remains the rendering of Christ's ignominious death on the cross as "one more sign of how one ought to behave

---

manifestation of Zarathustra's will to power, see *Z*, p. 164.

[83]   *HA*, pp. 5–6.
[84]   *UM*, p. 166.
[85]   *HA*, p. 144; *GM*, p. 27.
[86]   Ibid., p. 19.
[87]   *HA*, p. 94.
[88]   Ibid., p. 85.
[89]   *TI*, p. 174.

in relation to the authorities and laws of this world: *not to defend oneself.*[90] Subsequently, Christianity entails a most abominable acquiescence to mediocrity that is political, moral, and cognitive in scope. Nietzsche once claimed that this infusion of weakness and infirmity at the heart of Christian faith is an inevitable reflection of the sickly physiologies of Christianity's promulgators.[91] Moreover, he regarded faith itself as a direct embodiment of weakness, which is "needed most urgently where will is lacking."[92] Based on Nietzsche's strong conviction that "the unfree human being is a blemish upon nature and has no share in any heavenly or earthly comfort,"[93] he denounced Christianity for its "unnatural" preservation of inferiority. In addition to restraining the creative energies of the masters, the slaves tyrannize themselves with their self-flagellating ethics—"the morality of unselfing"[94]—and world-annihilating renouncements. Hence, Nietzsche charged, "The whole morality of the Sermon on the Mount belongs here; man takes a truly voluptuous pleasure in violating himself by exaggerated demands and then deifying this something in his soul that is so tyrannically taxing."[95] Contra Kierkegaard's claims, the main motivation behind such "volitional mutilation" is not love, but rather "the dangerous thrills of cruelty directed *against himself.*"[96] On account of its craven duplicity, Christianity becomes a haven for mediocrity at both the general and individual level of existence, enslaving all in its wake.

Kierkegaard

Affinity
Kierkegaard would not deny Nietzsche's accusation that Christianity seeks to reduce humankind to subservience. In fact, he would likely add that Nietzsche had underestimated the radical nature of "man's serfdom in respect to God, to whom every man not by birth, but by creation from nothing, belongs as a bondservant, and in such a way as no bondservant has ever belonged to an earthly master ... ."[97] Like Nietzsche, Kierkegaard was also a fierce opponent of mediocrity, regarding it as "far more dangerous than heresies or schisms, where there nevertheless is passion."[98] However, unlike Nietzsche, Kierkegaard identified mediocrity with the

---

[90]   *WP*, p. 103 [1887–88].

[91]   *GS*, p. 34.

[92]   Ibid., p. 289.

[93]   Ibid., p. 156.

[94]   *EH*, p. 67.

[95]   *HA*, p. 95.

[96]   *BG*, p. 160.

[97]   *WL*, p. 119.

[98]   *JP*, vol. 3, p. 177 [1854]. See also ibid., p. 179 [1855]; *TM*, p. 460 [1854]; *TA*, p. 39.

corrupted compromises of Christendom, which have obscured the heterogeneous excellence of the Gospel.[99]

Rebuttal

Anthropological wastage
The Danish theologian would probably have called attention to several crucial inconsistencies which characterize Nietzsche's understanding of humanity. First, for all of his unbridled enthusiasm for life and love of the world, Nietzsche was highly selective in his displays of affection. In his essay on Schopenhauer, Nietzsche once alluded to "the mankind most immediate to him" as "a feeble and worm-eaten fruit!"[100] His vision of spiritual evolution, entailing the production of a few exceptional specimens amidst a multitude of waste, requires the "squandering" of billions of individuals, something Nietzsche attributed to nature's "inexperience."[101] As Kierkegaard once observed, "[T]here are probably thousands times thousands of people to one genius etc.—always this enormous waste."[102] Judge William seemingly anticipated the Nietzschean project in deriding "an esthetic snobbery that thinks that accomplishing something in the world falls to the lot of a chosen few, that there are a few very talented individuals who accomplish something, that the rest of the people are *numerus* [ciphers], superfluities in life, extravagances of the creator."[103]

Loss of individuality
Second, this political favoritism neglects the individuality of millions of already deprivileged people. Ironically, in his fervor to undermine the free agency and subsequent moral accountability of human beings,[104] Nietzsche was unperturbed by this ensuing loss of individuality. This is particularly evident in his early writings, where the effacement of the self approximates Hegelian proportions.[105] By contrast, Kierkegaard's understanding of the will-transforming relationship between the individual and God presupposes a divine freedom of expression

---

[99]   *TM*, p. 200. See also *FS*, p. 188; *SD*, p. 124.

[100]   *UM*, p. 144.

[101]   Ibid., p. 177.

[102]   *TM*, p. 180.

[103]   *EO*, vol. 2, pp. 294–5.

[104]   Interestingly, Nietzsche once attributed this "freedom from sin" to Christ, which "everyone can now attain through science" (*HA*, p. 102).

[105]   In *Birth of Tragedy*, p. 18, he referred to "mystical self-negation" and "an ecstatic reality, which … seeks to destroy individuality and redeem it with a mystical sense of unity." See also ibid., p. 52. Individuality is also threatened both by his disintegration of the acting, thinking self, as well as the attribution of singular acts or thoughts to general, species-wide instincts and drives (*UM*, p. 131).

which lovingly respects the individual's choice to "curse God" or embrace him.[106] All people are equally important in the eyes of eternity. Although Nietzsche's *Übermensch* appears to be his highest homage to individuality, Kierkegaard contended that any formulation which envisions species-wide amelioration is a reversion to "the old paganism" which privileged race over individual, reducing individuals to mere "specimens."[107]

Slavish sentiments

Third, Kierkegaard might expand his previous point by highlighting the strange ambivalence which the "all-loving" philosopher exhibited towards most of the human race. Nietzsche once confessed, "*Disgust* at mankind, at the 'rabble,' has always been my greatest danger ... ."[108] For all of his emulation of the gentry, Nietzsche displayed a decidedly "unaristocratic" attitude towards the masses: given their superabundance of power and ego, the masters would hardly have responded with hatred or irritation, but rather indifference towards those "nonentities" which pose neither threat nor consequence to their position. This is splendidly illustrated in François Mauriac's *The Knot of Vipers*, when Louis, the rich lawyer, explains, "I never talk to servants. It is not that I am a difficult or unreasonable master, but simply that, for me, they don't exist. I don't see them."[109] By regarding "slaves" as a threat—and merely by regarding them at all—Nietzsche exposed his own decidedly bourgeois bias, an attitude which sometimes elided into the *ressentiment* which he attributed to slaves. In praise of a proto-Ayn Randian selfishness, Zarathustra exclaimed,

> Entirely hateful and loathsome to it is he who will never defend himself, who swallows down poisonous spittle and evil looks, the too-patient man who puts up with everything, is content with everything: for that is the nature of slaves. Whether one be servile before gods and divine kicks, or before men and the silly opinions of men, it spits at slaves of *all* kinds, this glorious selfishness.[110]

Moreover, by engaging in his own moral revaluation[111] and exposing the vices of slave morality and the virtues of master morality, the German philosopher was ironically adopting the hermeneutical tactics of the slaves themselves. Nietzsche's insistence upon personal moderation and self-control among masters would have further distanced him from the superabundant excesses that allegedly comprise the

---

[106]   *PV*, p. 81.

[107]   Ibid., p. 107.

[108]   *EH*, p. 19.

[109]   François Mauriac, *The Knot of Vipers*, trans. Gerard Hopkins (London, 1985), p. 183.

[110]   *Z*, p. 209. Judge William once criticized the move to aggrandize evil as an attempt "to have a little distinction from the common herd" (*EO*, vol. 2, p. 226).

[111]   For example, Nietzsche's "redemption" of redemption (*EH*, p. 80), or Zarathustra's blessing upon sensual pleasure, lust for power, and selfishness (*Z*, p. 206).

spirit of aristocracy.[112] Hence, Kierkegaard might observe that, for a champion of upper-class culture and mores, Nietzsche fights like a slave.[113]

Limited explanatory capacity

Fourth, Kierkegaard may also have taken Nietzsche to task over his definitions of human victory and mastery. Despite Nietzsche's personal preferences, the so-called slave classes managed to overcome their "vastly superior" masters and institute a cultural revolution whose impact has lasted for millennia. As Nietzsche acknowledged, "Never and nowhere has there hitherto been a comparable boldness in inversion, anything so fearsome, questioning and questionable, as this formula: it promised a revaluation of antique values."[114] Nietzsche attributed this surprising occurrence to both superior intellect and superior numbers of the slaves,[115] as well as the masters' own cruelty, treason, and ineptitude.[116]

Kierkegaard might respond by questioning the ability of Nietzsche's perspective to explain adequately the unfolding of history. It is no small irony that "the victory of Christianity over Greek philosophy" represented the "brutal injustice" that "something more crude and violent has triumphed over something more spiritual and delicate."[117] The Christian life view can explain such "evil tidings" via its account of sinful, rebellious humankind, but how can the "naturalist" account for such a glaring imbalance of "evil" over "good"— whether by Nietzsche's definitions or Christianity's—in a truly amoral and unteleological universe? Should not the odds have suggested an equal occurrence of both randomly appearing? If so, acceptance seems the appropriate response, not bitterness. Furthermore, given all of their heightened biological, spiritual, and cultural advantages, how can the masters appear so weak?[118] It is the strong who have become the "endangered species," who appear ludicrously vulnerable as they suckle from the Nietzschean "wet nurse":

> My man's fare, my succulent and strengthening discourse, is effective: and truly
> I did not feed them with distending vegetables! But with warriors' food, with
> conquerors' food: I awakened new desires. There are new hopes in their arms

---

[112]   *HA*, p. 85; *TI*, p. 53. For moderation as a chief tactic for "blending in with the crowd," see *SD*, pp. 63–4.

[113]   Kierkegaard would regard all human formulations as necessarily slavish attempts to subvert true "Master morality," since every individual "belongs to God in every thought, the most hidden, in every feeling, the most private, in every motion, the most inward" (*WL*, p. 119).

[114]   *BG*, p. 75.

[115]   *TI*, p. 87.

[116]   *GM*, pp. 17, 67. See also *EH*, p. 84.

[117]   *HA*, p. 57.

[118]   See, for example, *GS*, p. 131; *WP*, p. 363 [1888].

and legs, their hearts are stretching themselves. They are discovering new words, soon their spirits will breathe wantonness.[119]

Subsequently, Kierkegaard would seriously question the heuristic efficacy of Nietzsche's formulations: if the bonds of biology and culture are so strong, how could a generation of inferior lower classes, presumably impoverished physically, intellectually, and spiritually, and having docility inculcated in them for millennia, possibly rise *en masse* and invoke such a profoundly significant and long-lasting revolution against an aristocratic class who possessed such genetic and cultural advantages carefully crafted for centuries? How could the church have arisen from the battered remnants of scattered and disillusioned disciples who had just witnessed their master ignominiously undergo an agonizing death? The suggestion that they did so by engineering a system of untruth and psychological forgery which has persevered undetected for nearly two thousand years seems at least as "incredulous" as the suggestion that God willed it so. Nietzsche's view thus fails to account satisfactorily for the spectacular rise and continued "success" of the "slaves" in light of seemingly overwhelming historical disadvantages. If he were to cite the slaves' victory as an element of the uncontrollable nature of the design-less cosmos, Kierkegaard would likely question the basis for Nietzsche's confidence that his own philosophical projections can instigate such "seismologically" significant shifts despite the "fickleness" of fate.

The need for epistemological stability
Despite the "radical" challenge which Nietzsche's morality of mastery poses to Christianity, Kierkegaard might contend that his perspective embodies an antiquated, pagan conservatism which predicates a sociological immobility within classes. As Zarathustra exhorted, "Do not will beyond your powers: there is an evil falsity about those who will beyond their powers."[120] Moreover, Nietzsche's endorsement of a universe where philosophical influences may alter human destiny to some degree situates him firmly within the Western philosophical tradition. His presuppositions call to mind the moral autonomy of Kant and Hobbes, as well as Hegel's and Hume's optimism in humankind progressing "beyond faith."[121] Even his argument for privileging the strong based on observances in nature was voiced by Plato's Callicles.[122]

---

[119]   *Z*, p. 320.

[120]   Ibid., p. 300.

[121]   See also Keith Ansell-Pearson, *An Introduction to Nietzsche as Political Thinker* (Cambridge, 1997), p. 41: "Nietzsche's political theory makes the classic move of resting a theory of the political on a theory of nature … ."

[122]   *CI*, p. 529, n. 495. See Irving Zeitlin, *Nietzsche: A Re-Examination* (Cambridge, 1994), pp. 100–112.

Kierkegaard would also maintain that Nietzsche's optimism in human autonomy and its ability to bind itself to self-legislated laws is hopelessly unfounded.[123] By contrast, Kierkegaard asserted that it is only through the objective, immutable standards levied by an impartial and transcendent God—who is beyond bribe or manipulation—and divine empowerment to attain these standards, that human beings are able to become truly free from self-servitude, arbitrariness, and self-destruction. From this perspective, ultimate freedom for a select elite does not constitute genuine freedom, but rather slavery for all. Human freedom and the intrinsic worth of every individual is irreversibly rooted in the non-negotiable standard of measurement—God's holiness—and the universal opportunity for everyone to be enabled to meet its requirements in Christ if only each person is willing. The distorted desire to sever the self from relationship with the power in which it is established is, for Anti-Climacus, indicative of profound despair.[124] Without such eternal foundations, human beings succumb to "mediocrity's fancied peace of mind": "to become distinguished—precisely because the yardstick has been converted to our size."[125] Rather than avoiding mediocrity, by dispelling transcendence and its incontrovertible standard, Kierkegaard would charge that Nietzsche had unwittingly launched humankind on a flight deeper into mediocrity and, ultimately, slavery.

---

[123]   *JP*, vol. 1, p. 76 [1850]. Here, he was responding specifically to Kant's autonomous moral agency. Dietrich Bonhoeffer concurs, "But self-negation is also a way of self-affirmation. In so far as the logos [human reason] limits itself it also establishes itself with power" (*Christology*, trans. Edwin Robertson [London, 1981], p. 29).

[124]   *SD*, p. 99.

[125]   *FS*, p. 199. See also ibid., p. 96; *WL*, p. 127.

Chapter 7

Power in Principle: Comparing the Masters

The Tier of Authority: The Accusation of Power Mongering

Because Nietzsche dismissed all notions of transcendence in the material universe, his criticisms of Kierkegaard would revolve upon situating all Christian endeavor within the universal drive for power. Any pretense of love and selflessness would be regarded as spiritual subterfuge towards this all-encompassing goal.

Nietzsche

Church as power tool

Nietzsche contended that all human and biological life on the planet is directed towards a single purpose: the accumulation of power and its reconfiguration into larger units.[1] According to Nietzsche, Schopenhauer prepared the way for the nineteenth century to transcend a "valueless existence" through participation in "an exalted and transfiguring overall goal: to acquire power so as to aid the evolution of the *physis* and to be for a while the corrector of its follies and ineptitudes."[2] The human race advances to the degree that dangerously knowledgeable individuals—the "master free spirits"—defy societal limitations and establish an "experimental" precedent which radically shifts the horizons of potential and ushers in the arrival of the "superspecies."[3] Intermediary periods of cultural conventionality are valuable for constraining mutually hostile forces and providing sociological stability so that power bases can be consolidated under relatively peaceful conditions.[4]

As a product of human culture, the Christian church once played an eminent role in power consolidation, according to Nietzsche.[5] Spurning the example set by Christ, the church utilized his teachings and brutal execution as a foundation for a new system of religious tyranny.[6] Nietzsche was keen to point out the ludicrous

---

[1]   *BG*, pp. 44, 194; *GS*, pp. 175–6, 291–2; *GM*, pp. 56–7.

[2]   *UM*, p. 142.

[3]   *Z*, p. 100. See also *HA*, pp. 7–8.

[4]   Ibid., p. 168; *UM*, p. 150; *WP*, p. 340 [1888].

[5]   *UM*, p. 150.

[6]   *WP*, p. 116 [1887–88]. See also ibid., pp. 97–8 [1888]: "What did Christ *deny*? Everything that is today called Christian." The fact that similar criticism is leveled by Leo Tolstoy against the Russian Orthodox church suggests the validity of this protest across nineteenth-century Europe: "And to not one of those present, from the priest and the superintendent … did it occur that this Jesus Whose name the priest repeated in wheezy

hypocrisy evident within a church that "wages war, condemns, tortures, swears, hates," embodies nationalist prejudices, and still professes to follow Christ.[7] He savagely purred,

> What? A god who loves men, provided only that they believe in him, and who casts an evil eye and threats upon anyone who does not believe in this love? What? A love encapsulated in if-clauses attributed to an almighty god? A love that has not even mastered the feelings of honor and vindictiveness? How Oriental this is! "If I love you, is that your concern?" is a sufficient critique of the whole of Christianity.[8]

Although deriding its inconsistencies, Nietzsche also admired the church's ability to dominate without recourse to "brute" force:

> A church is above all a structure for ruling that secures the highest rank for the *more spiritual* human beings and that *believes* in the power of spirituality to the extent of forbidding itself the use of all the cruder instruments of force; and on this score alone the church is under all circumstances a *nobler* institute than the state.[9]

Nietzsche's relation to the church was not one of simple rejection. He recognized that the church had historically been a gymnasium for gentry to exercise power and practice their insouciance of superabundance. Unfortunately for the church, Luther—a man devoid of "instinct for power"—mistook as corruption "that *luxury* of skepticism and tolerance which every triumphant, self-assured power permits itself."[10]

Historically, Christianity's depiction of God as "king" and its endorsement of secular authority as divinely sanctioned had immense repercussions for the polity of the state. Nietzsche observed, "Men often deal with their princes in a similar way as with their God, since after all the Prince was often God's representative, or at least his high priest."[11] Subsequently, religions have their uses and Nietzsche duly protested "when they themselves want to be final ends and not means beside other means."[12]

---

tones such an endless number of times, praising Him with outlandish words, had expressly forbidden everything that was being done there ..." (*Resurrection*, trans. Rosemary Edmonds [London, 1966], p. 184).

  [7]   *WP*, p. 100 [1887–88].

  [8]   *GS*, p. 190. This last point occurs in Goethe's *Wilhem Meisters Lahrjahre*, where Philine says to Wilhelm, "If I love you, what does that matter to you?" (*TC*, p. 283, n. 32).

  [9]   *GS*, p. 313.

  [10]   Ibid., p. 311.

  [11]   *HA*, p. 220.

  [12]   *BG*, p. 87.

Within Kierkegaard's own formulations, Nietzsche would have observed a crucial inconsistency. If God's power is so heterogeneous and independent of "sensate authority," why do populist incursions on the Danish monarchy effect an erosion of divine power? Furthermore, was not Kierkegaard cunningly indebting God to his polemical services by acting as "an insignificant official who by any means, by slyness, by force (that is, spiritual force) must confiscate all illusions and seize those arrogant delusions based on effrontery toward God"?[13] Nietzsche would find this reliance upon "force"—"spiritual" though it may be—conclusive evidence that, contrary to Christianity's assertions, a ruse is a ruse by any other name.

The myth of Christian "selflessness"
Despite the church's doctrinal protestations to the contrary, Nietzsche contended that every ecclesiastical activity—from the imposition of moral judgments,[14] to the praise of worthy examples,[15] from the dissemination of teachings,[16] to the dispensation of "mercies"[17]—is a demonstration of sensate power. Nietzsche considered the Christian ethic of "selflessness" to be a ludicrous illusion for several reasons. First, even the best-intentioned philanthropist "has to do a *great deal* for himself in order to be able to do anything at all for the sake of others."[18] Second, the Christian's "selfless" existence is ironically predicated on "the continued existence of loveless egoists incapable of self-sacrifice" who supply the necessary objects for such "selfless" munificence.[19] Nietzsche argued that Christian virtue irrefragably thrives upon its dialectical relations with "unchristian" atrocities; consequently, "[T]he highest morality, in order to endure, would have virtually to *exact* the existence of immorality (by which, to be sure, it would cancel itself out)."[20] Finally, to the degree that such selflessness is a manifestation of "the ascetic ideal," it represents one of the most refined and totalitarian power constructs known to humankind.[21] Nietzsche concluded, "Never has a man done anything that was only for others and without any personal motivation."[22]

---

[13] *CD*, p. 385 [20 November 1847].

[14] *HA*, p. 62; *Z*, p. 136.

[15] *HA*, p. 123.

[16] Ibid., p. 154.

[17] Ibid., p. 184; *GS*, pp. 86, 88.

[18] *HA*, p. 92.

[19] Ibid.

[20] Ibid.

[21] *GM*, pp. 123–4. This accounts for some of Nietzsche's ambivalence towards the church: insofar as it was the inculcator and repository of the ascetic ideal, he admired the "rigorous" Christianity of earlier centuries (*TI*, p. 190). See *WP*, p. 95 [1887–88] for how its "subterranean conspiracy" rejuvenated "the politically weary and the indifferent."

[22] *HA*, p. 92. He cited Georg Lichtenberg and François La Rochefoucauld in support of this contention. In contrast to selflessness, Nietzsche advocated an overwhelming sense

Kierkegaard's Quest for Power

Nietzsche would probably adduce several of Kierkegaard's own statements on Christian authority and polemical joustings with the state church, the media,[23] rival philosophical and ethical systems,[24] and "the two great powers in society, envy and obtuseness"[25] to support his argument for the church's predominant preoccupation with power.[26] Kierkegaard once confessed his love of intellectual pugilism: "By nature I am so polemical that I really feel in my element only when surrounded by human mediocrity and scurviness."[27] Tellingly, he justified his stance on the basis that, "[a]lthough I am so thoroughly polemical and was so even in my youth, still Christianity is almost too polemical for me."[28] Bishop Mynster once accused Kierkegaard of "wanting to tyrannize" after he urged ecclesiastical leaders to rule more vigorously.[29] Kierkegaard even audaciously instructed his own king on how to rule with authority and "fight with 'the masses.'"[30]

Furthermore, from Nietzsche's viewpoint, Kierkegaard is guilty of committing noetic violence by constraining the amoral universe within artificial theological structures such as grace, providence, and judgment, thus exercising his own "will to power."[31] His sophisticated attempts to assist his readership, however indirectly, towards a closer relationship to God are merely subtle attempts at self-empowerment by gaining mastery over his audience. This is reflected in the duplicitous origins of indirect communication—Kierkegaard's wilful deception of a naive Regine Olsen to evade an undesirable engagement, a woman who "could be helped only by an untruth about me ... ."[32]

---

of "selffulness"—*"great love"* for self and world—in order to resolve the "great problems" of existence (*GS*, p. 283).

23   *TC*, p. 174 [1846].

24   For example, *JK*, p. 146 [1848]; *SW*, p. 230; *PF*, p. xiii; *CI*, p. 25.

25   *TM*, p. 92.

26   For key references to Christian "battles," self-conquering, and authority, see *TM*, pp. 143, 332; *JP*, vol. 1, p. 78 [1854]; *FS*, pp. 61, 129; *JP*, vol. 3, p. 243 [1851]; ibid., vol. 4, p. 186 [1851]; *PC*, pp. 76, 229, 361 [1850]; *WA*, p. 157; *PV*, pp. 123, 179 [1849], 203 [1849]; *JK*, p. 173 [1849]; *CD*, p. 321; *BA*, p. 232 [October 1848]; *EUD*, p. 258; *JP*, vol. 4, p. 462 [1847]; *FT*, p. 16; *EUD*, p. 281; *CI*, p. 319.

27   *TM*, p. 92. His feistiness was marked from an early age, as observed by his friend and academic mentor Poul Møller: "You are so thoroughly polemical that it is quite appalling" (ibid., p. 458 [1854]).

28   Ibid., p. 459 [1854].

29   *PC*, p. 364 [1851].

30   *JK*, p. 155 [1849].

31   *Z*, p. 136; *GM*, pp. 57–8.

32   Kierkegaard adopted a womanizing persona to facilitate her emotional break-up with him. *PV*, p. 249 [1850]. For the deception of pseudonymous writing, see *CD*, p. 386

Nietzsche would never have accepted Kierkegaard's "Socratic" disclaimer that he possessed no authority of his own but wrote with the mere intention of seeking personal edification.[33] Declarations of spiritual "bankruptcy" would not have dissuaded the Nietzschean power "creditor" from exhuming the hidden "vaults" of authority by which Kierkegaard sought to bankroll a resurgence against the political and ecclesiastical leadership of his day. Undoubtedly, Nietzsche would have been impressed by Kierkegaard's intellectual prowess, his solitude and strength of character, his abhorrence for the mediocrity of the masses, and his attempt to "make life difficult" for them.[34] However, Kierkegaard's ongoing struggles with despair—the contamination of "bad conscience" in Nietzsche's view—and his ultimate confinement within the insidious restraints of Christianity would have convinced Nietzsche that he, like Pascal, was yet another casualty of the pernicious slave morality of Christianity: "I do not read Pascal but *love* him, as the most instructive of all sacrifices to Christianity, slowly murdered first physically then psychologically, the whole logic of this most horrible form of inhuman cruelty ... ."[35]

Kierkegaard

Affinity

Unlike thousands of Nietzsche's contemporaries who masked their rebellion against God beneath the niceties and external conventions of religiosity, Kierkegaard would have lauded him for openly expressing his antagonism against divine authority. As a member of the "fallen" human race, Kierkegaard would claim that Nietzsche unavoidably participated in a tragic bid for freedom which severs humankind from its very source of life. According to Kierkegaard, the tragic assault on the heavens consists of quantifying God and translating his transcendental power into temporal terms, allowing individuals to co-opt "divine" power for sensate gains and objectives, to obfuscate divine power by marshalling sensate power in its "defence," or to dismiss it as antiquated superstition deemed irrelevant to contemporary life. God is thereby anthropomorphized into a cosmic "human," whose authority may be challenged, circumvented, appropriated, or altogether ignored.[36] Nobody would have been more in agreement with Nietzsche on the deplorable ways that the church, grace, and compassion had been used to buttress political power in state Lutheranism.

[20 November 1847]; *WL* [revised], p. 398; *BA*, p. 279 [1846–47]; *CUP*, vol. 1, p. 625; *TC*, pp. 195, 211, 227 [1848], 239 [1849]; *SW*, p. xii.

[33]   *EUD*, p. x. On irony and mockery as "comic power," see *SW*, p. 366. In *The Concept of Irony*, p. 228, Kierkegaard referred to the subjective detachment of the ironist as "negative freedom," "because he is not limited in another."

[34]   *CUP*, vol. 1, pp. 186–7; *JK*, p. 93 [1845]; *FT*, p. 121.

[35]   *EH*, p. 27.

[36]   *PC*, p. 104; *CD*, p. 384 [20 November 1847].

Rebuttal

Despair-turned-boredom

Kierkegaard insisted that divine power as embodied in Christ remains primarily incomprehensible to a non-Christian perspective prior to redemption.[37] By regarding Nietzsche's writings as reflections of sinful despair, Kierkegaard's initial response may have been to call attention to a fundamental ennui which restlessly seeks fulfillment in temporal externalities. The longing that "severity, force, slavery, peril in the street and in the heart, concealment, stoicism, the art of experiment and devilry of every kind, that everything evil, dreadful, tyrannical, beast of prey and serpent in man serves to enhance the species 'man' just as much as does its opposite …"[38] could not possibly have been originated from the tumult of the French Revolution or the One-Hundred-Year's War. Instead, it may suggest boredom, frustration, the feeble mutterings of an "existential shut-in" sitting at his desk as he gazes out the window through the "bars" of a deadening bureaucracy, pining for a war or similar adventitious cause to rescue him from the smothering meaninglessness of his life.

In a similar vein, I believe that Kierkegaard would have critiqued Nietzsche's Faustian quest for "dangerous knowledge" as aesthetic despair and over-romanticized idealism. As he commented in one upbuilding discourse, "Who would know how to speak about the delights of riches better than the one who lives on crumbs, who would describe power and might more glowingly than the person who sighs in bondage … ."[39] And yet chaos shows no favoritism in the aftermath it wreaks. Wide-scale devastation would likely weaken the very institutes which propagate the aristocrats. Kierkegaard would likely contend that Nietzsche has idealistically and tragically overestimated the possibilities of creation from devastation, reconfiguration from chaos.

Moreover, Nietzsche's fundamental principle of agonism in "nature" appears to contradict his professed opposition to anthropomorphizing the "natural universe."[40] Zarathustra once derided the "truth-tellers" of society:

---

[37]   *PF*, pp. 30–31; *EUD*, p. 379. Hence, "secular" accounts would evaluate Christ on the basis of his historical accomplishments and typically conclude that he had squandered his great potential (*PC*, p. 49; *EUD*, p. 91). The observer would ultimately be offended by the mere notion that "God proves to be the lowly, poor, suffering and finally powerless human being" (*PC*, p. 102).

[38]   *BG*, p. 72. See also *WP*, p. 33 [1888].

[39]   *EUD*, p. 93. See Pascal, p. 59: "Who indeed would think himself unhappy not to be king except one who had been dispossessed?" Miguel de Unamuno derides Nietzsche's philosophy as, "the doctrine of weaklings who aspire to be strong" (*The Tragic Sense of Life* [London, 1962], pp. 65–6).

[40]   This point is exquisitely made by Britain's philosophical jesters, Monty Python's Flying Circus, Episode #30, who parody a similar tendency in "nature" programming: while showing a photo of a wolf, a German voice intones: "Here we see an ant. This ant is

You first want to *make* all being conceivable: for, with a healthy mistrust, you doubt whether it is in fact conceivable. But it must bend and accommodate itself to you! Thus will your will have it ... . That is your entire will, you wisest of men; it is a will to power; and that is so even when you talk of good and evil and of the assessment of values.[41]

However, "nature" itself becomes a useful polemical construct for Nietzsche, and his own anthropomorphization of nature is manifest in certain statements: "Nature is in its depths much richer, mightier, happier, more dreadful ... ."[42] Nature's inherent drive for power seems suspiciously human, "all too human."

The idealized aristocracy
Another prominent feature of Nietzsche's concept of authority which would invite Kierkegaardian scrutiny is his romanticization of the nobility. Nietzsche envisioned an aristocracy whose magnanimity flows from "strong and godlike selfhood."[43] Such figures tower above a pygmied humankind: "The noble type of man feels *himself* to be the determiner of values, he does not need to be approved of, he judges 'what harms me is harmful in itself,' he knows himself to be that which in general first accords honour to things, he *creates values*."[44]

Kierkegaard would undoubtedly have endeavored to inject some realism into the reverie. Nietzsche's depictions of the chivalrous "knightly code" among the nobility appear more frequently in the medieval romances of Marie de France than in the turbulent pages of European history.[45] In *On the Genealogy of Morals*, he depicted the nobleman as a paragon of virility whose lordship over villages and value-systems alike radiates from a superabundance of health.[46] Nietzsche's highly selective idealization of the aristocracy as the purveyor of fine human

---

engaged in a life-and-death struggle with the wolf ..." (http://www.ibras.dk/Monty python/episode30.htm#6).

[41]   *Z*, p. 136.

[42]   *UM*, p. 221. See also ibid., p. 76, where he described "life" as "that dark, driving power that insatiably thirsts for itself."

[43]   *WP*, p. 209 [1887].

[44]   *BG*, p. 195.

[45]   See, for example, *GS*, p. 87: "[B]ut they are doubly obliging toward their *peers* whom it would be honourable to fight if the occasion should ever arise. Spurred by the good feeling of *this* perspective, the members of the knightly caste became accustomed to treating each other with exquisite courtesy." For "the charm of rareness, inimitableness, exceptionalness, and unaverageness—its aristocratic magic," see *WP*, p. 175 [1887–88]. Stephen Houlgate traces Nietzsche's "heroic" emphasis to Greek tragedy (*Hegel, Nietzsche and the Criticism of Metaphysics* [Cambridge, 1986], p. 195). See also Ian Burkitt, "Overcoming Metaphysics: Elias and Foucault on Power and Freedom," *Philosophy of the Social Sciences*, 23/1 (1993): 62.

[46]   *GM*, p. 19.

specimens—the repository of "collective self-esteem" which comprises "the great preparatory school for personal sovereignty,"[47] "[t]hose great forcing houses for strong human beings"[48]—conveniently overlooked the more pernicious themes of indulgence, cruelty, excess, treachery, indolence, and early death which befell many a noble. His paeans to these phantasmal figures resonate with sentimentality for a "golden" because idealized past.[49] By contrast, Kierkegaard's personal acquaintance with Danish monarchs likely tempered any temptations to over-idealize the aristocracy.[50]

One way Nietzsche might have responded to such criticism is by emphasizing that it is not the aristocrats themselves but their institutions which constitute the decisive factor in breeding forerunners of the *Übermensch*.[51] Hence, he regarded material security as

> *the source of a nobility of the blood.* Wealth necessarily produces an aristocracy
> of race, for it permits one to select the most beautiful women and to pay the best
> teachers; it allows a person to be clean, to have time for physical exercise, and,
> above all, to avoid dulling physical labour.[52]

In less exuberant moments, Nietzsche contended that the greatest specimens share a symbiotic connection with their times.[53] Hence, the "herd," too, must be protected from excessive damage at the hands of an overzealous, short-sighted "exception."[54]

Nietzsche himself knew that his genealogical assessments contained some inspired embellishment in attempt to press back Schopenhauerian pessimism and the overwhelming tides of mediocrity which were inundating nineteenth-century Europe. He once wrote,

> History shows: the strong races decimate one another: through war, thirst for
> power, adventurousness; the strong affects: wastefulness ... . [T]heir existence
> is costly; in brief—they ruin one another; periods of profound exhaustion and
> torpor supervene: all great ages are *paid for*—The strong are subsequently
> weaker, more devoid of will, more absurd than the weak average.[55]

---

[47]　*WP*, p. 406 [1887–88].

[48]　*TI*, p. 104.

[49]　See *GS*, pp. 117, 228, 346.

[50]　*JK*, p. 155 [1849].

[51]　*Z*, p. 110; *WP*, p. 463 [1887–88].

[52]　*HA*, p. 231.

[53]　*TI*, p. 108. See also *WP*, pp. 68 [1885], 215 [1888], 463 [1887–88].

[54]　*GS*, p. 131.

[55]　*WP*, pp. 462–3 [1888].

Nevertheless, Nietzsche's "*carpe deum*" strategy is effective so long as everyone does not strive to "seize the godhead," to live as conquerors, innovators, and thieves.[56] Perhaps this is one reason why Nietzsche addressed his books to a small but select audience, "the kind of people who alone matter: I mean those who are *heroic*."[57]

Enslaved to the outcome

Another of Kierkegaard's probable criticisms of Nietzsche's concept of authority strikes at the very heart of his philosophical project. By absolutizing temporal power and human ability to shape hermeneutically the world which they inhabit, the human being enslaves herself to "fate."[58] With the eradication of the transcendent Other, Kierkegaard argued that the individual is imprisoned between an unchangeable past and an uncertain future, confined to the domain of thieves, rot, rust, and the "slings and arrows of outrageous fortune" which constantly threaten to erode her basis of authority. This culminates in avarice, anxiety, and despair,[59] for she becomes, in Climacus' words, "a slave to the outcome."[60] Ironically, the more a person exchanges the "uncertainty" of spiritual freedom for the "certainty" of sensate power, the more she locates her self-worth in uncontrollable externals instead of a restored relationship with God, the more impoverished the self becomes, and the less power she is subsequently capable of wielding without succumbing to that power.[61] Because the Christian's identity and ultimate worth are rooted in the unshakable love of God, she is "freed" from external accomplishments, and Kierkegaard contended that not even death can negate or "cut short" her life's work if she has been living in obedience to God.[62]

In contrast to Nietzsche's ever-grasping will to power, Kierkegaard concurred with Plato that the best rulers are those who do not desire power, lest the tyrant become enslaved by his own lust for power or enter "a concealed relation of dependency on those whom he is supposed to rule … ."[63] Hence, Anti-Climacus stated that the man who relentlessly bases his self-worth upon temporal achievements—adhering to a Nietzschean "either/or," "Caesar or nothing"— demonstrates true weakness in failing to accept himself regardless of whether he becomes Caesar or not.[64] Kierkegaard contended that anything—including sensate

---

[56]   *GS*, p. 338.

[57]   Ibid., p. 235.

[58]   *CUP*, vol. 1, p. 137; *CA*, pp. 96–7. Here the classical Hellenistic despair inherent within Nietzsche's framework becomes evident. See also *EO*, vol. 1, p. 38.

[59]   *JP*, vol. 6, p. 202 [1855]; *CD*, p. 48; *EUD*, p. 27; *SW*, p. 466; *CA*, p. 61; *FT*, p. 15; *EUD*, p. 10.

[60]   *CUP*, vol. 1, p. 398.

[61]   *WL*, p. 252; *TA*, p. 7.

[62]   *EUD*, p. 142.

[63]   *TM*, p. 91.

[64]   *SD*, p. 49. See also *EUD*, p. 171.

authority—which is possessed as a result of "accidents of fortune" can never be confidently possessed.[65] For this reason, Kierkegaard emphasized, "All finite power makes [a being] dependent ... ."[66]

The lofty and "indifferent" power which Nietzsche praised, "which is conscious of no witness around it; which lies oblivious of the existence of any opposition; which reposes in *itself*, fatalistic, a law among laws,"[67] applies more to architecture than arch-dukes. Such security is poor comfort, according to Kierkegaard, in light of the incontestable power of God. Any sensate authority, which is necessarily dependent upon uncontrollable variables and must be continuously bolstered and maintained,[68] thereby entails "hard and heavy slavery."[69] From the perspective of eternity, monarchs and nobility possess no existential distinctions or privileges: they are as equally alienated from God and as much in need of redemption as any other human being.[70] Subsequently, Kierkegaard maintained that sensate leaders like the King lack any spiritual authority,[71] though they unwittingly retain their sensate authority "*by the grace of God*."[72] To the extent that the strong and wealthy protect the poor and promote justice among the nations, they are dutifully fulfilling their posts. However, as soon as rulers adopt a "pyramidical" mindset and subjugate their charges, Kierkegaard contended, "So God pushes over the pyramid and everything collapses—a generation later man begins the pyramid business again."[73]

Blindness to the limitations of sensate authority

Kierkegaard would probably press his offensive one step further and assert that Nietzsche was blind to the inherent limitations of sensate authority by his own desire for power. Nietzsche's totalizing reduction of human behavior and action to "instincts" and unconscious drives entails the promulgation of natural determinism: even the most strident ascetic measures and self-sacrifices are attributed to the innate instincts, which weaker humans are "too degenerate" to rein in by moderation.[74] Kierkegaard would indubitably challenge Nietzsche on his definition of "freedom" and ask whether it did not represent a most repressive kind of bondage:

---

[65]   *CD*, p. 225; *CUP*, vol. 1, p. 398.

[66]   *TM*, p. 391 [1846]. See also *EUD*, pp. 29–30; *FT*, p. 41; and *EUD*, p. 201: "[A]ll external power is powerless."

[67]   *TI*, p. 85.

[68]   *EUD*, p. 317.

[69]   *EUD*, p. 181.

[70]   Because God's power is qualitatively heterogeneous, God shows complete impartiality as to whether a king or a beggar becomes a Christian, since none can "assist God's cause" (*TM*, p. 43).

[71]   Ibid., p. 113; *WA*, p. 100.

[72]   *JP*, vol. 4, p. 135 [8 August 1839].

[73]   Ibid., p. 194 [1854].

[74]   *TI*, p. 53.

For what is freedom? That one has the will to self-responsibility. That one preserves the distance which divides us. That one has become more indifferent to hardship, toil, privation, even to life. That one is ready to sacrifice men to one's cause, oneself not excepted. Freedom means that the manly instincts that delight in war and victory have gained mastery over the other instincts—for example, over the instinct for "happiness."[75]

Because human nature is inextricably connected with its sociological context, according to Nietzsche individuals are thus conditioned by cultural as well as biological determinants.[76] He is, however, somewhat equivocal as to whether nature or nurture gains predominance. Although his entire philosophical project is founded upon the prospect of assisting "nature" using proper guidance, Nietzsche remained intensely sceptical of any reformation of "tainted" biological factors.[77] Within his doctrine of eternal recurrence, humankind is encircled by a cosmic "hamster wheel" which perpetually spins without going anywhere—a curious incongruence for a thinker who endorsed "becomings." According to Anti-Climacus, Nietzsche's motto of *amor fati* in a God-less universe would entail a most tragic abrogation of human life and liberty, for "[t]he determinist, the fatalist, is in despair, and in despair he has lost his self because for him everything is necessity."[78] Kierkegaard would likely focus upon two specific components of Nietzsche's theological "blindspots" regarding the shortcomings of sensate power.

Querying control
Kierkegaard would first contend that Nietzsche's position is highly unrealistic in its optimism concerning human capacities to transmute personal and societal contexts. Though Nietzsche held no utopian illusions as to the contributions of the aristocrats for their contemporaries, the nobility provided long-term benefits insofar as they advanced the species towards a spiritual freedom unimpeded by obsolete mores and conventions. This optimism is paralleled by what Kierkegaard would deem an exaggerated hopefulness in humankind's ability to master its darkest instincts once they have been unleashed.[79] In response to Nietzsche's insistence that the noble leader can liberate himself from all pettiness and excel

---

[75]   Ibid., pp. 103–4.

[76]   See, for example, ibid., p. 102.

[77]   *EH*, p. 18: "[A]ll the *concealed* dirt at the bottom of many a nature, perhaps conditioned by bad blood but whitewashed by education, is known to me almost on first contact."

[78]   *SD*, p. 70.

[79]   See, for example, *WP*, p. 503 [1885] and p. 207 [1885–86]: "But putting them [the affects] into service ... may also mean subjecting them to a protracted tyranny (not only as an individual, but as a community, race, etc.). At last they are confidently granted freedom again: they love us as good servants and go voluntarily wherever our best interests lie."

at "self-control and self-outwitting,"[80] Kierkegaard would insist, "No matter how strong a person is, no person is stronger than himself."[81] Subsequently, Nietzsche's sentiment is an impossible and inane expectation, "the marvel unheard of in heaven or on earth or under the earth—that something that is in conflict with itself can in this conflict be stronger than itself!"[82]

To Nietzsche's question,

> Is a state of affairs unthinkable in which the malefactor calls himself to account and publicly dictates his own punishment, in the proud feeling that he is thus honouring the law which he himself has made, that by punishing himself he is exercising his power, the power of the law-giver?[83]

Kierkegaard would have undoubtedly answered with a stentorian affirmative. Because, by Nietzsche's own admission, the "born aristocrats of the spirit" have nothing to prove—"The wish to create incessantly is vulgar, betraying jealousy, envy, and ambition ..."[84]—Kierkegaard might validly ask what motivation would instigate such pivotal and widespread spiritual revolutions. Both men envisioned a liberating independence from external pressures and accomplishments for genuine heroics. Climacus explained, "[I]n the process he [the ethical hero] perhaps would produce a great effect in the external world, but this would not occupy him at all, because he would know that the external is not in his power and therefore means nothing either *pro* or *contra*."[85] However, according to Kierkegaard, Nietzsche's vision fails precisely by throwing the person back on her own strength to achieve this independence, whereas the Christian is freed from basing her identity upon the uncontrollable throes of temporality precisely because she knows that her self-worth and identity are founded entirely upon God.

Questioning the breeder
The second element which indicates that Nietzsche was blind to the limits of temporal power is his ambitious presumption that one can deliberately mould the entire species and hasten the arrival of a "higher" race of bipedal behemoths.[86] Nietzsche explained, "Breeding, as I understand it, is a means of storing up the tremendous forces of mankind so that the generations can build upon the work of their forefathers—not only outwardly, but inwardly, organically growing out of them

---

[80]   *BG*, p. 122.
[81]   *EUD*, p. 18.
[82]   Ibid., p. 128.
[83]   *NR*, p. 234.
[84]   *HA*, p. 126.
[85]   *CUP*, vol. 1, pp. 135–6. See also *BA*, p. 157.
[86]   *GM*, pp. 66–7. See also Nietzsche's distinction between "stolid metronomes for the slow spirit" and "*We others*" in *GS*, p. 131.

and becoming something stronger … ."[87] Zarathustra's intention to "walk among men as among fragments of the future" and "compose into one and bring together what is fragment and riddle and dreadful chance" presupposes a transcendence and power of divine proportions.[88] Assuming that such a brash undertaking is even possible in theory, why should Nietzsche be the one to engineer the psychological "genome" of the human species?

Such an aspiration appears inconsistent with the aspersions Nietzsche cast towards the imposition of cause-and-effect frameworks upon the world. How can he labor to effect a constructive impact upon the entire race when he, along with Kierkegaard, recognizes that a person has no guarantee that her smallest action will produce the desired effect in light of the world's dynamic complexities?[89] According to Nietzsche's revisioned understanding of history—a paradoxical undertaking given his scepticism that such hermeneutical endeavors are inherently flawed and untruthful, as Douglas Smith points out[90]— Christianity was a kind of "brace" which once stabilized European society:

> Protracted unfreedom of spirit, mistrustful constraint in the communicability of ideas, the discipline thinkers imposed on themselves to think within an ecclesiastical or courtly rule or under Aristotelian presuppositions, the protracted spiritual will to interpret all events according to a Christian scheme and to rediscover and justify the Christian God in every chance occurrence—all these violent, arbitrary, severe, gruesome and antirational things have shown themselves to be the means by which the European spirit was disciplined in its strength, ruthless curiosity and subtle flexibility … .[91]

But now, according to Nietzsche, humankind has outgrown its "school-master" and the support-turned-strait-jacket needs to be removed. Here, Kierkegaard might interject objections to another methodological inconsistency: if Nietzsche truly believed the conquistador creed that "that which does not kill us makes us stronger,"[92] how could he hope to breed a super-being if he deprived his protégés of the very adversarial stimuli needed to test and develop the superiority of "master

---

[87]   *WP*, p. 215 [1888].

[88]   *Z*, p. 161.

[89]   As Mr. A declared, "It also seems to me that with cause and effect the relation does not hold together properly. Sometimes enormous and *gewaltige* [powerful] causes produce a very *klein* [small] and insignificant little effect, sometimes none at all; sometimes a nimble little cause produces a colossal effect" (*EO*, vol. 1, p. 25). Kierkegaard was also aware of hermeneutical games played by the will. Subsequently, in the wake of 1848, he wrote, "[P]eople must take a few days to fool one another into thinking that what occurred is what they wanted" (*WA*, p. 228 [1848]).

[90]   *GM*, p. xxv.

[91]   *BG*, p. 111.

[92]   Ibid., p. 155; *TI*, p. 33.

spirits"? Furthermore, if the world is truly in a state of flux and becomings as Nietzsche suggested, Kierkegaard might also ponder why the will to power as a foundational principle of life seems invulnerable to transition.

Moreover, if all truth is conditional and all morality and principles are self-serving and power-enhancing, Kierkegaard might fairly ask why anyone should bother listening to Nietzsche's "truths," since his formulations enjoy no privileged status in a world where all truth is merely will to power. It seems strange that Nietzsche should object vociferously when the majority of people refuse to acknowledge his truth-claims about universal untruth.[93] What is the basis of Nietzsche's own philosophical authority if, indeed, "[o]ne seeks a picture of the world in that philosophy in which we feel freest; i.e., in which our most powerful drive feels free to function. This will also be the case with me!"[94]—particularly when the greatest freedom, apart from that of the philosophical architect of the human race, is allotted to a small, excessively privileged elite? In light of his notebook writings, one must ask who determines a "miscarried life" and how society "ought to prevent them,"[95] who possesses the "genuine charity" to dictate which human sacrifices must be made "for the good of the species."[96]

Even if Nietzsche could somehow arrogate such moral authority to himself, even if the strong were to thrive under Nietzsche's philosophical regimen, the so-called "supermen" would ultimately remain in bondage to one person—the noble "architect of the future," Nietzsche himself.[97] At times, the *Übermensch* pales beneath the shadow of the mighty philosopher-king:

> For every elevated world one has to be born or, expressed more clearly, *bred* for it: one has a right to philosophy—taking the word in the grand sense—only by virtue of one's origin; one's ancestors, one's "blood" are the decisive thing here too. Many generations must have worked to prepare for the philosopher; each of his virtues must have been individually acquired, tended, inherited, incorporated, and not only the bold, easy, delicate course and cadence of his thoughts but above all the readiness for great responsibilities, the lofty glance that rules and looks down, the feeling of being segregated from the mob and its duties and virtues, the genial protection and defence of that which is misunderstood and calumniated, be it god or devil, the pleasure in and exercise of grand justice,

---

[93]   *BG*, p. 36. As Rüdiger Safranski observes, although he rejected free will, "Nietzsche would keep right on judging human affairs as though people did have a choice and could make decisions ..." (*Nietzsche: A Philosophical Biography*, trans. Shelly Frisch [New York, 2003], p. 176).

[94]   *WP*, pp. 224–5 [1883–88].

[95]   Ibid., p. 389 [1888].

[96]   Ibid., p. 142 [1888].

[97]   *UM*, p. 94. Nietzsche playfully prognosticated this paradox: "I have a terrible fear I shall one day be pronounced *holy* ..." (*EH*, p. 96).

the art of commanding, the breadth of will, the slow eye which seldom admires, seldom looks upward, seldom loves ... .[98]

The philosopher alone understood the true value of the herd and protected their wanton destruction by short-sighted "exceptions."[99] He alone appreciated the need to restrict the flow of aristocratic blood and values to the elite and knew why horrible misunderstandings must follow when class divisions are transgressed.[100] Nietzsche himself easily surpassed the limited brilliance of the "higher men":

> Very rarely does a higher nature retain sufficient reason for understanding and treating everyday people as such; for the most part, this type assumes that its own passion is present but kept concealed in all men, and this belief even becomes an ardent and eloquent faith. But when such exceptional people do not see themselves as the exception, how can they ever understand the common type and arrive at a fair evaluation of the rule?[101]

Nietzsche perhaps recognized the irony of his philosophical supremacy in *Beyond Good and Evil* where he admitted that not all slavery is bad: "[I]t seems that slavery, in the cruder and in the more refined sense, is the indispensable means also for spiritual discipline and breeding."[102] If Nietzsche's project entails a newer and more sophisticated slavery as a means of advancing the species, Kierkegaard would likely identify his promise of spiritual "freedom" as merely a rhetorical ploy for masking a more ingenuous mode of tyranny as little entitled to the epithet "liberty" as the Christian legalism Nietzsche justifiably denigrated.

The myth of master power

It is highly feasible that Kierkegaard's greatest attack upon Nietzsche would be to question the very existence of "master power" *per se* on account of its dialectical interdependence upon so-called "slave power" and its vulnerability to change. Kierkegaard contended that government is "an indulgence" whose powers teeter precariously on the ignorance or passivity of its "subjects."[103] Master power is arguably a form of harnessed slave power benefiting a chosen few.[104] For this reason, Kierkegaard compared democracy with tyranny in that both amount to

---

98   *BG*, pp. 145–6.

99   *GS*, p. 131.

100   *BG*, pp. 136–7. See also *WP*, p. 461 [1888].

101   *GS*, p. 78.

102   *BG*, p. 112.

103   *WA*, p. 215 [1848].

104   *CD*, p. 128. For the support of a leader as nationalistic self-celebration of his supporters, see *WA*, p. 82.

rule by fear of men: the difference is merely numerical, and the power basis of all forms of government including monarchies[105] is "always 'the people.'"[106]

The paradox of "master power" is also evident when one considers Nietzsche's assertion that a "great spirit" must prove himself against opponents who are evenly matched. If such a spirit can defeat all potential challengers, he must despair and fall into ruin, since he has deprived himself of the source of his strength—the existence of worthy because equally powerful threats. As Anti-Climacus observed, "[A] master who is a self directly before slaves, indeed really ... is not a self—for in both cases there is no standard of measurement."[107] Kierkegaard contended, "If a capability is actually to be a capability, it must have opposition, because if it has no opposition, then it is either all-powerful or something imaginary."[108] Moreover, if a mighty tyrant were to arise and successfully implement a new morality, the tyrant invariably makes life existentially easier for slaves and aristocrats alike insofar as he removes their responsibility to think for themselves, thus volitionally weakening the *Übermensch* "stock" and subsequently "demoralizing" men.[109]

Nietzsche probably would have responded that subjugating an opponent does not destroy the threat they pose: "[T]here is in commanding an admission that the absolute power of the opponent has not been vanquished, incorporated, disintegrated. 'Obedience' and 'commanding' are forms of struggle."[110] However, Kierkegaard might counter by asking whether these never-ending battles for supremacy will permit that stable *status quo* of prosperity by which the species accumulates its collective energy for the surge of future extraordinary specimens. Moreover, Nietzsche's concept of power relies upon external resistances:[111] foes to fight, conventions to revoke, an unsuspecting "bovine" populace to corral. "Freedom" is largely dependent upon ongoing hostilities between the self and the other.[112] The paradox of a "great" man who is paralysed by the absence of conflict is cogently depicted by Charlotte Brontë when Jane Eyre observes of St. John Rivers:

> Well may he eschew the calm of domestic life; it is not his element: there his
> faculties stagnate—they cannot develop or appear to advantage. It is in scenes of

---

[105]   *JP*, vol. 3, p. 486 [1854]; *JK*, p. 234 [1854]; *JP*, vol. 4, p. 148 [1848]; ibid., vol. 4, p. 141 [1847]; *EUD*, p. 316; *CUP*, vol. 1, p. 610.

[106]   *JP*, vol. 4, p. 146 [1848].

[107]   *SD*, p. 111. See also *CD*, p. 209. Judge William argued that one who defines himself by conflict is never at peace and never "inside himself" since his focus is always turned outwards (*EO*, vol. 2, p. 143).

[108]   *EUD*, p. 318.

[109]   For a similar charge that the Jesuits weakened men by placing "superhuman" ascetic demands upon themselves, see *JP*, vol. 3, pp. 421–2 [1850].

[110]   *WP*, p. 342 [1885].

[111]   *EH*, p. 17.

[112]   *WP*, p. 493 [1887–88].

strife and danger—where courage is proved, and energy exercised, and fortitude tasked—that he will speak and move, the leader and superior.[113]

Enduring peace may require a whole new strength of its own.

Perhaps Nietzsche projected something of himself onto Schopenhauer when he once explained,

> [L]et us not underestimate the fact that Schopenhauer ... *needed* enemies to remain in good spirits; that he loved grim, green galling words; that he raged for the sake of raging, out of passion; that he would have fallen ill, become a *pessimist* ... without his enemies, without Hegel, woman, sensuality, and the whole will to existence, the will to endure.[114]

Even Nietzsche's "systematic ingratitude"—to employ Tanner's apt phrase[115]—cannot negate one's dependence on those upon whom one treads. Arguably, Nietzsche even needed Christianity, an opponent "ennobled" by his antagonism: "[T]o attack is with me a proof of good will, under certain circumstances of gratitude. I do honour, I confer distinction when I associate my name with a cause, a person: for or against—that is in this regard a matter of indifference to me."[116] In light of this essential reliance upon externality in general and "slave power" in particular, Nietzsche's delineation of "master power" is, from Kierkegaard's perspective, simply unfounded. Hence, the Danish theologian would concur with Mephistopheles:

> No more! That privilege I gladly waive,
> Of hearing about tyrant versus slave ... .
> They fight, they say, dear freedom's cause to save;
> But, seen more clearly, slave is fighting slave.[117]

The myth of slave power

In order to approximate Kierkegaardian standards, this hypothetical critique must be pressed still further, beyond the far-ranging abstraction of superspecies-enhancements to bear upon the existential circumstances of "that single individual." Whereas "master power" is mythical, given the inextricable interconnectedness of human action and influence regardless of class, "slave power" is equally mythical for Kierkegaard, since all people—irrespective of rank or status—exhibit the hallmark of aristocratic indulgence: the ability to transform others into nonentities

---

[113]   Charlotte Brontë, *Jane Eyre* (London, 1996), p. 438.

[114]   *GM*, p. 85.

[115]   *EH*, p. x.

[116]   Ibid., pp. 17–18.

[117]   Johann Wolfgang von Goethe, *Faust*, trans. Philip Wayne (2 vols, London, 1949), vol. 2, p. 104.

through sheer spite and/or indifference.[118] Distancing oneself from "undesirables" may be an aristocratic ideal,[119] yet Kierkegaard denounced its universal practice:

> Whether in the enjoyment of his haughtiness and pride one openly gives other people to understand that they do not exist for him, whether in the nourishment of his arrogance one wants them to be sensitive to this by demanding an expression of slavish subjection from them, or whether stealthily and secretly, simply by avoiding any contact with them ... one expresses that they do not exist for him—these are basically one and the same things. The inhumanness and unChristianness of this does not consist in the manner in which it is done but in wanting to deny one's relationship in the human race with all men, with absolutely every man.[120]

Kierkegaard proceeded to explore "passive aggression" as one subtle means by which the underprivileged slave can nullify the existence of the mightiest master, thus demonstrating "the strength of weakness."[121] The weakest invalid can commit spiritual murder by giving up the hated one as hopeless and consequently "taking possibility away from him."[122]

Meanwhile, the strongest tyrant cannot force an individual to do anything, according to Kierkegaard: the most he can do is to threaten death, which further undermines his power by immortalizing the "victim" with the mantle of martyrdom, as well as publicly legitimating his opponent as a serious threat which demands immediate and extreme measures.[123] Because the locus of the martyr's power is internal, her resolve is not eroded by external pressure; however, the tyrant, whose power is based externally upon oppositions and achievements, is ultimately weakened by the removal of external opponents like the martyr. The martyr, subsequently, demonstrates her superiority by forcing the tyrant's hand in having her killed.[124] Even if the tyrant succeeds in arrogating all power from his subjugated populace, he inadvertently fuels future rebellion by augmenting the means by which the "powerless" may attain power—a growing sense of desperation and will to power.[125]

---

[118]   *WL*, p. 85.

[119]   *WL* [revised], p. 411.

[120]   *WL*, p. 84. See also *JP*, vol. 4, p. 140 [1846].

[121]   *WL*, p. 277.

[122]   Ibid., p. 240.

[123]   For this reason, he advised King Christian VIII that the best course of action against scandal-mongers was to ignore them and thus de-legitimize their boasts (*JK*, p. 155 [1849]). Constantin made a similar point of how a "powerful" man is rendered ludicrous by oppressing a woman (*SW*, p. 51).

[124]   See *WA*, pp. 72–4.

[125]   *JP*, vol. 4, p. 141 [1847]; *TA*, p. 108. Hence, Quidam commented, "A person who is in desperate need always has supernatural powers ..." (*SW*, p. 387).

Though sensate power appears risible when analyzed within the temporal world alone, its foreboding power and relevance, for Kierkegaard, is paradoxically revealed only in conjunction with eternity. The power to exclude and existentially nullify the other is not merely demonstrated when an individual shuns other people—it is characteristic of every individual's degenerate attitude towards God. Regardless of intention, both the societal "master" and "slave" are unified in the fundamental revolt of creature against Creator.[126] According to Kierkegaard, every individual naturally strives to live a life free from divine authority. Her appropriation of sensate power to secure this end becomes a thieving from eternity, an arrogant arrogation of authority after "deposing" God.[127] "Slave" power is, therefore, an illusion, since every individual regardless of position wields the most eternally influential "master" power in existence—the ability to say "no" to God. Because of the way in which God lovingly holds back his omnipotence to safeguard the freedom of his creations, Kierkegaard maintained that "a person's selfishness" becomes God's greatest "opponent": "There is only one who can hinder God, him who indeed is eternally strongest, in becoming the strongest—this one is the person himself."[128]

A personal defence

As for the accusation that Kierkegaard was cunningly accumulating power for himself through the influence he sought to exert over Christendom, the Danish thinker would have protested that he did everything possible to eschew the acquisition of fame or following. His perennial aloofness, pseudonymous subterfuge, avoidance of neatly packaged dogmatic decrees, periodic disavowals of personally possessing apostolic authority or Christian "excellence," and public notoriety in the wake of *The Corsair* scandal thoroughly prevented his acquisition of sensate prominence, since "one single person can never literally become a physical power."[129] With regards to his writings and expertise on genuine Christian belief, Kierkegaard would have maintained that he was only doing his duty as a truth-witness, constantly reminding himself as much as others of the need for humility and service "not by domineering and wanting to force others to obey God, but by unconditionally obeying as an individual ... ."[130] If Nietzsche misinterpreted Kierkegaard's true motives, it was merely because he, too, like the Danish masses, was "not able to conceive of an intelligent man not coveting status and power."[131]

---

126   *FS*, p. 64.

127   See *EUD*, p. 193: "If human beings want to resemble God by ruling, they have forgotten God; then God has departed and they are playing the rulers in God's absence."

128   *CD*, p. 129. See also *PC*, p. 77 and *EUD*, p. 226: "[T]here is truly only one eternal object of wonder—that is God—and only one possible hindrance to wonder—and that is a person when he himself wants to be something."

129   *TM*, p. 77.

130   *WL*, pp. 121–2.

131   *TC*, p. 217.

The ultimate empowerment

Contrary to the universal practice of negating the meaningful existence of others through animosity or indifference, Kierkegaard emphasized that, because every individual is equidistant from the opportunity of a salvific relationship with God, "the possibility of the good exists at every moment for the other person."[132] The alteration of external conditions to redistribute temporal power allocation is, for Kierkegaard, irrelevant for alleviating the true spiritual plight of individuals. He cited the recent horrors of the French Revolution as an excruciating reminder that radical changes to societal conditions can neither end cruelty nor rehabilitate the human heart.[133] The only means of true empowerment is spiritual freedom, the humble acknowledgement that all individuals stand equally prodigal and helpless yet equally valued and loved before God.[134]

According to orthodox Christianity, "God exists and is the only master ... ."[135] On account of the limitations of sensate authority, Kierkegaard insisted that God alone, whose power is qualitatively other and therefore incontestable, can truly free a human being without enslaving her through obligation, threat of the gift's removal, or a slavish dependency upon the gift itself. Because love, "the strongest power in a man,"[136] is universally available to all who are willing, God may truly liberate the individual from the tyranny of the foulest ruler or the cruelest fate, abolishing slavery to the outcome and rendering God's followers "more than conquerors."[137] Subsequently, Kierkegaard proclaimed, "In suffering, bold confidence is able to take power from the world and has the power to change scorn into honor, victory into downfall!"[138] According to Kierkegaard, Nietzsche was right to declare that human beings are "destined" to rule;[139] however, this rule is not founded upon sensate power and oppression of the other, but rather upon eternal love and service to the other.[140]

Both Kierkegaard and Nietzsche were probably aware of the paradox of sacrilege, that the "gods" are only worth robbing so long as they remain the treasuries of value and significance in society. In light of this dialectical dependency, Kierkegaard might ask how long "hatred, envy, covetousness, and lust for domination" can remain "life-conditioning emotions"[141] after love, peace, and harmony have all but disappeared. Furthermore, Nietzsche once admitted

---

[132]   *WL*, p. 239.

[133]   Ibid., p. 89.

[134]   Nietzsche specifically blamed Christianity for the "crazy" concept of "equality of souls before God" (*WP*, p. 401 [1888]).

[135]   *WL*, p. 122.

[136]   Ibid., p. 160.

[137]   *JP*, vol. 4, p. 401 [1851]; *CD*, p. 400 [1848]; *EUD*, p. 303.

[138]   Ibid., p. 331.

[139]   *BG*, p. 151.

[140]   *EUD*, p. 189; *EUD*, p. 84.

[141]   *BG*, p. 53.

that one can never destroy an enemy if one is to be continuously strengthened by ceaseless conflict, even an enemy as despised as Christianity: "The continuance of the Christian ideal is one of the most desirable things there are—even for the sake of ideals that want to stand beside it and perhaps above it—they must have opponents, strong opponents, if they are to become *strong*."[142] Without a robust church to rebel against, the victory becomes hollow and the detractor may be left with an unnerving ambiguity as to whether he is truly rebelling against Christianity or aligning himself with a righteously indignant "remnant," who— albeit inadvertently—assists the prophetic call for reform.

---

[142] *WP*, p. 197 [1887]. See also *HA*, p. 240.

Chapter 8
Conclusions: Expanding the Dialogue

Strengths

Both Nietzsche and Kierkegaard must be commended for their brilliant and scintillating critiques of nineteenth-century excesses, their passion against mediocrity and theoretical abstraction, their insistence that, whatever it means to be human, it inevitably involves "a process of becoming,"[1] their honesty to confront the brutalities, suffering, and incongruities of existence, their recognition of the uses and abuses of a personal hermeneutic by which people "fool one another into thinking that what occurred is what they wanted,"[2] and their integrity to resist the *status quo*, whether political, intellectual, or ecclesiastical.

In particular, Friedrich Nietzsche justly challenged the stagnancy and hypocrisy inherent in a self-proclaimed "Christian" continent which brazenly sanctioned modes of power and affluence in blatant contradiction of the life and teachings of its founder.[3] His exposure of subtler uses of coercion such as language, the hermeneutical redaction of history—whether national or personal—and the deleterious dehumanization of the "less fortunate" under the guise of "Christian charity"[4] is both provocative and poignant. Nietzsche's exuberance for the "natural" world and willingness to explore marginalized topics such as passion and sexuality are both admirable and daring, offsetting an unhealthy existential escapism which often masquerades as "sound" Christian theology. He lucidly expounded the dangers of overemphasizing an abstract, disembodied transcendence: "For there is nothing at all we could state about the metaphysical world except its differentness, a differentness inaccessible and incomprehensible to us. It would be a thing with negative qualities."[5] Thus, he offered a cogent reminder that Christianity is a historically embodied and "incarnational" religion in more ways than one. His aversion to delusion and earnestness for truth ironically paralleled the efforts of many who identified with the robust center of Christian tradition—including

---

[1] *SD*, p. 60.

[2] *WA*, p. 228 [1848].

[3] *WP*, pp. 97–8 [1888]; *TI*, p. 160.

[4] See *GS*, p. 86: "We benefit and show benevolence to those who are already dependent on us in some way (which means that they are used to thinking of us as causes); we want to increase their power because in that way we increase ours, or we want to show them how advantageous it is to be in our power; that way they will become more satisfied with their condition and more hostile to and willing to fight against the enemies of *our* power."

[5] *HA*, p. 18.

Søren Kierkegaard—who would have heartily approved of such uncompromising and singular vigor.[6]

Both Nietzsche and Kierkegaard provided invaluable assistance in preserving the importance of the individual in the face of collectivist pressures which sought harmony and homogeneity at the expense of particularity. However, Kierkegaard unequivocally grounded human well-being, freedom, and identity upon the unchangeable and incontestable love and freedom of God, while emphasizing the qualitative "chasm" of heterogeneity which separates God from creation. At the same time, he exposed the implicit dangers of immanence, wherein humankind re-casts God in its own image and thereby faces an "all-too-human" autocrat, whose power and freedom—being merely quantitatively different—must therefore rival, oppress, and/or be supplemented by our own. His penetrating analysis of the limitations of sensate authority and the church's catastrophic compromise in enforcing spiritual goals with sensate power is both brilliant and timely. Ultimately, Kierkegaard would argue that the formulations of "master power" and "slave power" are themselves constructs for masking alienation from and avoidance of God.

Shortcomings

Nietzsche

Methodological inconsistencies
The greatest difficulty with the tenability of Nietzsche's position centers on the glaring inconsistencies of his variegated threads of thought. Despite his suspicion of the hermeneutical "shell-games" of history and the contention that he was born "ahead of his time,"[7] Nietzsche formulated his own historical schemas and clearly emulated past proclivities:

> The seventeenth century is aristocratic, imposes order, looks down haughtily on the animalic, is severe against the heart, not cozy, without sentiment, "un-German," averse to what is burlesque and what is natural, inclined to generalizations and sovereign confronted with the past—for it believes in itself. Much beast of prey *au fond*, much ascetic habit to remain master. The century of strong will; also of strong passion.[8]

In contrast to seventeenth-century "Aristocratism," the eighteenth century was characterized by "Feminism," "Rousseau, rule of feeling, testimony of the

---

[6] "We need dynamic personalities, unselfish persons who are not immersed and exhausted in endless consideration for job, wife, and children" (*BA*, p. 224 [1847]).

[7] *EH*, p. 39.

[8] *WP*, p. 59 [1887].

sovereignty of the senses, mendacious," while the nineteenth century revolved upon "Animalism": "Schopenhauer, rule of craving, testimony of the sovereignty of animality, more honest but gloomy."[9] Despite his aversion to piecemeal philosophy,[10] Nietzsche himself was highly selective in his emphasis upon seventeenth-century "aristocratism," eighteenth-century emotional epiphanies, and nineteenth-century "institutionalization" of instinct. Though he delighted in "deconstructing" previous philosophies—"[T]he philosopher believes that the value of his philosophy lies in the whole, in the building: posterity discovers it in the bricks with which he built and which are then often used again for better building ..."[11]—the disassembly of his own thought was insufferable, as reflected in his denunciation of "Zarathustra's apes."[12]

Although Nietzsche vehemently opposed Christianity as "sickness" and "up till now mankind's greatest misfortune"[13]—a blatant contradiction of his assertions that rendering moral judgments is the greatest injustice[14]—he also endorsed it as a useful "Machiavellian" means for securing political stability,[15] and based many of his formulations upon Lutheran doctrines.[16] Despite his abhorrence of slaves "levelling" all exceptionality in the world, in one monumental revaluation he flattened all human value systems, civilizations, arts, knowledge, love, and science into instinctual maneuvers for attaining power.

---

[9]   Ibid., pp. 58–9 [1887].

[10]   *BG*, p. 40; *Z*, p. 142.

[11]   *NR*, p. 33.

[12]   *Z*, pp. 195–7; *EH*, p. 96.

[13]   *TI*, p. 181.

[14]   *NR*, pp. 71–2.

[15]   *BG*, p. 86; *TI*, p. 184. On Christianity's usefulness for creating a more docile slave, see *WP*, p. 127 [1887–88].

[16]   In his introduction to *Thus Spoke Zarathustra*, R.J. Hollingdale identifies six major parallels: "*amor fati*" with the Lutheran acceptance of God willing all events in life; "eternal recurrence" with Christianity's affirmation of life and the unchangeable nature of God; "will to power" with God's inner grace which leads to outer victories; "living dangerously" with the radical nature of Jesus' challenge to the religious conventions of his day; the "Great Noontide" as the Second Coming of Christ; and the "*Übermensch*" with a model of God Himself (*Z*, pp. 28–9). I would also posit a strong dose of "remnant" theology, the belief that only a portion but not the whole shall be saved, and "messianic" theology, a characteristic feature of the destined *Übermensch*, who would, in effect, "redeem" the entire chain of historical unfoldings. He also borrowed heavily from Christian asceticism, particularly in his insistence that self-mastery lies at the heart of any "higher man" (*TI*, p. 104). For a pronounced parallel with Luther on hermeneutics as faith, see *Selections from His Writings*, ed. John Dillenberger (New York, 1962), pp. 63–4: "[I]n all things I can find profit toward salvation so that the cross and death itself are compelled to serve me and to work together with me for my salvation. This is a splendid privilege and hard to attain, a truly omnipotent power, a spiritual dominion in which there is nothing so good and nothing so evil but that it shall work together for good to me, if only I believe."

While Nietzsche deplored the Hegelian banishment of the natural world and the Christian negation of "natural man," he employed a personal hermeneutic which ultimately minimizes the world as aesthetic construct and apparently negates the human race itself—"the experimental material, the tremendous surplus of failures"[17]—in his focus on breeding the superspecies. In doing so, Nietzsche focused on generalities such as "the species" and "the race," leaving little room for the individual in his grand formulations.[18] His naturalistic embrace of the amoral cosmos and his nascent social constructionism which collapses ontology into human subjectivity and universalizes uniquely human power struggles seem highly incongruous.

Yet another inconsistency lies in Nietzsche's aversion to infinity as a threat to the material universe, which he ironically sought to "infinitize" through endless hermeneutical interpretations: "[T]he world has become 'infinite' for us all over again, inasmuch as we cannot reject the possibility that *it may include infinite interpretations*."[19] While he championed release from outdated conventions and oppressive superstitions, he bound the human majority with the shackles of determinism—both biological and sociological—via a loveless, goalless "fate," banishing humankind to perpetual revolutions on a cosmic "carousel" under the auspices of "true freedom." In his critique of Nietzsche, Miguel de Unamuno suggests, "And why does the lion laugh? I think he laughs with rage, because he can never succeed in finding consolation in the thought that he has been the same lion before and is destined to be the same lion again."[20]

Furthermore, while he advocated endorsement of a plurality of perspectives and rejected the illusion of arriving at "the truth," Nietzsche became curiously irate when his unique perspective did not receive privileged status.[21] The Heraclitean effort to preserve existential "flux" by withstanding the solidification of all "becomings" into "beings" seems far more "superhuman" than Nietzsche admitted. To the extent that humans are expected to accept their allotted positions in society as either *Übermensch* forebears or aristocratic facilitators, Nietzsche's

---

[17]   *WP*, p. 380 [1888].

[18]   Ludwig Feuerbach traces the classical roots of this approach: "The idea of man as an individual was to the ancients a secondary one, attained through the idea of the species. Though they thought highly of the race, highly of the excellences of mankind, ... they nevertheless thought slightly of the individual" (*The Essence of Christianity*, trans. George Eliot [New York, 1957], p. 151).

[19]   *GS*, p. 336.

[20]   Miguel de Unamuno, *The Tragic Sense of Life* (London, 1962), pp. 110–11.

[21]   This criticism may be somewhat unfair. See Maudemarie Clark, who argues that he is not rejecting "truth" *per se* but "metaphysical truth" ("Nietzsche, Friedrich," in Edward Craig [ed.], *Routledge Encyclopaedia of Philosophy* [10 vols, London, 1998], vol. 6, p. 848). She emphasizes that perspectivism is a claim about knowledge, not truth (ibid., p. 849).

views rest upon the "naive" presumption, according to Climacus, that "if only the objective truth stands firm, the subject will be ready and willing to slip it on."[22]

Nietzsche's optimism in the rise of new and stronger configurations of power from the ashes of conflict and animosity, and his confidence that he can chisel new behaviors and attitudes into human "bedrock" despite the seeming imperviousness of "bad blood"[23] seem audacious at best and contradictory at worst. On the one hand, he espoused the ineluctability of cosmic movements such as eternal recurrence while, on the other hand, the formulations of a single man, such as Kant, can apparently derail the astoundingly "fragile" inexorability of the natural universe's drive towards developing quintessential units of power—or at least delay it.[24] The fact that the "telos-less" cosmos in general and the preeminent "masters" in particular require the designs of a philosophical architect and "defender of the fate" is rather paradoxical, particularly when the strength of the forebears is predicated upon the existence of powerful opponents such as "Christianity" and its so-called "slave morality," which Nietzsche strove so valiantly to neutralize. This vociferous opponent of transcendence risked violating his own tenet in his derision of Christianity; for, if humankind truly inhabits a "natural" universe, does Nietzsche not posit an otherworldly heterogeneity when he criticizes the Christian faith as "unnatural"? Indeed, how can anything be "unnatural" in a universe where there is nothing but nature, and from what Archimedean point does Nietzsche presume to distinguish between the two?

The incongruities in Nietzsche's thought are legion. While he longed to preserve the present from the denigration of tyrannical historical traditions, he curiously drew upon a sentimentalized golden past of aristocratic supremacy in order to usher in a glorious future. While he expounded an Epicurean enthusiasm for the Dionysian delights of corporeal existence, he also advocated a Stoic detachment in order to transcend the impact of externals.[25] He vigorously denied the efficacy of human powers of judgment and conscious free will, while at the same time championing the victor's cry, "I willed it thus!" Nietzsche was either insidiously inconsistent or he possessed the greatest—and wickedest—sense of humor of any philosopher.

Theological double agent?
In order to consolidate the significant incongruities inherent in Nietzsche's thought, one must walk an epistemological tightrope between the extremities of ontological conservatism, which fossilizes truth, and a rampaging nihilism, which utterly vaporizes it. The theorist must articulate Nietzsche's insistence upon the commensurability between external and internal power without enslaving the

---

[22]   *CUP*, vol. 1, p. 37.

[23]   *EH*, p. 18.

[24]   *WP*, p. 64 [1887].

[25]   On his view of socialization as antithetical to self-creation, see Morwenna Griffiths, *Feminisms and the Self: The Web of Identity* (London, 1995), p. 124.

individual to the outcome. Ironically, Nietzsche's substantial inconsistencies may be stabilized within a Judaeo-Christian reference point. While Nietzsche regarded himself as an "outsider" confronting the corruption within Christian morality, he bore a marked resemblance to the biblical prophets.[26] Exposing hypocrisy, complacency, and indolence, Nietzsche charged that matters of truth and virtue do not lead to material advantages and prosperity but, in fact, are detrimental to one's earthly well-being.[27] Though he himself rigorously disputed its motives, Nietzsche recognized that the pursuit of genuine virtue leads to self-debasement and loss, not personal aggrandizement and temporal successes.

Nietzsche also played the prophet when denouncing humankind's ability to judge based on appearances of actions, recognizing that the intentions behind a morally courageous act are often ignoble—stubbornness, close-mindedness, cowardice, pride, selfishness.[28] Because of the opaque nature of the human heart, Nietzsche insisted that judgment must be suspended or at least tempered by an awareness of the judge's hermeneutical biases and limitations.[29] With his uncanny "nose" for spiritual mediocrity and an almost "priestly" concern for purity, he relentlessly reminded Christendom that their poor excuse for piety—their "religion of comfortableness"[30]—is a pathetic substitute for authentic moral courage, which relinquishes the safe havens of conventionality and abandons high ease for high seas. From his prophetic platform, Zarathustra exhorted, "And whatever harm the wicked may do, the harm the good do is the most harmful harm ... . For the good—*cannot* create: they are always the beginning of the end:—they crucify him who writes new values on new law-tables ... ."[31] Nietzsche predicted woe and suffering for the spiritually self-assured, who lackadaisically loitered around a lower-case Christianity, and sternly ordered them to "move along."

In retrospect, some of Nietzsche's most virulent attacks were not directed at Christianity *per se*, but rather at its corruption in Christendom—a *status quo* spirituality of complacency and decadence grown powerful to the point of undermining the development of human excellence for which Nietzsche longed:

> I have the greatest respect for the ascetic ideal, *in so far as it is honest*! As long as it believes in itself and refrains from farcical play-acting! But I dislike all

---

[26]   Though Michael Tanner would add, "A prophet of the apocalypse" (*Nietzsche* [Oxford, 1994], p. 32). Intriguingly, one of Nietzsche's deconstructive metaphors was echoed by Jeremiah: "Is not my word like fire, says the Lord, and like a hammer that breaks a rock in pieces?" (Jeremiah 23:29). See *WP*, p. 544 (1885). Lou Salomé regarded his greatest "intellectual disposition" to be his "religious genius" (*Nietzsche*, trans. and ed. Siegfried Mandel [Urbana and Chicago, 2001], p. 24).

[27]   *GS*, p. 92.

[28]   Ibid., p. 264.

[29]   Ibid., p. 265.

[30]   Ibid., p. 270.

[31]   *Z*, pp. 229–30.

these coquettish little bugs—whose insatiable ambition is to give off the smell of the infinite, until ultimately the infinite smells of bugs ... .[32]

At times, Nietzsche gives the impression of a young warrior who, after years of relentless training, has arrived to challenge a highly vaunted champion, only to confront a hermeneutical "has been" who has grown weak from resting on his laurels. Perhaps the church failed Nietzsche the most by its inability to "put up a fight" in the wake of his devastating criticisms. Arguably, Nietzsche even sought to strengthen Christianity by incinerating its dross for his own purposes of furnishing a fitter mettle against which to steel future generations of "higher men": "I have declared war on the anemic Christian ideal (together with what is closely related to it), not with the aim of destroying it but only of putting an end to its tyranny and clearing the way for new ideals, for *more robust* ideals ... ."[33] Subsequently, Nietzsche's true enemies were not "the most serious Christians," who "have always been well disposed towards me,"[34] but the "one kind of enemy who is capable of causing the ascetic ideal real *harm*: those play-actors who act out this ideal—for they arouse suspicion."[35] Kierkegaard could not have agreed more.

Kierkegaard

Temporal shortcomings

Like Nietzsche, Kierkegaard's problems stem from the extremities of cognitive range and stridency of "pitch." Although his insistence upon the incommensurability between internality and externality is a powerful deterrent against hypocrisy, it threatens to reduce Christianity to a private, quietist religion if not conjoined to a determined, proactive resolve for passionate involvement in society, something Anti-Climacus emphasized when guarding against spiritual indolence:

> The earnestness of life is not all this pressure of finitude and busyness with livelihood, job, office, and procreation, but the earnestness of life is to *will* to be, to *will* to express the perfection (ideality) in the dailyness of actuality, to *will* it, so that one does not to one's own ruin once and for all busily abandon it or conceitedly take it in vain as a dream—what a tragic lack of earnestness in both cases!—but humbly wills it in actuality.[36]

To the degree that Kierkegaard solely emphasized a faith that is supremely focused "inwards" upon one's relationship with God, his position is susceptible to

---

[32]   *GM*, p. 132.

[33]   *WP*, p. 197 [1887].

[34]   *EH*, p. 18.

[35]   *GM*, p. 134.

[36]   *PC*, pp. 189–90.

Feuerbach's criticism: *"Nature, the world, has no value, no interest for Christians. The Christian thinks only of himself and the salvation of his soul."*[37]

Kierkegaard's position is also not without its incongruities: on one level, he emphasized the sinfulness of humankind and natural aversion to the truth, yet he upbraided the bulk of Christendom—who allegedly were not genuine Christians—for secularizing the Kingdom of God and employing the sensate powers of wealth, reason, or government to aid or abet Christian aims. He himself was not able to model faultlessly this restraint, relying upon his privileged education, brilliant mind, and rich inheritance to sequester himself from vocational pursuits and write his long, sophisticated treatises which constituted an integral part of his Christian witness. By deploying his use of irony, keen rational abilities, polemical prowess, and literary skills, he, too, can be accused of committing the "sin of Uzzah" and, reaching out to steady the apparently precarious "ark of God,"[38] thus "weakening" Christianity by the very act of "defending" it.[39] Furthermore, if sensate authority truly poses no threat to spiritual authority, a sceptic can question the need for Kierkegaard's highly spirited polemics in the first place.[40]

Although he strove against sensate power, Kierkegaard was eventually worn down by the constant affliction and scorn he invoked, some of it intentionally, lapsing into further bitterness and isolation despite acknowledging the importance of love and neighbor. At the height of polemical frenzy, Kierkegaard committed the very infraction he railed so forcefully against throughout his authorship: quantifying God within human limitations and standards. In *The Moment*, he presented an astonishingly "human" description of God's waning patience, when he stated that the worst punishment is for God "not to will to be aware ... of the nothing that you are. For an omnipotent being it must, if one may speak this way, be an immense

---

[37]   Feuerbach, p. 287.

[38]   II Samuel 6:6–7.

[39]   Kierkegaard might have justified his use of reason as necessary to clear away faulty reasoning and "till the existential soil" in preparation for the "seed" of revelation since, in the paradoxical words of Climacus, "[T]he maximum of any eventual understanding [of revelation] is to understand that it cannot be understood" (*CUP*, vol. 1, p. 214). Earlier, Climacus justified apologetics on the basis that it elucidated the God-concept, in addition to demarcating the qualitative leap which separates revelation from all other human knowledge (*PF*, p. 43). Climacus was not a "fideist" in the sense that the understanding has no role to play in faith—human reason simply cannot supply the positive content of faith, but it can approach the near edge of the qualitative "chasm" which separates God and creation, though only under the transforming influence of divine grace.

[40]   Kierkegaard's defense, though easily misunderstood by the sceptic, is brilliantly articulated by Joe Jones: "Defending such concepts is not an attempt to make them plausible before the court of immanent human understanding. Rather, defense involves clarifying the concepts over against their illegitimate cousins, against the counterfeit substitutes, against the vain and trivializing uses which deflect and obscure the true character and point of Christian faith" ("Some Remarks on Authority and Revelation in Kierkegaard," *Journal of Religion*, 57/3 [1977]: 246).

effort to be obliged to look after a nothing, to be aware of a nothing, to be concerned about a nothing."[41] He similarly appeared to anthropomorphize God's love when he once compared "petty prayers"—prayers for attaining "worldly" aims rather than their banishment—to the unwarranted badgering of an exasperated doctor by parents who repeatedly summon him for every "imaginary" symptom of their child.[42] However, such references are still exceptions to the predominant theme of unconditional divine love which remains prevalent throughout his corpus, and the fact that God loves sinful individuals inspired greater wonderment for Kierkegaard than God's ability to create the universe *ex nihilo*.[43]

Reconnections

In order to expand upon Kierkegaard's insights, one must relentlessly press his thought in the direction of community and commitment to relationality, lest a well-intentioned attitude of love atrophy into strategic isolation or abstraction.[44] Theologically, this could be accomplished by emphasizing the relational nature of the Gospel, preserving Kierkegaard's central focus upon the individual's relationship with God while re-articulating the communal nature of God himself in the persons of the Trinity, as well as the essential role of the Holy Spirit operating in the life, unity, and actions of the Christian church. A fuller statement of Trinitarian theology, ecclesiology, and pneumatology would highlight the valuable contributions which Kierkegaard makes to Christian thought while demonstrating the real and practical nature of the Gospel's power to unite and restore that which is alienated and damaged.

One must also challenge the subtle power play behind "indirect teaching," combined with his epistemological flirtation with deception, to avoid undermining the importance of truth for the Christian.[45] There are three levels of divine "deception" in Kierkegaard's writing: first, the "inevitable" distortions of truth

---

[41]   *TM*, p. 307.

[42]   *CD*, p. 168.

[43]   Ibid., p. 128.

[44]   I disagree, however, with Michael Matthis' contention that Kierkegaard has subsumed "the other" "as an idea within the self" ("Kierkegaard and the Problem of the Social Other," *Philosophy Today*, 38/4 [1994]: 419), a position espoused by Martin Buber (George Connell and C. Stephen Evans [eds], *Foundations of Kierkegaard's Vision of Community: Religion, Ethics, and Politics in Kierkegaard* [New Jersey and London, 1992], pp. vii–ix). For the positives and problems of Kierkegaard's "open-ended" conception of the individual, see Alastair Hannay, *Kierkegaard* (London, 1982), pp. 326–8.

[45]   Christopher Norris accuses him of functionally endorsing Nietzsche's devaluation of truth ("Fictions of Authority: Narrative and Viewpoint in Kierkegaard's Writing," *Criticism*, 25/2 [1983]: 105). Although Norris is overstating his case, Nietzsche could have easily adduced Kierkegaard's duplicity in support of his view that the will to truth, when pursued in all earnestness, nihilistically exposes the fictitious nature of its truth claims.

which occur when it is communicated in a world saturated by untruth;[46] second, Jesus' "deceptive" use of political terminology and playing upon Israel's nationalistic expectations during the triumphal entry into Jerusalem;[47] third, Anti-Climacus posited "a necessary educational guile" whereby God—presumably temporarily—does not inform the believer of the inevitable suffering which will ensue when serving truth in a world of untruth.[48] Anti-Climacus justified deception on the basis that it was not "true" deception if it "deceived" a person "into the truth."[49] In *Stages on Life's Way*, Quidam justified the use of deception to break off his engagement with Quaedam, "provided I have not my welfare in mind but hers."[50] Quidam linked this "teleological suspension of the ethical principle of speaking the whole truth" with Christ's decision to withhold the entire truth from his disciples prior to his betrayal and execution because "as yet they cannot bear it."[51] However, it is significant that Kierkegaard later rejected his deployment of indirect communication and all but abandoned pseudonymous composition.[52]

---

[46]   See, for example, *TM*, p. 414 [1851]; *BA*, p. 170; *FT*, p. 185. The Incarnation is "deceptive" insofar as it constitutes "the absolute unrecognizability, when one is God, then to be an individual human being," entailing "the greatest possible distance, the infinitely qualitative distance, from being God, and therefore it is the most profound incognito" (*PC*, pp. 127–8).

[47]   *WA*, pp. 61–2. He softened this stance in *FS*, p. 61: "If he [Jesus] works for it [truth] with all his might, then he is working himself toward certain downfall. On the other hand, if he introduces the whole truth too quickly, his downfall will come too soon. Consequently, working against himself, he must for a time seem to enter into illusions in order to ensure the downfall all the more thoroughly."

[48]   *PC*, p. 186.

[49]   Ibid., p. 190. For use of the "pious fraud," see *PV*, p. 7. On the "aesthetic writings" as "deception," see ibid., p. 77; *UD*, p. 123; *FT*, p. 359 [1844].

[50]   *SW*, p. 230. Is it possible that Kierkegaard became entangled in his own disguises? This is plausible if Meier Goldschmidt's assessment is accurate: "[T]here had come to be something about him that gave him the appearance of standing at a distance, observing ironically, like one who with conscious superiority—a superiority that seemed to be based both on his intellect and his reputed wealth—could understand everything, also all cares and sorrows, and give the word but not share it. That could, in fact, be a pretense that would vanish if one followed him into his cubbyhole, but who could do that, and how much trouble do we take in that respect with regard to each other before it is too late? Egotistically preoccupied as we generally are ..." (*TC*, pp. 147–8). The deliberate sabotaging of Quidam's engagement for the spiritual "benefit" of his fiancée bore more than a passing resemblance to Kierkegaard's dis-engagement from Regine Olsen insofar as he "played the cad" in order to "ease" her suffering—a point to which *The Corsair* gleefully alluded (ibid., pp. 118–19). On Kierkegaard's admission of his heightened powers of "dissimulative art" from an early age, see *PV*, p. 79.

[51]   *SW*, p. 230.

[52]   In an 1848 journal entry, he described "the arts of the maieutic" as an "unchristian way ... even though useful for a time and relatively justified simply because Christendom has become paganism" (*CD*, p. 422 [1848]).

Although one must realistically confront the fractured realities of human existence, the heterogeneity of God's freedom and power must be reflected by Christian resistance to deception as a means of confronting deception if divine victory is as certain as Kierkegaard would insist.

Relevance for Contemporary Power Issues

A thorough analysis of the implications of Nietzsche's and Kierkegaard's thought for contemporary discussion on the issues of power lies beyond the scope of this book; however, a few general observations may be offered. In the highly charged political landscape of the twenty-first century, both Nietzsche and Kierkegaard can serve as models for rigorously self-scrutinizing one's personal, ethical position for underlying biases, self-interest, and blind spots. They also provide a timely critique of liberal democracy, particularly for proponents who are advocating worldwide democraticization and consumer-based egalitarianism as a panacea for systemic problems of tyranny, poverty, injustice, and material inequities. As Timothy Jackson observes, "No external power (neither Adam's sin nor God's grace) can compel a moral choice …"[53]—to which one might add trade embargos, constitutional amendments, and preemptive strikes. In light of the subtleties of self-empowerment under a façade of humanitarianism, these two thinkers provide a cogent reminder that assisting others must always be undertaken amidst sensitive dialogue between helper and "helpee," recognizing the dangers of exchanging material poverty for spiritual impoverishment. Moreover, epistemological humility must ensure that provisional understandings are not tragically imbued with the ominous certainties of fundamentalism, religious or otherwise.

Both men also provide poignant reminders of how quickly human structures of power—whether political, economic, or ecclesiological—may be "deified" and incorporated into a new or existing *status quo*, how easily the name of "God" can be invoked to sanction national interests or institutionalized injustices, and how susceptible theological formulations may be to hierarchical "corrosion."[54] However, in light of the volatile and belligerent conditions in many regions of the world wracked by power imbalances, Nietzsche's attempt to subsume all human activity within a matrix of agonistic power relations appears reductionistic and ultimately unhelpful for arriving at more constructive means of mediating human differences within the framework of social justice.[55] Such a presupposition

---

[53] Timothy Jackson, "Arminian Edification: Kierkegaard on Grace and Free Will," in Alastair Hannay and Gordon Marino (eds), *The Cambridge Companion to Kierkegaard* (Cambridge, 1998), p. 251.

[54] See Rosemary Radford Ruether, *Sexism and Godtalk: Towards a Feminist Theology* (London, 1989), p. 28.

[55] On the absence of social justice from his account of "creative, aristocratic polity," see Keith Ansell-Pearson, *An Introduction to Nietzsche as Political Thinker* (Cambridge,

may easily undermine mutual trust and promote an atmosphere of suspicion and cynicism, leveling all overtures of peace, munificence, and good will as unmitigated self-interest.

The implications of Kierkegaard's Christian world view seem particularly dire from a non-Christian perspective: he does not dilute his pessimism towards human beings' natural receptivity to truth and justice, and many will take offence at his delimitation of "sinful" humankind's ability to recognize and will the good, not to mention his Christocentric exclusivism.[56] Nevertheless, his "existence-communication" is permeated by themes of grace and divine enabling which neither whitewashes atrocities nor evades the "Golgothas" of fallen creation. Furthermore, Kierkegaard's critique of human folly and fallibility is extended to both rich and poor, male and female, subverting the hidden power dynamics within the relationship between empowered oppressor and impotent victim.[57] Accordingly, the weakness of sensate power holders is exposed, along with the surreptitious potential strength of the marginalized, and everyone regardless of time, culture, or privilege is truly responsible to God for herself and for each other.

By emphasizing the qualitative difference which separates God from humankind, Kierkegaard addresses the theological fallacy of human identity being annihilated or impinged upon by God, which often arises when human concepts of sensate power are projected onto God. Much of the modern political milieu resonates with Nietzsche's cry: "[H]e who wants to become free has to become so

---

1997), p. 51.

[56] Proponents of "autonomy over heteronomy" (Daphne Hampson, "On Autonomy and Heteronomy" in Daphne Hampson [ed.], *Swallowing a Fishbone? Feminist Authors Debate Christianity* [London, 1996], p. 2), a "politics of difference," or "basic self-determination" (Christine Gudorf, "Probing the Politics of Difference: What's Wrong with an All-Male Priesthood?," *Journal of Religious Ethics*, 27/3 [1999]: 380, 385) will deride his criticism of political reform. His distinction between Christian and non-Christian capacity for truth would be regarded by some feminists as "the kyriarchally dualistic way of thinking" (Mary Hunt, "Designer Theology: A Feminist Perspective," *Zygon*, 36/4 [2001]: 746). However, to the degree that all remain sinners in desperate need of divine grace, the dualism of "us" and "them" is dissipated. Furthermore, as Himani Bannerji argues, a "politics of difference" as espoused by multiculturalism may harbor its own essentialist biases ("The Paradox of Diversity: The Construction of a Multicultural Canada and 'Women of Colour,'" *Women's Studies International Forum*, 23/5 [2000]: 548), or subvert constructive political action altogether (Lynne Segal, "Only Contradictions on Offer," *Women: A Cultural Review*, 11/1 [2000]: 27). It is safe to say that Kierkegaard's severe polemical tone directed towards a society rationalizing indulgence under "Christian" pretences would be radically modified were Kierkegaard to address himself to a multicultural, post-Christian era.

[57] On the "passive complicity" of a victimized society, see David Tombs, "Crucifixion, State Terror, and Sexual Abuse," *Union Seminary Quarterly Review*, 53/1–2 (1999): 91. On the universal ability to exert "power over," see Sarah Coakley, "Kenosis and Subversion: On the Repression of 'Vulnerability' in Christian Feminist Writing," in Daphne Hampson (ed.), *Swallowing a Fishbone? Feminist Authors Debate Christianity* (London, 1996), p. 107.

through his own actions and that freedom falls into no one's lap like a miraculous gift."[58] Conversely, Kierkegaard asserted that human freedom is not threatened by divine omnipotence, but founded upon it as a free and loving gift which neither diminishes the Giver nor enslaves the recipient. On account of the Incarnation, Kierkegaard's emphasis does not lead to an abstract, inaccessible, unknowable transcendence. Because of God's unlimited power, made readily available to all earnest seekers, promise is wedded to the paradoxical command to love thy neighbors in the central figure of Christ, who is both human exemplar and divine Enabler.[59] Although Kierkegaard's perspective remains intrinsically Christian, his insights into the devastating compromise of spiritual authority bolstered by sensate power is illuminating for proponents of all religions who seek to impact the world around them.

The importance of the neighborly "other" for Kierkegaard also provides grounds for practical engagement, as opposed to the "tepidity" of Nietzsche's *amor fati* where the line between universal affirmation and resignation is all-too-thin.[60] Due to the inseparable connection between Kierkegaard's christocentric theology and his socio-political outlook, his position is more resistant to appropriation by fascist or tyrannical agendas.[61] Moreover, his heightened sensitivity to issues of authority, epistemological humility in vigilantly supplying correctives in response to ever-changing contextual imbalances while extending hermeneutical suspicion to one's own views,[62] and cognizance of the unsettling ease with which the "learner" may be obstructed from finding her personal, unique, existential response to truth claims by even the most solicitous "instructor" render Kierkegaard a particularly

---

[58] *UM*, p. 252.

[59] This two-fold focus obviates a self-centered focus on personal actualization, as articulated by James Torrance: "More important than our experience of Christ is the Christ of our experience" (*Worship, Community & the Triune God of Grace* [Downers Grove, 1996], p. 34). Stephen Houlgate observes that "Nietzsche ignores the immense importance of divine incarnation in Christian belief" (*Hegel, Nietzsche and the Criticism of Metaphysics* [Cambridge, 1986], p. 40).

[60] Tanner, p. 68. Tanner contends that Nietzsche's book on transvaluation was unfinished "because in the end Nietzsche found himself at a loss" (ibid., p. 77).

[61] Houlgate, p. 196, contends that Nietzsche's ethically suspect concept of "an aristocratic, tragic society" opens the door for such abuses. Miroslav Volf derides "the Nietzschean kind of affirmation of life, which is a paradise for the strong but a hell for the weak, because it celebrates the way things are, which is to say the way the strong have made them to be" (*Exclusion and Embrace: A Theological Exploration of Identity, Otherness, and Reconciliation* [Nashville, 1996], p. 108). Michele Nicoletti observes that German theologians such as Erik Peterson regarded Kierkegaard as a source of solace and support in opposing Nazism ("Politics and Religion in Kierkegaard's Thought: Secularization and the Martyr," in George Connell and C. Stephen Evans [eds], *Foundations of Kierkegaard's Vision of Community: Religion, Ethics, and Politics in Kierkegaard* [New Jersey and London, 1992], p. 192).

[62] *JK*, p. 127 [1847].

well-suited and prolific dialogue partner for marginalized and marginalizing individuals.[63] Recent centuries have painfully shown how a macrocosmic focus on species-wide amelioration all-too-easily sacrifices individuals and social justice upon the idealistic altars of deified "progress." However, both thinkers may rightly receive censure for endorsing governance by an educated elite—those who serve a well-defined "idea"[64]—over more democratic rule, and their ambivalence and/or animosity towards egalitarian tendencies which could be detrimentally ensconced within oppressive ideologies.

A canny observer might ask whether Kierkegaard's view of the world steeled in sinful rebellion against its Creator-God is any less agonistic than Nietzsche's perspective. But the Danish theologian would promptly assert that God, in his omnipotence, knows neither genuine threat nor defeat. Moreover, this rebellion is itself posited upon a perpetually upheld and uplifting foundation of divine love and freedom, which establishes the worth and identity of every human being in history while providing the requisite acceptance, forgiveness, and empowerment which every potentate and pauper, standing equally hapless and helpless in the sight of God, desperately needs. Kierkegaard's perspective may prove to be invaluable for those striving to hold together the existential tensions of celebrating unity in the face of disparity and difference in the face of conformity.[65]

Concluding Summary

One final task remains: to address the introductory question whether there is such a thing as Christian power versus non-Christian power. Given his adamant monism, Nietzsche would heartily disagree: Christians, like all biological organisms, remain inextricably involved in expanding their personal power bases and minimizing the competition. Kierkegaard, however, would cite the Incarnation as proof and promulgation of a qualitatively "Other" power expressed

---

[63]   See Wanda Warren Berry, "Finally Forgiveness: Kierkegaard as a 'Springboard' for a Feminist Theology of Reform," in George Connell and C. Stephen Evans (eds), *Foundations of Kierkegaard's Vision of Community: Religion, Ethics, and Politics in Kierkegaard* (New Jersey and London, 1992), pp. 212–13: "Kierkegaard's emphasis on freedom is the anthropological corollary of his emphasis on God as 'Possibility,' and is fundamental to any theology of liberation." For feminist rejections of "power-over," see Mary Holmes, "Second-Wave Feminism and the Politics of Relationships," *Women's Studies International Forum*, 23/2 (2000): 239; Elizabeth Johnson, *She Who Is: The Mystery of God in Feminist Theological Discourse* (New York 1992), p. 169; Elisabeth Schüssler Fiorenza, *Bread Not Stone: The Challenge of Feminist Biblical Interpretation* (Boston, 1984), p. 143.

[64]   *CD*, p. 321.

[65]   On the challenges and failures of the modern multicultural liberal state to address these tensions, see Charles Taylor, "The Politics of Recognition," in Amy Gutmann (ed.), *Multiculturalism: Examining the Politics of Recognition* (Princeton, 1994), pp. 37–9.

in acts of divine self-limitation for the empowerment of all. Such power is not exclusively "Christian," but "the power of God for the salvation of everyone who believes ... ."[66]

The preceding two chapters examined three nexus of a reconstructed dialogue between Friedrich Nietzsche and Søren Kierkegaard. With regard to cosmology, Nietzsche accused Kierkegaard of negating an amoral, "telos-free" universe and escaping to an imaginary other-world of eternity. He was, thus, guilty of existential cowardice. Paradoxically, Kierkegaard leveled the same charge against Nietzsche, on the grounds that Nietzsche was negating a moral, telos-ful universe by escaping to an imaginary other-world of human rebellion. Both assertions are valid within their particular contexts: it takes genuine courage to doubt—*pace* Nietzsche— when "faith" is fashionable, but it also takes genuine courage to believe—*pace* Kierkegaard—when "doubt" is dominant.[67]

On their understanding of human identity and purpose, Nietzsche accused Kierkegaard of complicity in the proliferation of "slave" values and subsequent mediocrity, which obfuscate human instincts and growth. In response, Kierkegaard accused Nietzsche of complicity in the promulgation of "master" values and subsequent mediocrity, which obfuscate human freedom and spiritual advancement, asserting that it is only through Christ that universal slavery to "the laws of the flesh and of the drives"[68] and an inescapable determinism of individual, societal, and cosmic proportions is unmasked and ultimately transformed.

Regarding their concepts of power, Nietzsche contended that the church in general and Kierkegaard in particular exemplified human endeavors to consolidate personal power and minimize external threats through such duplicitous constructs as "selflessness" and "divine love." By contrast, Kierkegaard contended that humanity in general and Nietzsche in particular exemplified autonomous rebellion against divine authority, seeking to justify personal control and minimize existential accountability before God through such duplicitous constructs as "master power" and "slave power."

Nietzsche would have been right to protest that, in posing behind a cloud of feigned unknowing, Kierkegaard was cunningly able to exert a formidable influence in an attempt to "deceive his reader into the truth."[69] As earnest polemicists, both men unapologetically declared war against the illusions which, they believed, blinded nineteenth-century Europe, wielding considerable intellectual and rhetorical power in the process. But whereas Nietzsche sought to turn the "slave-ruled" world upside-down with his "dangerous knowledge" and initiate a new era of extraordinaries, Kierkegaard sought to avoid ineffectual societal "renovations" by testifying to and through suffering for the Gospel and the necessary offense and denigration it occasions in a world of revolt against God. Despite certain

---

[66]   Romans 1:16.

[67]   See *CUP*, vol. 1, pp. 364–5.

[68]   *CI*, p. 301.

[69]   *PV*, p. 7.

inconsistencies, however, Kierkegaard's comprehension of the limitations of sensate authority and his poignant attempts to sever deplorable alliances with spiritual authority demonstrate internal coherence. By contrast, Nietzsche's formulation of power remains—from start to finish—a clash of contradictions, and demonstrates the inherent shortcomings of basing human independence and well-being on an exclusively anthropocentric foundation of power masking impotence, the myth of mastery.

Bibliography

Primary Sources

Kierkegaard, Søren, *The Book on Adler*, trans. and eds Howard V. Hong and Edna H. Hong (Princeton: Princeton University Press [1846] 1998).
———, *Christian Discourses: The Crisis and a Crisis in the Life of an Actress*, trans. and eds Howard V. Hong and Edna H. Hong (Princeton: Princeton University Press [1848] 1997).
———, *The Concept of Anxiety: A Simple Psychologically Orienting Deliberation on the Dogmatic Issue of Hereditary Sin*, trans. and ed. Reidar Thomte with Albert B. Anderson (Princeton: Princeton University Press [1844] 1980).
———, *The Concept of Irony: With Continual Reference to Socrates*, trans. and eds Howard V. Hong and Edna H. Hong (Princeton: Princeton University Press [1841] 1989).
———, *Concluding Unscientific Postscript to Philosophical Fragment: A Mimical-Pathetical-Dialectical Compilation, An Existential Contribution by Johannes Climacus*, trans. and eds Howard V. Hong and Edna H. Hong (2 vols, Princeton: Princeton University Press [1846] 1992).
———, *The Corsair Affair and Articles Related to the Writings*, trans. and eds Howard V. Hong and Edna H. Hong (Princeton: Princeton University Press [1846] 1982).
———, *Eighteen Upbuilding Discourses*, trans. and eds Howard V. Hong and Edna H. Hong (Princeton: Princeton University Press [1843] 1990).
———, *Either/Or*, trans. and eds Howard V. Hong and Edna H. Hong (2 vols, Princeton: Princeton University Press [1843] 1987).
———, *Fear and Trembling/Repetition*, trans. and eds Howard V. Hong and Edna H. Hong (Princeton: Princeton University Press [1843] 1983).
———, *For Self-Examination/Judge For Yourself*, trans. and eds Howard V. Hong and Edna H. Hong (Princeton: Princeton University Press [1851] 1993).
———, *The Journals of Kierkegaard: 1834–1854*, trans. and ed. Alexander Dru (London: Fontana Books, 1958).
———, *The Moment and Late Writings*, trans. and eds Howard V. Hong and Edna H. Hong (Princeton: Princeton University Press [1855] 1998).
———, *Philosophical Fragments/Johannes Climacus, or De Omnibus Dubitandum Est: A Narrative*, trans. and eds Howard V. Hong and Edna H. Hong (Princeton: Princeton University Press [1844] 1985).
———, *The Point of View*, trans. and eds Howard V. Hong and Edna H. Hong (Princeton: Princeton University Press [1851] 1998).

————, *Practice in Christianity*, trans. and eds Howard V. Hong and Edna Hong (Princeton: Princeton University Press [1850] 1991).

————, *The Sickness Unto Death: A Christian Psychological Exposition for Edification and Awakening by Anti-Climacus*, trans. Alastair Hannay (London: Penguin Books [1849] 1989).

————, *Søren Kierkegaard's Journals and Papers*, trans. and eds Howard V. Hong and Edna H. Hong (6 vols, Bloomington: Indiana University Press, 1967–78).

————, *Stages on Life's Way: Studies by Various Persons*, trans. and eds Howard V. Hong and Edna H. Hong (Princeton: Princeton University Press [1845] 1988).

————, *Two Ages: The Age of Revolution and the Present Age: A Literary Review*, trans. and eds Howard V. Hong and Edna H. Hong (Princeton: Princeton University Press [1846] 1978).

————, *Upbuilding Discourses in Various Spirits*, trans. and eds Howard V. Hong and Edna H. Hong (Princeton: Princeton University Press [1847] 1993).

————, *Without Authority: The Lily in the Field and the Birds of the Air*, trans. and eds Howard V. Hong and Edna H. Hong (Princeton: Princeton University Press [1849] 1997).

————, *Works of Love: Some Christian Reflections in the Form of Discourses*, trans. and eds Howard V. Hong and Edna H. Hong (New York: Harper & Row [1847] 1962).

————, *Works of Love: Some Christian Reflections in the Form of Discourses*, Revised edn, trans. and eds Howard V. Hong and Edna H. Hong (Princeton: Princeton University Press [1847] 1995).

Nietzsche, Friedrich, *Beyond Good and Evil: Prelude to a Philosophy of the Future*, trans. R.J. Hollingdale (London: Penguin Books [1886] 1990).

————, *The Birth of Tragedy: Out of the Spirit of Music*, trans. Shaun Whiteside (London: Penguin Books [1872, 1886] 1993).

————, *Ecce Homo: How One Becomes What One Is*, trans. R.J. Hollingdale (London: Penguin Books [1888] 1992).

————, *The Gay Science: With a Prelude in Rhymes and an Appendix of Songs*, trans. Walter Kaufmann (New York: Vintage Books [1882, 1887] 1974).

————, *On the Genealogy of Morals: A Polemic*, trans. Douglas Smith (Oxford: Oxford University Press [1887] 1998).

————, *Human, All Too Human*, trans. Marion Faber and Stephen Lehmann (London: Penguin Books [1878, 1886] 1984).

————, *A Nietzsche Reader*, trans. R.J. Hollingdale (London: Penguin Books [1977] 1979).

————, *Thus Spoke Zarathustra*, trans. R.J. Hollingdale (London: Penguin Books [1883–84, 1886] 1976).

————, *Twilight of the Idol/The Antichrist*, trans. R.J. Hollingdale (London: Penguin Books [1888/1895] 1990).

————, *Untimely Meditations*, trans. R.J. Hollingdale (Cambridge: Cambridge University Press [1873–76] 1997).

————, *The Will to Power*, trans. Walter Kaufmann and R.J. Hollingdale (New York: Vintage Books [1901] 1968).

Secondary Sources

Agonito, Rosemary, *History of Ideas on Women: A Source Book* (New York: Perigee Books, 1977).

Aiken, David W., "The Decline from Authority: Kierkegaard on Intellectual Sin," *International Philosophical Quarterly*, 33.1 (1993): 21–35.

Ansell-Pearson, Keith, *An Introduction to Nietzsche as Political Thinker* (Cambridge: Cambridge University Press [1994] 1997).

Armstrong, Paul B., "Reading Kierkegaard—Disorientation and Reorientation," in Joseph H. Smith (ed.), *Kierkegaard's Truth: The Disclosure of the Self* (New Haven and London: Yale University Press, 1981), 23–50.

Athanasius, "Orations Against the Arians, Book I," in William G. Rusch (trans. and ed.), *Sources of Early Christian Thought: The Trinitarian Controversy* (Philadelphia: Fortress Press, 1980), 63–129.

Babich, Babette E., "Self-Deconstruction: Nietzsche's Philosophy as Style," *Soundings*, 73.1 (1990): 105–16.

Bannerji, Himani, "The Paradox of Diversity: The Construction of a Multicultural Canada and 'Women of Colour,'" *Women's Studies International Forum*, 23.5 (2000): 537–60.

Barfield, Owen, *History in English Words* (London: Faber and Faber Ltd. [1953] 1962).

Barnes, Julian, *Early Greek Philosophy* (London: Penguin Books, 1987).

Barth, Karl, *Dogmatics in Outline*, trans. G.T. Thomson (London: SCM Press, 1957).

Bergmann, Peter, *Nietzsche: The Last Antipolitical German* (Bloomington and Indianapolis: Indiana University Press, 1987).

Berry, Wanda Warren, "Finally Forgiveness: Kierkegaard as a 'Springboard' for a Feminist Theology of Reform," in George B. Connell and C. Stephen Evans (eds), *Foundations of Kierkegaard's Vision of Community: Religion, Ethics, and Politics in Kierkegaard* (New Jersey and London: Humanities Press, 1992), 196–217.

Bettenson, Henry and Chris Maunder (eds), *Documents of the Christian Church* (Oxford: Oxford University Press [1943] 1999).

Bonhoeffer, Dietrich, *Christology*, trans. Edwin Robertson (London: Collins Fount Paperbacks [1933] 1981).

Brandes, Georg, *Friedrich Nietzsche*, trans. A.G. Chater (London: William Heinemann [1889] 1914).

Brandt, Joan, "The Power and Horror of Love: Kristeva on Narcissism," *Romantic Review*, 82.1 (1991): 89–104.

Brobjer, Thomas H., "Notes and Discussions of Nietzsche's Knowledge of Kierkegaard," *Journal of the History of Philosophy*, 41.2 (2003): 251–63.

Brontë, Charlotte, *Jane Eyre* (London: Penguin Books [1847] 1996).

Burkitt, Ian, "Overcoming Metaphysics: Elias and Foucault on Power and Freedom," *Philosophy of the Social Sciences*, 23.1 (1993): 50–72.

Carr, Karen L., "Nietzsche on Nihilism and the Crisis of Interpretation," *Soundings*, 73.1 (1990): 85–104.

Clark, Maudemarie, "Nietzsche, Friedrich," in Edward Craig (ed.), *Routledge Encyclopaedia of Philosophy* (10 vols, London: Routledge, 1998), vol. 6, 844–61.

Coakley, Sarah, "Kenosis and Subversion: On the Repression of 'Vulnerability' in Christian Feminist Writing," in Daphne Hampson (ed.), *Swallowing a Fishbone? Feminist Theologians Debate Christianity* (London: SPCK, 1996), 82–111.

Connell, George B. and C. Stephen Evans (eds), *Foundations of Kierkegaard's Vision of Community: Religion, Ethics, and Politics in Kierkegaard* (New Jersey and London: Humanities Press, 1992).

Cope, Charlotte, "Freedom, Responsibility, and the Concept of Anxiety," *International Philosophical Quarterly*, 44.4 (2004): 549–66.

Cutting, Pat, "The Levels of Interpersonal Relationships in Kierkegaard's *Two Ages*," in Robert L. Perkins (ed.), *International Kierkegaard Commentary* (Macon: Mercer University Press, 1984), 73–86.

Davey, Nicholas, "Nietzsche, Friedrich," in Stuart Brown, Diané Collinson and Robert Wilkinson (eds), *One Hundred Twentieth-Century Philosophers* (London: Routledge, 1998), 139-43.

Detwiler, Bruce, *Nietzsche and the Politics of Aristocratic Radicalism* (Chicago and London: The University Press of Chicago, 1990).

Dooley, Mark, *The Politics of Exodus: Kierkegaard's Ethics of Responsibility* (New York: Fordham University Press, 2001).

Dostoyevsky, Fyodor, *The Brothers Karamazov*, trans. David McDuff (London: Penguin Books, [1879–80] 1993).

Dunning, Stephen N., "Who Sets the Task? Kierkegaard on Authority," in George B. Connell and C. Stephen Evans (eds), *Foundations of Kierkegaard's Vision of Community: Religion, Ethics, and Politics in Kierkegaard* (New Jersey and London: Humanities Press, 1992), 18–32.

Esquith, Stephen L. and Nicholas D. Smith, "Slavery," in William Craig (ed.), *Routledge Encyclopaedia of Philosophy* (10 vols, London: Routledge, 1998), vol. 8, 803–7.

Evans, C. Stephen, *Kierkegaard's "Fragments" and "Postscript": The Religious Philosophy of Johannes Climacus* (New Jersey: Humanities Press, 1983).

———, "Realism and Antirealism in Kierkegaard's *Concluding Unscientific Postscript*," in Alastair Hannay and Gordon D. Marino (eds), *The Cambridge Companion to Kierkegaard* (Cambridge: Cambridge University Press, 1998), 154-76.

Ferreira, M. Jamie, "Faith and the Kierkegaardian Leap," in Alastair Hannay and Gordon D. Marino (eds), *The Cambridge Companion to Kierkegaard* (Cambridge: Cambridge University Press, 1998), 207–34.

Feuerbach, Ludwig, *The Essence of Christianity*, trans. George Eliot (New York: Harper Torchbooks [1841] 1957).

Fiorenza, Elizabeth Schüssler, *Bread Not Stone: The Challenge of Feminist Biblical Interpretation* (Boston: Beacon Press, 1984).

Foucault, Michel, *Power/Knowledge: Selected Interviews and Other Writings: 1972–1977*, ed. Colin Gordon (London: The Harvester Press, 1988).

———, *Religion and Culture by Michel Foucault*, ed. Jeremy R. Carrette (Manchester: Manchester University Press [1980] 1999).

Gardiner, Patrick, *Kierkegaard: A Very Short Introduction* (Oxford: Oxford University Press [1988] 2002).

———, "Kierkegaard, Soren Aabye (1813–55)," in Edward Craig (ed.), *Routledge Encyclopedia of Philosophy* (10 vols, London: Routledge, 1998), vol. 5, 235–44.

Gemes, Ken, "Postmodernism's Use and Abuse of Nietzsche," *Philosophy and Phenomenological Research*, 62.2 (2001): 337–60.

Goethe, Johann Wolfgang von, *Faust*, trans. Philip Wayne (2 vols, London: Penguin Books [1801, 1832] 1949).

Golomb, Jacob, "How to De-Nazify Nietzsche's Philosophical Anthropology?," in Jacob Golomb and Robert S. Wistrich (eds), *Nietzsche, Godfather of Fascism? On the Uses and Abuses of a Philosophy* (Princeton: Princeton University Press, 2002), 19–46.

———, "Kierkegaard's Ironic Ladder to Authentic Faith," *Philosophy of Religion*, 32 (1991): 65–81.

———, "Nietzsche on Authority," *Philosophy Today*, 34.3 (1990): 243–58.

———, and Robert S. Wistrich (eds), *Nietzsche, Godfather of Fascism? On the Uses and Abuses of a Philosophy* (Princeton: Princeton University Press, 2002).

Green, Leslie, "Power," in Edward Craig (ed.), *Routledge Encyclopaedia of Philosophy* (10 vols, London: Routledge, 1998), vol. 7, 610–13.

Griffiths, Morwenna, *Feminisms and the Self: The Web of Identity* (London: Routledge, 1995).

Gudorf, Christine E., "Probing the Politics of Difference: What's Wrong with an All-Male Priesthood?," *Journal of Religious Ethics*, 27.3 (1999): 377-405.

Habermas, Jürgen, *The Philosophical Discourse of Modernity*, trans. Frederick Lawrence (Cambridge, MA: The MIT Press, 1987).

Hamilton, Christopher, "Kierkegaard on Truth as Subjectivity: Christianity, Ethics, and Asceticism," *Religious Studies*, 34 (1998): 61–79.

Hampson, Daphne, "On Autonomy and Heteronomy," in Daphne Hampson (ed.), *Swallowing a Fishbone? Feminist Theologians Debate Christianity* (London: SPCK, 1996), 1–16.

————, (ed.), *Swallowing a Fishbone? Feminist Theologians Debate Christianity* (London: SPCK, 1996).

Hannay, Alastair, *Kierkegaard* (London: Routledge & Kegan Paul, 1982).

———— and Gordon D. Marino (eds), *The Cambridge Companion to Kierkegaard* (Cambridge: Cambridge University Press, 1998).

Hegel, Georg W.F., *The Phenomenology of Mind*, trans. J.B. Baillie (2 vols, London: Swan Sonnenschein & Co., Ltd., 1910).

Hirsche, Elizabeth and Gary A. Olson, "'Je-Luce Irigaray': A Meeting with Luce Irigaray," *Hypatia: Special Issue: Feminist Ethics and Social Policy*, 2 (1995): 93–114.

Hollingdale, R.J., *Nietzsche* (London and Boston: Routledge & Kegan Paul, 1973).

Holmer, Paul, "About Being a Person: Kierkegaard's *Fear and Trembling*," in Robert L. Perkins (ed.), *Kierkegaard's Fear and Trembling: Critical Appraisals* (Tuscalosa: The University of Alabama Press, 1981), 81–99.

Holmes, Mary, "Second-Wave Feminism and the Politics of Relationships," *Women's Studies International Forum*, 23.2 (2000): 235–46.

Houlgate, Stephen, *Hegel, Nietzsche and the Criticism of Metaphysics* (Cambridge: Cambridge University Press, 1986).

————, "Power, Egoism and the 'Open' Self in Nietzsche and Hegel," *Journal of the British Society for Phenomenology*, 22.3 (1991): 120–38.

Hunt, Mary E., "Designer Theology: A Feminist Perspective," *Zygon*, 36.4 (2001): 737–51.

Hustwitt, Ronald, "Adler and the Ethical: A Study of Kierkegaard's *On Authority and Revelation*," *Religious Studies*, 21.3 (1985): 331–48.

Irigaray, Luce, *An Ethics of Sexual Difference*, trans. Carolyn Burke and Gillian G. Gill (London: The Athlone Press [1984] 1993).

————, *Speculum of the Other Woman*, trans. Gillian G. Gill (Ithica: Cornell University Press [1974] 1992).

Irwin, William, "Philosophy and the History of Philosophy: On the Advantage of Nietzsche," *American Catholic Philosophical Quarterly*, 75.1 (2001): 25-43.

Jackson, Timothy, "Arminian Edification: Kierkegaard on Grace and Free Will," in Alastair Hannay and Gordon Marino (eds), *The Cambridge Companion to Kierkegaard* (Cambridge, 1998), p. 251.

Johnson, Elizabeth A., *She Who Is: The Mystery of God in Feminist Theological Discourse* (New York: Crossroad, 1992).

Jones, Joe R., "Some Remarks on Authority and Revelation in Kierkegaard," *Journal of Religion*, 57.3 (1977): 232–51.

Jones, Serene, "This God Which Is Not One: Irigaray and Barth on the Divine," in C.W. Maggie Kim, Susan M. St. Ville, and Susan M. Simonaitis (eds), *Transfigurations: Theology and the French Feminists* (Minneapolis: Fortress Press, 1993), 109–41.

Josephus, Flavius, *The Jewish War*, trans. G.A. Williamson (London: Penguin Books, 1959).

Kain, Philip J., "Nietzschean Genealogy and Hegelian History in *The Genealogy of Morals*," *Canadian Journal of Philosophy*, 26.1 (1996): 123–48.

Kaufmann, Walter, *Nietzsche: Philosopher, Psychologist, Antichrist*, 4th edn (Princeton: Princeton University Press, 1974).

Keeley, Louise Carroll, "Subjectivity and World in *Works of Love*," in George B. Connell and C. Stephen Evans (eds), *Foundations of Kierkegaard's Vision of Community: Religion, Ethics, and Politics in Kierkegaard* (New Jersey and London: Humanities Press, 1992), 96–108.

Kirmmse, Bruce H., *Kierkegaard in Golden Age Denmark* (Bloomington and Indianapolis: Indiana University Press, 1990).

———, "'Out With It!': The Modern Breakthrough, Kierkegaard and Denmark," in Alastair Hannay and Gordon D. Marino (eds), *The Cambridge Companion to Kierkegaard* (Cambridge: Cambridge University Press, 1998), 15–47.

Kodalle, Klaus-M., "The Utilitarian Self and the 'Useless' Passion of Faith," in Alastair Hannay and Gordon D. Marino (eds), *The Cambridge Companion to Kierkegaard* (Cambridge: Cambridge University Press, 1998), 397–410.

Koontz, Gayle Gerber, "The Liberation of Atonement," *Mennonite Quarterly Review* 63 (1989): 171–92.

Levinas, Emmanuel, "The Trace of the Other," in Mark C. Taylor (ed.), *Deconstruction in Context: Literature and Philosophy* (Chicago: University of Chicago Press, 1986), 345–59.

Löwith, Karl, *From Hegel to Nietzsche: The Revolution in Nineteenth-Century Thought*, trans. David E. Green (London: Constable, 1965).

Lowrie, Walter, *A Short Life of Kierkegaard*, 2nd edn (Princeton: Princeton University Press, 1965).

Luther, Martin, *Documents of Modern History*, ed. E.G. Rupp and Benjamin Drewery (London: Edward Arnold, 1979).

———, *Selections from His Writings*, ed. John Dillenberger (New York: Doubleday, 1962).

Lynch, Richard A., "Mutual Recognition and the Dialectic of Master and Slave: Reading Hegel Against Kojève," *International Philosophical Quarterly*, 41.1 (2001): 33–48.

Machiavelli, Niccolò, *The Prince*, trans. George Bull (London: Penguin Books [1514] 1981).

Mandelbaum, Maurice, *History, Man & Reason: A Study in Nineteenth-Century Thought* (Baltimore & London: Johns Hopkins University Press, 1974).

Matthis, Michael J., "Kierkegaard and the Problem of the Social Other," *Philosophy Today*, 38.4 (1994): 419–39.

Mauriac, François, *The Knot of Vipers*, trans. Gerard Hopkins (London: Penguin Books [1932] 1985).

Milbank, John, "Can a Gift Be Given? Prolegomena to a Future Trinitarian Metaphysic," *Modern Theology*, 11.1 (1995): 119–61.

Moltmann, Jürgen, *God in Creation: An Ecological Doctrine of Creation*, trans. Margaret Kohl (London: SCM Press Ltd., 1985).

————, *The Trinity and the Kingdom of God: The Doctrine of God*, trans. Margaret Kohl (London: SCM Press Ltd., 1981).

Monty Python's Flying Circus. http://www.ibras.dk/Monty python/episode30. htm#6.

Mooney, Edward F., "Understanding Abraham: Care, Faith, and the Absurd," in Robert L. Perkins (ed.), *Kierkegaard's Fear and Trembling: Critical Appraisals* (Tuscalosa, AL: The University of Alabama Press, 1981), 100–114.

Nehamas, Alexander, *Nietzsche: Life as Literature* (London and Cambridge, MA: Harvard University Press, 1985).

Nicoletti, Michele, "Politics and Religion in Kierkegaard's Thought: Secularization and the Martyr," in George B. Connell and C. Stephen Evans (eds), *Foundations of Kierkegaard's Vision of Community: Religion, Ethics, and Politics in Kierkegaard* (New Jersey and London: Humanities Press, 1992), 183–95.

Norman, Richard, *Hegel's Phenomenology: A Philosophical Introduction* (New Jersey: Humanities Press, 1981).

Norris, Christopher, "Fictions of Authority: Narrative and Viewpoint in Kierkegaard's Writing," *Criticism*, 25.2 (1983): 87–107.

Oakley, Francis, "The Absolute and Ordained Power of God in Sixteenth- and Seventeenth-Century Theology," *Journal of the History of Ideas*, 59.3–4 (1998): 437–61.

Parsons, Susan F., "Conceiving of God: Theological Arguments and Motives in Feminist Ethics," *Ethical Theory and Moral Practice*, 4 (2001): 365–82.

Pascal, Blaise, *Pensées*, trans. A.J. Krailsheimer (London: Penguin Books, [1670] 1966).

Pattison, George, *Kierkegaard, Religion, and the Nineteenth-Century Crisis of Culture* (Cambridge: Cambridge University Press, 2002).

Peperzak, Adriaan T., "Philosophy-Religion-Theology," *International Journal for Philosophy of Religion*, 50 (2001): 29–39.

Perkins, Robert L., "Climacan Politics: Person and Polis in Kierkegaard's *Postscript*," in Robert L. Perkins (ed.), *International Kierkegaard Commentary: Concluding Unscientific Postscript to 'Philosophical Fragments'* (Macon: Mercer University Press, 1997), 33–52.

————, "Envy as Personal Phenomenon and as Politics," in Robert L. Perkins (ed.), *International Kierkegaard Commentary: Two Ages* (Macon: Mercer University Press, 1984), 107–32.

————, "For Sanity's Sake: Kant, Kierkegaard, Father Abraham," in Robert L. Perkins (ed.), *Kierkegaard's Fear and Trembling: Critical Appraisals* (Tuscalosa: The University of Alabama Press, 1981), 43–61.

————, "Habermas and Kierkegaard: Religious Subjectivity, Multiculturalism, and Historical Revisionism," *International Philosophical Quarterly*, 44.4 (2004): 481–96.

————, (ed.), *International Kierkegaard Commentary: Two Ages* (Macon: Mercer University Press, 1984).

————, "Kierkegaard's Critique of the *Bourgeois* State," *Inquiry*, 27.2 (1984): 207–18.

———— (ed.), *Kierkegaard's Fear and Trembling: Critical Appraisals*. Tuscalosa: The University of Alabama Press, 1981).

Pippin, Robert B., "Nietzsche's Alleged Farewell: The Premodern, Modern and Postmodern Nietzsche," in Bernd Magnus and Kathleen M. Higgins (eds), *The Cambridge Companion to Nietzsche* (Cambridge: Cambridge University Press, 1996), 252–78.

Plantinga, Alvin, *The Twin Pillars of Christian Scholarship* (Grand Rapids: Calvin College, 1990).

Plekon, Michael, "Kierkegaard the Theologian: The Roots of His Theology in *Works of Love*," in George B. Connell and C. Stephen Evans (eds), *Foundations of Kierkegaard's Vision of Community: Religion, Ethics, and Politics in Kierkegaard* (New Jersey and London: Humanities Press, 1992), 2–17.

————, "Towards Apocalypse: Kierkegaard's *Two Ages* in Golden Age Denmark," in Robert L. Perkins (ed.), *International Kierkegaard Commentary: Two Ages* (Macon: Mercer University Press, 1984), 19–52.

Pletsch, Carl, "The Self-Sufficient Text in Nietzsche and Kierkegaard," *Yale French Studies*, 66 (1984): 160–88.

Poole, Roger, "The Unknown Kierkegaard: Twentieth-Century Receptions," in Alastair Hannay and Gordon D. Marino (eds), *The Cambridge Companion to Kierkegaard* (Cambridge: Cambridge University Press, 1998), 48–75.

Quinn, Philip L., "Kierkegaard's Christian Ethics," in Alastair Hannay and Gordon D. Marino (eds), *The Cambridge Companion to Kierkegaard* (Cambridge: Cambridge University Press, 1998), 349–75.

Rae, Murray, *Kierkegaard's Vision of the Incarnation: By Faith Transformed* (Oxford: Clarendon Press, 1997).

Rice, Martin P., "Dostevskii's *Notes from Underground* and Hegel's 'Master and Slave,'" *Canadian-American Slavic Studies*, 8.3 (1974): 359–69.

Richardson, John, *Nietzsche's System* (New York and Oxford: Oxford University Press, 1996).

Rosenthal, Bernice Glatzer, "Nietzsche: Impact on Russian Thought," in Edward Craig (ed.), *Routledge Encyclopaedia of Philosophy* (10 vols, London: Routledge, 1998), vol. 6, 862–7.

Ruether, Rosemary Radford, *Sexism and Godtalk: Towards a Feminist Theology* (London: SCM Press [1983] 1989).

Rumble, Vanessa, "Eternity Lies Beneath: Autonomy and Finitude in Kierkegaard's Early Writings," *Journal of the History of Philosophy*, 35.1 (1997): 83–103.

Safranski, Rüdiger, *Nietzsche: A Philosophical Biography*, trans. Shelly Frisch (New York: W.W. Norton & Company [2000] 2003).

Salomé, Lou, *Nietzsche*, trans. and ed. Siegfried Mandel (Urbana and Chicago: University of Chicago Press [1894] 2001).

Schacht, Richard, *Nietzsche* (London: Routledge & Kegan Paul, 1983).

Schönbaumsfeld, Genia, "No New Kierkegaard," *International Philosophical Quarterly*, 44.4 (2004): 519–34.

Segal, Lynne, "Only Contradictions on Offer," *Women: A Cultural Review*, 11.1–2 (2000): 19–36.

Slee, Nicola, "The Power to Re-Member," in Daphne Hampson (ed.), *Swallowing a Fishbone? Feminist Theologians Debate Christianity* (London: SPCK, 1996), 33–49.

Søe, N.H., "Christ," in Niels Thulstrup and M. Mikulová Thulstrup (eds), *Bibliotheca Kierkegaardiana: Theological Concepts in Kierkegaard* (16 vols, Copenhagen: C.A. Reitzels Boghandel, 1980), vol. 5, 55–70.

Solzhenitsyn, Aleksandr, *One Day in the Life of Ivan Denisovich*, trans. Ralph Parker (London: Penguin Books [1962] 2000).

Soskice, Janet Martin, "Turning the Symbols," in Daphne Hampson (ed.), *Swallowing a Fishbone? Feminist Theologians Debate Christianity* (London: SPCK, 1996), 17–32.

Stack, George J., *Kierkegaard's Existential Ethics* (Tuscalosa: The University Press of Alabama, 1977).

Stern, Robert and Nicholas Walker, "Hegelianism," in Edward Craig (ed.), *Routledge Encyclopedia of Philosophy* (10 vols, London: Routledge Press, 1998), vol. 4, 280–302.

Strong, Tracy B., *Friedrich Nietzsche and the Politics of Transfiguration* (Berkeley, Los Angeles and London: University of California Press, 1975).

Tanner, Michael, *Nietzsche* (Oxford: Oxford University Press, 1994).

Taylor, Charles, "The Politics of Recognition," in Amy Gutmann (ed.), *Multiculturalism: Examining the Politics of Recognition* (Princeton: Princeton University Press, 1994), 25–73.

Taylor, Mark C., "Christology," in Niels Thulstrup and M. Mikulová Thulstrup (eds), *Bibliotheca Kierkegaardiana: Theological Concepts in Kierkegaard* (16 vols, Copenhagen: C.A. Reitzels Boghandel, 1980), vol. 5, 167–206.

Tolstoy, Leo, *Resurrection*, trans. Rosemary Edmonds (Penguin: London, [1899] 1966).

Tombs, David, "Crucifixion, State Terror, and Sexual Abuse," *Union Seminary Quarterly Review*, 53.1–2 (1999): 89–109.

Torrance, James B., *Worship, Community & the Triune God of Grace* (Downers Grove: IVP, 1996).

Unamuno, Miguel de, *The Tragic Sense of Life* (London: The Fontana Library, [1921] 1962).

Volf, Miroslav, *Exclusion and Embrace: A Theological Exploration of Identity, Otherness, and Reconciliation* (Nashville: Abingdon Press, 1996).

Washbourn, Penelope, "Authority or Idolatry? Feminine Theology and the Church," *The Christian Century* (October 1975): 961–4.

Westphal, Merold, "Abraham and Hegel," in Robert L. Perkins (ed.), *Kierkegaard's Fear and Trembling: Critical Appraisals* (Tuscalosa: The University of Alabama Press, 1981), 62–80.

————, "Kierkegaard and Hegel," in Alastair Hannay and Gordon D. Marino (eds), *The Cambridge Companion to Kierkegaard* (Cambridge: Cambridge University Press, 1998), 101–24.

————, "Kierkegaard's Politics," *Thought*, 55.218 (1980): 320–32.

————, "Kierkegaard's Religiousness C: A Defense," *International Philosophical Quarterly*, 44.4 (2004): 535–48.

————, "Kierkegaard's Sociology," in Robert L. Perkins (ed.), *International Kierkegaard Commentary: Two Ages* (Macon: Mercer University Press, 1984), 133–54.

————, "Kierkegaard's Teleological Suspension of Religiousness B," in George B. Connell and C. Stephen Evans (eds), *Foundations of Kierkegaard's Vision of Community: Religion, Ethics, and Politics in Kierkegaard* (New Jersey and London: Humanities Press, 1992), 110–29.

White, Richard, "The Return of the Master: An Interpretation of Nietzsche's 'Genealogy of Morals,'" *Philosophy and Phenomenological Research*, 48.4 (1988): 683–96.

Whittaker, John H., "Kierkegaard on the Concept of Authority," *International Journal for Philosophy of Religion*, 46 (1999): 83–101.

Yalom, Irvin D., *When Nietzsche Wept* (New York: Basic Books, 1992).

Zeitlin, Irving M., *Nietzsche: A Re-Examination* (Cambridge: Polity Press, 1994).

Ziolkowski, Eric J., "Don Quixote and Kierkegaard's Understanding of the Single Individual in Society," in George B. Connell and C. Stephen Evans (eds), *Foundations of Kierkegaard's Vision of Community: Religion, Ethics, and Politics in Kierkegaard* (New Jersey and London: Humanities Press, 1992), 130–43.

Index

Søren Kierkegaard and Friedrich Nietzsche are referred to as SK and FN throughout the index, except in their own main entries where their names are spelled out.